GAY PARTIES
For All Occasions

Alphabet Drama -305

GAY PARTIES

FOR ALL OCCASIONS

E. O. HARBIN

ABINGDON COKESBURY

New York   Nashville

GAY PARTIES FOR ALL OCCASIONS

SET UP, PRINTED, AND BOUND BY THE
PARTHENON PRESS, AT NASHVILLE,
TENNESSEE, UNITED STATES OF AMERICA

Dedicated to

A GREAT TRIO

The Generalissimo (*that's Mabel, my wife*), Captain Trouble (*that's Tommy, my son*), and General Nuisance (*that's Mary Elizabeth, my daughter*). The Captain, the General, and I, Colonel Can't-Take-It, were, in our younger days, "The Three Musketeers."

PREFACE

PARTIES ARE MOST FUN—

    when they are gay parties.
    when they are built around some clever idea or theme.
    when everyone participates.
    when informality and friendliness prevail.

Such parties require careful planning. The larger the crowd, the more definite and careful must be the preparation. The parties in this book are offered as suggestions of things that can be done. Modify them or amplify them to suit your particular situation.

Emphasis has been placed on suggestions for family parties and family recreation, although there are games and parties for all age groups. These suggestions are so arranged that they can be used by a single family or by groups of families working together in the church, club, or community in big family night programs.

More games are listed for the parties than will be needed ordinarily, and in some cases a still larger choice is offered by references to my previous book, *The Fun Encyclopedia*.

E. O. HARBIN

CONTENTS

9

CHAPTER I

Family Night Parties

Family Party Invitation

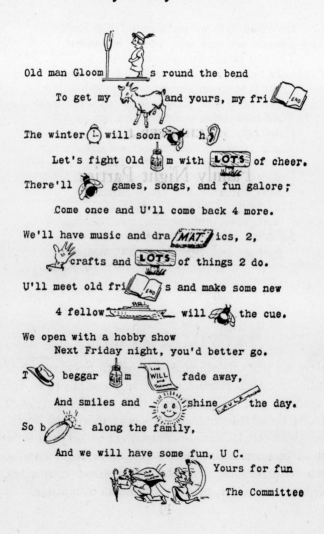

Old man Gloom   s round the bend

    To get my   and yours, my fri

The winter (L) will soon   h

    Let's fight Old   m with LOTS of cheer.

There'll   games, songs, and fun galore;

    Come once and U'll come back 4 more.

We'll have music and dra MAT ics, 2,

    crafts and LOTS of things 2 do.

U'll meet old fri   s and make some new

    4 fellow   will   the cue.

We open with a hobby show

    Next Friday night, you'd better go.

T   beggar   m WILL   fade away,

    And smiles and   shine   the day.

So b   along the family,

    And we will have some fun, U C.

                    Yours for fun

                    The Committee

Family Night Parties

Old man Gloom waits round the bend
To get my goat and yours, my friend.
The wintertime will soon be here;
Let's fight Old Gloom with lots of cheer.
There'll be games, songs, and fun galore;
Come once and you'll come back for more.
We'll have music and dramatics, too,
Handcrafts and lots of things to do.
You'll meet old friends and make some new
   For fellowship will be the cue.
We open with a hobby show
   Next Friday night, you'd better go.
That beggar Gloom will fade away,
   And smiles and sunshine rule the day.
So bring along the family,
   And we will have some fun, you see.

Yours for Fun
The Committee

LET'S HAVE A CIRCUS

Here is a party in which all groups can co-operate. Entire families can work together and have a glorious time. It can be made a community, church, club, or school affair. If it is to be elaborate, then many weeks should be spent in getting ready for it. Various committees would need to function—a program committee, a general arrangements committee (decorations, site, etc.), a costume committee, a side-show committee, perhaps a publicity committee.

13

Different groups should be made responsible for certain features of the circus, such as the circus animals, the side shows, the parade, the refreshments, the circus ring features, the clowns. The more people you have working, the better.

The plans can be greatly simplified, if necessary. A small program committee, in this case, would have charge of the circus, and many of the activities could be rather impromptu. However, even for such a spontaneous affair there should be very careful planning by the committee. Program ideas, program organization, materials and equipment for various

acts, decorations, and other matters should be carefully considered and arrangements made for all those matters that need attention before the program gets under way.

THE RINGMASTER. The ringmaster, as master of ceremonies, is an important factor in making the circus a success. If he has the "gift of gab," it will be helpful. Enthusiasm and mental alertness are necessities. "Ladies and gentlemen, this is the greatest show on earth! It's stupendous! It's colossal! It's gigantic! It's the most magnificent performance you will ever see!"

THE BARKERS. Good, noisy barkers for the side shows will give the proper atmosphere. The show could begin with these showmen extolling the virtues of their offerings, all at the same time—"Have your palm read!" "See the greatest animal show on earth!" "See the mighty midget, marvel of the ages!" "See the magnificent monkey who talks like a human!" (A mirror reflects the image of the customer as he steps into this show.)

THE CLOWNS. Whoever heard of a circus without clowns? Their humorous, whimsical antics add to the fun. Flip-Flop, Flim-Flam, Flu-Flu, Gab-Gab, and Jo-Jo the child clown should work out some good clown acts, which they rehearse. Their "stuff" is not likely to be funny if they trust only to spur-of-the-moment ideas.

TRAINED ANIMALS. With a little work and ingenuity some remarkable animals can be created.

GARY-THE-GIRAFFE. Sew black spots on a yellow blanket or burlap. Use a broomstick as the base for a neck and make a papier-mâché head. Glue a small magnet at the mouth, leaving the points of the magnet exposed. The giraffe could then pick up a handkerchief which has a piece of tin glued on the top side. Two persons.

ELLIE-THE-ELEPHANT. Use a gray blanket and make a head of gray paper. Pin on large ears, white cardboard tusks, and a stuffed trunk. Two persons.

WALLIE-THE-WALRUS. Wear a brown wool wig, a long, fuzzy, brown wool mustache, white or brown work gloves, and a baggy brown coat. One person.

DOTTIE-THE-DRAGON. Glue long sheets of green crepe paper together and make a head of green and red crepe

15

paper. Half a dozen persons walk in winding formation under this covering.

HORACE-THE-HORSE. Use a corrugated box for the body. Cut a hole in the box to make it fit over the body of the rider and rest on his hips. The body may be tied to the rider's waist. Cover the horse's body with a crepe-paper or cambric canopy so that the rider's legs and feet are not visible. A head and neck can be made of wrapping paper, or the head of a hobbyhorse may be used.

The animals may perform various stunts—balancing, rolling over dead, answering questions by shaking their heads or pawing their feet. Dottie-the-Dragon may end the act by coming on the scene and chasing the others away. One of the clowns could appear as the dragon killer and score a triumphant victory with a wooden sword.

CHARIOT RACE. Make cardboard chariots with stick horses attached. No wheels are used. The chariot driver stands inside the chariot frame, holding the chariot in place by a wooden brace. Cover frame with crepe paper to conceal the driver's legs and feet. After the drivers finish a stirring race, clowns come on with kiddy cars, tricycles, and wheelbarrows. They do a burlesque race that ends in a wreck.

THE FIRE. Feature a Clown Fire Department arriving in great confusion. The fire may be sparklers or a synthetic fire made with an electric light globe and red paper or cellophane. The clowns drag in a stepladder. They climb up and then back down to the fire, and use atomizers with great gusto.

IM AND UN, THE BALANCE TWINS. Tight-rope walkers de luxe. Place a wide, heavy plank on several boxes, twelve to eighteen inches from the floor. On the plank stretch a small rope, heavy cord, or wire. Use a ladder to help the balance twins into place even though the climb is only one or two feet from the floor. The twins do the various tightrope-walking stunts—balancing with a pole or parasol, stooping to pick up a handkerchief, going down to one knee, turning, etc. The clowns look on in amazement, applaud vigorously, and then do a burlesque of the act.

SAMSON II. A weight-lifting act. Samson II lifts large empty cans painted black and marked "500 Pounds," "1000 Pounds." The clowns try to lift the weights after Samson II finishes. They strain, but cannot budge them. Then the child clown, Jo-Jo, comes on and carries all of the weights off with the other clowns in pursuit.

SIDE SHOWS. Madam Gypsem, the gypsy palmist; Lotta Baloney, the Fat Lady (a fat man made up); the Swimming Match (a match in a pan of water); The Last of the Race (the letter "E"); the Wild Boy; Remains of Old Greece (candle grease); the Snake Charmer. Your imagination may suggest other and better ones.

THE CIRCUS ZOO. The animals are displayed in tiny toothpick and cardboard cages. Each exhibit is numbered. Provide each guest with a piece of paper and a pencil. On the paper they are to identify the animals being shown. The guessing feature may be eliminated if desired. In this case the exhibits would be labeled.

EXAMPLES. 1. A tiny doll with no clothes. (Bear.) 2. A

17

small piece of chain. (Lynx.) 3. The letters "M-O-N" and a key. (Monkey.) 4. A bow tie and the letters "G-E-R." (Tiger.) 5. A small doll lying prone. (Lion.) 6. A wiener. (Dog.) 7. A lock of hair. (Hare.) 8. A small candle. (Tapir —taper.) 9. A lump of dough. (Doe.) 10. The letter "U." (Ewe.) 11. A paper or candy heart. (Hart.) 12. An Easter or Christmas seal. (Seal.) 13. A piece of chamois. (Chamois.) 14. A jack and a picture of a man greeting another man—"Hi, Al!" (Jackal.)

PROGRAM OUTLINE. 1. Side shows. 2. Parade. 3. Ring features.

Impromptu Circus Suggestions

FREAK MIXER. Pin on the back of each guest a slip of paper on which is written the name of some freak in the circus. A quick way to do this in a large crowd is to give each person a slip of paper and a pin. No one is to see what is written on the slip. Each player then pins a title on some other player's back. If this method is not used, have a committee do the job. In a crowd of one hundred people there would be ten of each title. Suggestions: Fat Lady, Snake Charmer, Giant, Dwarf, Tattooed Man, Human Pincushion, Bearded Lady, Sword Swallower, Fire Eater, Half Man–Half Woman, Dog-faced Boy.

Each person tries to discover what he represents by asking questions of others and by listening to remarks made about him. As soon as he discovers who he is, the slip is taken off his back and pinned on his front.

CIRCUS ACTS. As soon as all players are identified, they group themselves according to their titles—the Giants in one part of the room, the Dwarfs in another, and so on. Each group is now given fifteen or twenty minutes to arrange a suitable act.

Thus the Half Man–Half Woman group may prepare the Romeo and Juliet stunt (below). The Giant group could make a giant by putting one man on the shoulders of another man and covering the two with a blanket or sheet. Other creative ideas will evolve as the group plans. The element of surprise is important. Therefore it would be well if each group could meet in a place by itself to prepare for its act.

It can readily be seen that some preparty planning on the part of the host or committee would add to the success of this affair. Costume and make-up materials should be made available. An idea or two to some of the groups for their acts may be needed. If so the leader or the committee should be ready with some hints and suggestions.

CIRCUS MIXER. Write on slips of paper, one for each guest, the names of various circus acts—animals, clowns, freaks, bareback riders, tightrope walkers, band, trapeze performers, Wild-West show, etc. Pin these slips on backs of guests. Each is to find out what he is. Then persons bearing the same titles are grouped together.

CIRCUS PERFORMANCE. Each group is allotted thirty minutes to get up its part of the circus. Again preparation beforehand by a committee or by the leader would pay dividends. Blankets, sheets, drapes, stockings, hats, broomsticks, boots, crepe paper, newspapers, pins, and make-up materials should be made available for possible creative efforts of the various groups.

ROMEO AND JULIET. One person dresses so that half of his body represents a man and the other half represents a woman. This effect may be achieved by dressing as a man and then covering one side of the body with a woman's outfit—shoes, dress, half-hat, etc. With make-up draw a mustache on the man's side and rosy cheeks, cupid's

19

bow, and wig (if available) on the woman's side. Several persons may perform the stunt. The Half Man–Half Woman stands with his side toward the audience, changing rapidly and rhythmically to the other side as he sings the song. On "Romeo" turn the man's side to the audience; on "Juliet," the woman's side. The words are sung to the tune "Long, Long Ago."

Come, now, and listen to my tale of woe
    Of Romeo and Juliet;
Cribbed out of Shakespeare and reeking with woe,
    Oh, Romeo and Juliet!
Ne'er was a story so mournful as that one;
If you have tears, now prepare to get at one.
Romeo's the slim one and Juliet's the stout one;
    Oh, Romeo and Juliet!

I am the hero of this little tale,
    I'm Romeo! I'm Romeo!
I am that highly susceptible male,
    I'm Romeo! I'm Romeo!
Ne'er did a lover e'er do as I did,
When his girl into eternity slided,
I took cold poison, and I suicided;
    I'm Romeo! I'm Romeo!

I am the heroine of this tale of woe,
    I'm Juliet! I'm Juliet!
I am the lady who mashed Romeo,
    I'm Juliet! I'm Juliet!
Locked in the prison, no pickax to force it,
Gloomy old hole, without room to stand or sit,
I up and stabbed myself right through the corset;
    I'm Juliet! I'm Juliet!

This of our tale is the short and the long,
    Of Romeo and Juliet;

This is the moral of our little song,
    Of Romeo and Juliet.
Lovers, we warn you, always be wary,
Don't buy your drinks of an apothecary,
Don't stab yourselves in the left pulmonary,
    Like Romeo and Juliet.

FAMILY CIRCUS

A single family can adapt the circus idea for its own home. Get a ten-cent-store book of animal pictures. Cut them out, mount them, and use as table decorations. It would be easy to make a tiny circus tent of red and white construction paper for a table centerpiece. Toy balloons could be used to decorate the dining-room and living-room walls.

The "Circus Zoo" idea could be used as a party feature.

GAMES. Hidden animals; feeding the elephant (tossing peanuts into a megaphone); making words out of the word "elephant" (dad and son versus mother and sis).

REFRESHMENTS. Clown-face cookies and pink lemonade.

A CHINTSOYA PARTY

If you're five or if you're fifty,
    If you're twenty or seventy-five,
Here's a party that's a nifty,
    You'll be glad that you're alive!

So pack your troubles, never mind them,
    Join us in two hours of fun;
Chintsoya's golden hours you'll find them,
    Bring dad and mom and sis and son.

21

The idea for this party is adapted from suggestions by the Rev. David J. Cathcart, a pastor in Florida. The idea, with him, grew out of the fun his intermediates got out of a sort of scavenger hunt, in which they worked in teams of four or five. They gathered such things as a piece of grass twelve inches long, a red leaf, a piece of glass ("not hard to find around our buildings"), a sandspur, something alive (ant, moth, spider, or mosquito), etc.

CHINTSOYA. Cathcart's group used the word "chintsoya" for their party; the nine letters stand for children, intermediates, seniors, older youth, and adults. Similar word combinations can be made by other groups, using the same idea. Have each person at the party write on a slip of paper what he thinks the word means. Any person in on the secret must remain quiet. This is a party in which various age groups can co-operate, and it ought to result in a better spirit of unity in your group.

THE HUNT IS ON. Divide the group into teams of four or five persons, perhaps one from each age group on each team. The teams are given the following list of things to gather from persons present. (Players are not confined to their own team in making the collection. Anyone on the place may be canvassed for the necessary articles.) 1. A finger ring. 2. A safety pin (any size). 3. Hairpin (bobby pin will do). 4. Straight pin. (Yes, just an ordinary pin.) 5. Four pennies. (You might get them back.) 6. A lipstick (any color). 7. A shoestring. (Yes, the string without the shoe.) 8. A key (key on a ring will do). 9. An earring. 10. A man's necktie. (No, we don't want the man— just the tie.)

Each team hustles to get its list completed. Everyone co-operates with everyone else in producing the necessary articles when approached and when the articles are available.

"I must confess it looks dumb, but I was amazed at how much fun the teams had," said Dave. And why not? It ought to be hilarious. Try it in your own group.

WHOSE IS IT? As the guests arrive, one person is assigned the task of listing characteristics or articles of jewelry or apparel that are distinctive. These are turned in early and typed copies are made so that each team of four or five persons can have a list. The object of the game is to put down the name of the person by each of the distinctive items. If this requires some personal investigation and checking, so much the better. The list used by Cathcart's group was as follows: 1. Butterfly pin. 2. Flowered necktie. 3. Pearl-cluster earring. 4. Ruby ring. 5. Shoe with four eyes. 6. Widow's peak. 7. Peasant embroidery. 8. Someone wearing a "V." (One of the girls had a "V" on an ankle chain.) 9. Dress with ten buttons.

In a large crowd several "spotters" could work at the job of listing distinctive things. If a typewriter is not available, have several people help in making the necessary number of lists.

OTHER GAMES PLAYED. In addition to these events the following games may be played: Name Lotto or Human Bingo; Sit and Sing (an object is hidden in plain sight while all are out of the room; when you see the object, you sit and sing); Who Is the Leader?; "Wink"; Know Your Numbers (page 283).

A COMMENCEMENT PARTY

Quituater, graduater, brother, sister, bum,
Doctor, lawyer, merchant chief, everybody come.

You'll see such a commencement as you never saw before.
There'll be fun aplenty, fun a rarin', fun galore.
Commencement party   Date and time

This is a party for the whole family, to be sponsored by
the church or club. When members of the group are graduating from high school or college, recognition of these persons by some appropriate word or gift can be featured.

SETTING. Arrange the room like a schoolroom—
teacher's desk or table, blackboard (perhaps with a cartoon
of teacher on it), maps, posters with nonsensical advice
such as "Brush your teeth before putting them away for
the night."

The teacher should be in caricature—old-fashioned garb,
hairdo extraordinary, large horn-rimmed spectacles. This
person should be carefully selected far in advance of the
party so as to allow adequate time for preparation. Much
of the success of the party depends on this teacher. Clever-
ness, ability to keep things moving, and a keen sense of
what is appropriate are essential qualities.

Program Outline

The party begins when the teacher rings the bell.

GROUP SINGING. The teacher calls on "the music
teacher" to lead a rousing sing—folk songs, stunt songs,
and school songs.

SPECIAL MUSIC. Solo, duet, trio, or quartet by
selected members. If this can be an expertly performed
number, fine. If not, make it contribute to the fun by some
burlesque, such as announcing that the song will be sung
backwards. The singers then turn their backs on the audience and sing. Or the song may be sung upside down. The

singers kneel or sit behind a blanket or sheet. They have shoes on their hands, which are held up above the blanket as they sing.

DEMONSTRATION OF READING. Select unsuspecting people from the audience for this demonstration. Bring them to the front and give them tongue twisters to read, like "She sells sea shells by the seashore."

ARITHMETIC. Call twenty people to the front. Line them up in two teams of ten each. Give each team three-by-six-inch cards on which are printed numbers from 1 to 9 to distribute among their team members. The teacher calls problems in addition, subtraction, or multiplication. The first side to arrange the answer in front of its group scores a point. For instance if the teacher calls "Three times twelve!" the side getting its 3 and 6 arranged properly in front of its line will score.

GEOGRAPHY QUIZ. Select persons or teams from the crowd, or call questions and let anyone who thinks he knows the answer whisper it to three or four persons. They must then all yell the answer in unison. This can be done by sides. The questions should be carefully prepared. State nicknames (example: what is the Empire State?), state flowers, state capitals, and other ideas could be used.

CALISTHENICS. Try something like "Hands on your hips" (*The Fun Encyclopedia*, page 261). Or put the group through a burlesque calisthenics drill.

RECESS. Teacher rings the bell for recess. Have game committee ready to use this period for group games— marches, folk games, parlor volleyball. If space does not permit moving about, use some action songs and quiet games. Arrange a refreshment stand where people can get some orangeade and cookies.

25

SPELLING BEE. The bell rings and everyone comes back to school for the fun de luxe of the evening. Conduct an old-fashioned spelling bee, or use some such idea as dumb spelling (where spellers make signs for certain letters), or spelldown, or living alphabet.

DRAMATICS. Have some group prepare some good short stunt or skit. Suggestions: "The Lover's Errand" (in *Easy Blackouts*, published by Baker); "A Few Words" (in *Four Plays for Two People*, published by The Dramatic Publishing Company); "The Crooked Mouth Family" (The *Fun Encyclopedia*, page 537). Or break up into two or more groups and have each prepare an impromptu dramatization of a nursery rhyme, or prepare and present a charade.

AWARDS. Call up some prominent people in the group and make some nonsensical awards. Pin cardboard "medals" on them. "The Best Speller" will be given some very difficult words to spell. Before he gets under way, the teacher interrupts with "That's fine! You're awarded the medal for being the town's best speller." So it would be for history, geography, music, etc.

CLOSING SING. "Home on the Range," "Old Folks at Home," "Swing Low, Sweet Chariot," and "Jacob's Ladder."

PROGRESSIVE PARTY WITH HOMEMADE GAMES

Here is a party for indoors or outdoors, for a big crowd or a little one. It may be adapted for use in a family group. All of the equipment can be easily constructed by any group.

Select ten to fifteen of the games, depending on the

number of guests. Type simple rules for playing and scoring each game on four-by-six-inch cards. Number the cards consecutively and place them with the games at their various places.

Divide the guests into groups of about four each. Supply each player with a score card. Number the groups and have them start playing games corresponding to the group number. After that they take the games in order. Thus the fifteens will progress to one, the ones to two, the twos to three, etc. This progression continues until each group has played every game. Request that each group leave all equipment ready for the next group. At the close, total individual and group scores.

This party, after getting started, will run itself. There will be no necessity for whistle blowing or bell ringing.

CLOTHESPIN DROP. Equipment: One quart milk bottle, five clothespins, kitchen chair.

Game: Player kneels on the chair, resting right forearm on back of chair, and endeavors to drop clothespins, one at a time, into the milk bottle, which is on the floor back of the chair.

Score: Ten points for each pin dropped into the bottle. Double score if all are in.

RING ITS NECK. Equipment: Catchup or pop bottle, brass or wooden curtain ring suspended from the end of a two-foot stick with twenty inches of string.

Game: Try to get the ring over the neck of the bottle which stands on the floor. The player holds the stick at the end opposite from where the string is fastened.

Score: 100 points if done in 15 seconds or less.
       75 points—15 to 30 seconds.
       50 points—30 to 45 seconds.
       25 points—45 to 60 seconds.

BEAN SHOOTER. Equipment: Soda straw, five penny-box safety matches, and a small pan.

Game: From a distance of about four feet from the pan, which is placed on top of a table, each player tries to blow his matches into the pan by placing them one at a time in the end of the soda straw and blowing.

Score: Ten points for each match in the pan. Double the score if all are in.

BOTTLE TENPINS. Equipment: Ten pop, catchup, or similar bottles set up in tenpin fashion, and large rubber ball.

Game: Roll the ball from a distance of ten to twenty feet and try to knock bottles down.

Score: Allow ten points for each pin knocked down. Double the score if all are knocked over on the first trial. Each player has a second trial.

PEANUT JACKSTRAWS. Equipment: Drinking glass of size used in serving iced tea and enough peanuts with hulls to fill the glass.

Game: Each player in turn inverts the glass of peanuts on the table top and slowly lifts it, leaving the peanuts in a compact heap. By using the fingers he removes as many peanuts as possible without moving any of those in the heap. He is through when a peanut moves.

Score: Ten points for each peanut successfully removed.

RING THE CHAIR LEG. Equipment: One kitchen or folding chair and five rubber rings constructed from bath hose. (Cut hose in lengths that will give desired diameter when formed into a ring. Insert a wooden dowel of proper diameter and length into the ends of the hose forming the ring. Tack to prevent pulling out. Tape over joint.) The rings should measure eight, seven, six, five, and four inches in diameter, respectively.

Game: Invert the chair and toss the rings from a distance of eight to twelve feet one at a time, endeavoring to ring one of the chair legs.

Score: 100, 75, 50, 25, 10 points respectively, from the smallest to the largest ring.

RING AND HOOK. Equipment: A post with a large hook attached at about five feet from the ground. A curtain ring tied to a long string and suspended four or five feet away from the hook. There should be enough string to make it possible for the ring to drop over the hook.

Game: Pull the ring back and try to swing it, pendulum style, so as to catch on to the hook.

Score: Ten trials for each player with ten points for each successful attempt.

MUFFIN-PAN POLO. Equipment: One six-compartment muffin pan. This may be painted with shellac. Five wooden cubes about one inch square.

Game: Toss the cubes into the compartments at a distance of from six to ten feet.

Score: Ten points for each cube remaining in the pan. Double the score if a player gets them all in. Or number each side of the cubes, as follows: 0, 5, 10, 15, 20, 25. In this case the score is the total of sides up.

DROP IT. Equipment: One small pan and five toothpicks or matches for each player.

Game: Set the pan on a chair or stool and by holding the matches in the following manner try to drop them into the pan: First one dropped from the chin. Second one dropped from the mouth. Third one dropped from the nose. Fourth one dropped from the right eye. Fifth one dropped from the left eye. In each case the match is held in the hand.

Score: 10 points for each match in the pan. Double score for getting all in.

SNAP SHOT. Equipment: One twelve-by-twenty-four-inch cardboard. Draw a rectangle six inches wide and four inches deep at one end. Make a cross mark at the other end for a shooting point. Five small disks (checkers, broomstick disks, or Crokinole disks).

Game: Place one disk on each corner of the rectangle. The fifth disk is placed at the cross. Shoot this disk with the finger as in Crokinole, and try to make it land inside the rectangle without displacing the disks on the corner.

Score: Five trials. Ten points for each successful trial. Double if a perfect score is made.

BELL RINGER. Equipment: A small bell suspended in a wire hoop ten or twelve inches in diameter and a five-cent rubber ball or tennis ball.

Game: Suspend the hoop from an open doorway or other suitable place to within four or five feet from the floor. From a distance of eight to fifteen feet toss the ball through the hoop without ringing the bell.

Score: Five trials. Ten points if it goes through the hoop. Twenty points if it goes through without ringing the bell.

CANDLE BLOWING. Equipment: Place ten small candles on a board or cardboard about eight inches square, in positions similar to tenpins. Place on table.

Game: Player is seated about two and a half or three feet from the table. With his mouth on a level with the tops of the candles he tries to blow them out.

Score: Two trials, if necessary. Ten points for each candle blown out. Double score if all are blown out on first trial.

PLUMB BALL. Equipment: One golf ball or rubber sponge ball suspended from the ceiling or other convenient place to within three inches of the floor. Ten five-inch pieces of broom handle or toy tenpins set up tenpin fashion.

30

The ball is suspended to hang directly in front of the head pin.

Game: Draw the ball back and release it. Do not throw.

Score: Ten points for each pin down on first trial. Double score if all are knocked down. Second trial, if necessary, to knock down remaining pins.

EGG-CRATE BOWLING. Equipment: One six-compartment egg carton or muffin pan, golf ball or small wooden or rubber ball, one piece of heavy cardboard, press-board, or plywood about eight inches wide and the length of the carton or pan.

Game: Set the carton or pan flat on a table. Place the board against one edge of the carton so as to form an incline. Roll the ball from a distance of six to ten feet so it will go up the incline and land in a compartment of the carton or pan.

Score: Five trials. Ten points for each successful attempt. Double the score if all are in. Or values may be indicated in each compartment.

BOUNCE BALL. Equipment: A wastepaper basket and one or more old tennis balls. A large rubber ball may be used, if desired. A chair.

Game: From a distance of ten feet bounce the ball on the floor and over the chair into the basket.

Score: Five trials. Ten points for each success. Double score for perfect record.

FAMILY JAMBOREE

> Daddy and mother,
> Sister and brother,
> And all of the family,
> We now do invite
> On next Friday night
> To a grand big jamboree.

31

PLANS

Make this family night. Invite all of the families in the group.

Plan to do three things: (a) Build a finer spirit of understanding between the young people and the adults of the group. (b) Develop a spirit of fellowship through the entire membership. (c) Stimulate home and family recreation.

Plan an exhibit of materials for home recreation. Homemade games (Chinese checkers, nine-men's morris, fox and geese, skittles, etc.); bought games (anagrams, logomachy, authors, lotto, dominoes, checkers, chess, old maid, etc.); books and pamphlets helpful in home recreation (the public library could help you here). Include an exhibit of outdoor equipment—badminton, croquet, horseshoes, etc.

Plan for some demonstrations of family fun—games, handicrafts, puppet shows, informal dramatics, family music (a family orchestra or family singing around the piano), storytelling.

GAMES FOR ALL

SQUIRREL-IN-A-NEST. Divide into groups of three or four each. All but one of these players take hold of hands to form the nest. The other player gets inside and becomes the squirrel. Designate three or more players as squirrels without a home. When the leader blows a whistle, all squirrels must leave their homes and find another nest. In the scramble the extra players probably get a home, forcing others out, who in turn become squirrels without a home.

OCEAN WAVE. Players are seated in a circle, with one chair vacant. An extra player stands at center and calls, "Slide right!" or "Slide left!" He then makes an effort to get a vacant seat. Players keep sliding to the right or to the left, as directed. As soon as a seat is vacant next to a player, he must slide into it before the extra player can occupy it. If the player who is "It" gets a seat, the player responsible must take his place at center. Thus if the group is sliding to the right, the player to the left of the seat obtained by "It" is the one responsible.

FAMILY POP-SACK RELAY. Line up two teams, each composed of several family groups. At the opposite end of the room are two chairs, each with empty paper sacks on them. At the signal to go, the father and son on each team run to the chair. The son picks up a sack, blows it up, and bursts it on father's back. As soon as this is done, they run back to the starting line and touch off mother and daughter. They repeat the same process, the daughter blowing up and bursting the sack. Next come little sister and brother. Then uncle and aunty, and perhaps grandma and grandpa. The first team to finish wins. The family groups may be manufactured for the occasion.

FAMILY HANDICAP RELAY. Line up family teams. At the opposite side of the room set up an Indian club or bottle for each team. Around each club place a barrel hoop covered with crepe paper, or a wire hoop will answer the purpose. The racers walk backward by couples to the Indian club. There the man picks up the hoop and passes it over the body of the woman. She steps through the hoop and then replaces it over the Indian club. Then the couple walks forward to the starting line and touches off the next couple. If the club is knocked down, it must be set up before the couple can proceed.

FAMILY GRAND MARCH. Line up all men and boys on one side according to height. Line up all women and girls on the other side of the room in the same manner. Conduct a grand march with the pianist playing "She'll

33

Be Coming 'Round the Mountain." After they come down by couples, add variety by calling such orders as "Step high," "Chins up," "Bend knees," etc.

FAMILY CENSUS. End the grand march by coming down center by fours. Then march half of the group to one side of the room and the other half to the other. Here they line up facing one another. One side is named the Bumstead family, and the other the Gumps. Two census takers stand in the middle of the floor. When they call "The Bumsteads move," all Bumsteads must cross to the other side of the room. The census takers tag as many as they can. Each person tagged helps the census takers in tagging others. Continue until most of the players have been tagged.

CHARADES. Have the Bumsteads and the Gumps work out several charades, each for the other side to guess.

INFANTRY (Inn-fan-tree). Presented in three scenes. *Scene 1:* A hotel desk with guests registering. *Scene 2:* A girl fanning or a baseball "fan" telling about his favorite ballplayers. *Scene 3:* A couple sitting on the floor and talking about the shade of the old apple tree, to a humming accompaniment of "In the Shade of the Old Apple Tree."

GALVESTON. Presented in one scene. A girl appears wearing a vest.

Other suggestions are: Handicap (hand-eye-cap), cabbage (cab-age), airplane (air-plain), Arkansas (ark-can-saw), Milwaukee (mill-walk-key), runabout, buccaneer (buck-can-ear).

FAMILY STUNTS. Give to each of several groups a nursery rhyme to dramatize. After five minutes of preparation they get busy. "Mary had a little lamb," "Peter, Peter, pumpkin eater," "Mary, Mary, quite contrary," "Little Jack Horner," etc.

34

A GOOD FAMILY PLAY. Who Gets the Car To-night? by Christopher Sergel. Three men, two women, fifteen minutes. (Dramatic Publishing Co.) A cast can do a walking rehearsal of this excellent comedy on a problem of family life after several rehearsals.

HAND PARTY

Listen, Handsome, we're inviting you to our Hand Party. Be there on time, and don't hand us any sass! Date, time and place. (Print on hand cut from paper.)

SHAKE HANDS. Use one or more handshaking plans, such as: (a) Tie a paper sack on the right hands of all guests and make them shake hands until they wear the sack out. (b) Use the secret handshaker plan, in which you give pennies to certain people in your crowd. The thirteenth person to shake hands with the holder of the penny gets the penny to keep until a thirteenth person has shaken hands with him. (c) Circle or spiral handshake.

HANDCRAFTS. Make this party a springboard for introducing the group to some sort of Hobby-Night program. Have several sample handcrafts that can be practiced at the party, such as spatter-painting and soap carving. If soap carving is done, be sure to cover the floor with newspapers so the soap shavings will not spoil the floor. An exhibit of handcrafts may be put on display. Posters could be displayed to encourage the group to take up some hobbies. Definite announcement should be made about the beginning of a Hobby-Night program.

STAGEHANDS. Put on a simple play or panto-mime. For example, put on a play without words, in which the whole message is put across by the use of the hands. There could be three characters—the boy, the girl, and the father. (a) They meet. Business of beckoning, waving, etc.

The boy waves to the girl, she beckons, they talk in pantomime. (b) They fall in love. Business of holding hands, sighing. (c) Enter Papa. Thumbs the boy out. Scolds girl. Curtain.

FAMOUS HANDS. Give your various members of the group slips of paper. On each slip is written some character who makes a well-known use of his hands. Each person presents his portrayal in pantomime while the group guesses what he represents. The following are suggested: (a) Umpire. (b) Traffic cop. (c) Prosecuting attorney. (d) Porter. (e) Prize fighter. (f) Speaker or preacher. (g) Hitchhiker. (h) Musician (pianist, violinist, banjo player, saxophonist, flute player). (i) Fisherman. (j) Ballplayer (catcher, pitcher, first baseman, infielder, outfielder, football or basketball player). (k) Orchestra leader. (l) Gum-chewing typist. (m) Soda jerker. (n) Physician.

HANDS TELL. Secure someone or several persons who know something about palmistry and have them read palms for the group. You may have a special room or tent where this is done.

HAND PUPPETS. Make some paper-sack hand puppets, or use regular hand puppets and put on a short hand-puppet show. If the paper-sack idea is used, the group can make the hand puppets right on the spot. They could be divided into several groups and each group could put on a very brief puppet show.

HAND PICKED. Have the girls stand behind a curtain with only their hands showing. Let the boys select their partners, one at a time, from the hands that are shown. To determine the order in which the boys have the opportunity of choosing, let them draw numbers. When a boy takes hold of a hand, the girl comes out from behind the screen.

HANDOUT. Partners will then get in line for refreshments.

A HOBBY PARTY

Hobbies to ride,
Hobbies to ride,
Come in a walk,
A trot, or a glide.

Dust off your brain,
Give it a chance,
Your power to live
You will enhance.

Lay plans for this event a month or so ahead. Line up hobby demonstrators and other people for various parts of the program. Gather together the best hobby exhibit you can possibly get. Advertise with posters, clever announcements, special invitations. The latter could perhaps be written on cutout hobbyhorses.

HOBBY EXHIBIT. Gather collections and the results of creative hobbies—stamp collections, coin collections, doll collections, spatter prints, needlework, paintings, carvings, books on various hobbies, etc. Organize your hobby exhibit so that the various kinds of hobbies are grouped together. Print cards to label the various exhibits, with the name of the exhibitor prominently displayed. See that each exhibitor gets back what belongs to him.

HOBBY DEMONSTRATIONS. Have some hobbies demonstrated. For instance have someone making pottery, or doing clay modeling. Someone also could be doing spatter painting, soap carving, wood turning or carving, plaster casting, and the making of masks. In one such affair

37

a young man was demonstrating chip carving. Be careful to get persons who can put on good demonstrations of the various hobbies. Poor work will not encourage persons to want to follow up.

One of the demonstrations could be in the nature of a puppet show by someone who makes puppets a hobby. Other possibilities would be a good demonstration of the possibilities in reading poetry, or reading plays. A demonstration book club discussion would fit in nicely, or perhaps there are some who make dramatics a hobby and would be glad to put on a dramatic skit of some sort. Or there may be some who make music a hobby and who could aid the group by some demonstration in that area.

HOBBY OPPORTUNITIES.   Give everyone in the party an opportunity to try his hand at some hobby. Several simple hobbies that could be used for this purpose would be spatter painting, finger painting, block printing and soap carving. For source material on these hobbies see "Fun With Hobbies," in *The Fun Encyclopedia*, page 71; *Handicrafts and Hobbies for Pleasure and Profit*, by Marguerite Ickis; and *Handicraft*, by Lester Griswold. A pamphlet that would be helpful in the discussion of hobbies would be *Care and Feeding of Hobby Horses*, by Calkins. A pamphlet on soap carving can be obtained from Procter & Gamble, Cincinnati, Ohio, for 10c. Look in the ten-cent store for inexpensive books on hobbies such as "Seeing Stars," "Talking Leaves," books on birds and flowers.

HOBBY-LOBBY.   Get some hobby fans to appear before the group in a panel discussion on hobbies. Or get some one person who has an interest in a hobby or hobbies to demonstrate before the group and talk to the group about a particular hobby, such as astronomy, photography, nature lore, and the like.

Prepare for a discussion on possibilities of following up a hobby party with a hobby program for adults and young adults. Have your plans pretty well worked out so you can announce dates, time, place, and leaders.

One church put on a three-month hobby school and got expert leaders for various hobbies such as dramatics, music, woodwork, weaving, and the like.

FUN-SHOP FUN

How about a "Fun-Shop Fun" series? Here's the idea: Meet once a week for several weeks or meet for a series of consecutive nights to collect, repair, repaint, and construct games, puzzles, toys, and scrapbooks to donate to some children's home, home for the aged, hospital, or mission project.

BUILDING INTEREST. (1) Get all the facts you can about the needs of the particular group or groups for whom the project is promoted. Personal observation, interviews, and correspondence will reveal these needs to you. (2) Present the needs to your club or group. (3) Be specific in telling your group what you want them to do (giving of old games and toys that can be refurbished, plans for making games, dates of the Fun-Shop Fun series, etc.). (4) Sell them on the pure fun of such a venture. Service can be thrilling fun. (5) Canvass the town, the community, and the church for toys and games. (6) See that every member gets an insistent and cordial invitation to help in the project. (7) Line up the people with special abilities to aid in the Fun Shop—painters, woodworkers, etc.—even though you have to go outside your membership to get them. They will be invaluable in supervising the work of making and repairing games and toys. (8) Use posters, post cards, letters, and special announcements.

PLANS. (1) Have all materials on hand at the place of meeting—wood, tools, paint, and all other necessary equipment. (2) Fix up a tool rack, if possible, and see that all tools are replaced after using. (3) Protect floors, tables, and furnishings from injury. Use newspapers, beaverboard, and other protective coverings as needed. (4) Be careful to return all borrowed equipment to owners. (5) Organize your group into working crews—painters, repairers, makers of new games, etc.

PROGRAM. (1) Sing a bit. (2) Workshop period. (3) One good game and a goodnight prayer.

WHAT GAMES TO MAKE. Beanbag boards, peg boards, table polo, box hockey, Chinese checkers, etc. Specialize in games that can be readily learned by the groups for whom they are intended.

FAMILIES HAVE FUN

The Rev. Floyd Olson, pastor of the Methodist church at Troy, New York, put on a successful family-night program using the theme "Families Have Fun."

For tiny tots there was a nursery. For the children there were movies. For the rest there were some interesting booths, where there were exhibits and demonstrations, as follows:

MIMEOGRAPHING IS FUN. Evening programs made on the spot.

BABIES HAVE FUN. Toys and ideas that keep babies happy.

GIRLS HAVE FUN. Exhibits of cooking and sewing skills.

BOYS HAVE FUN. Exhibits of boys' sports and hobbies.

YOUTH HAVE FUN. Demonstration of plastic-bracelet making.

40

RECORDING IS FUN. Two booths where persons could have their own voices recorded.

BOOKS ARE FUN. An exhibit of books for all ages.

MEN HAVE FUN. Molding figures, shell-loading equipment, fishing tackle, copper craft.

WOMEN HAVE FUN. Buttons, rugs, knitting, sewing, etc.

ART IS FUN. Production of photographic prints explained and demonstrated. The sound-slide set "Is Your Family Fun?" was shown in the auditorium during the evening.

FAMILY RECREATION

FAMILY BAND. One family occasionally spends the period between the evening meal and the children's bedtime in a rhythm band concert. They have an assortment of "instruments"—a triangle, tambourine, gourd, some bells, and a set of sticks that came from an old play pen. When each person has chosen an "instrument," the young son starts a record and they all keep time to it. It's lots of fun. A group of six to a dozen people could have fun with this idea, especially if they tried to develop finesse in orchestral effects.

OTHER IDEAS. Family and neighborhood picnics; family hobbies; family play spaces; observance of religious feast days and other holidays with family-centered activities, family-centered games, musicales, and entertainments in the churches; home rumpus room; home workshop; back-yard playground.

Why not a big Family Party quarterly?

CRAFETERIA. In line with these suggestions it might not be amiss to call attention to an experiment tried by Howard Tanner of the Handcrafters, Waupun, Wisconsin. He called it a "Crafeteria." Several families were

41

invited into his home. On tables about the room various kinds of craft materials were displayed and suggestions offered as to what could be done with each medium. Each family selected one or more projects and began to work on them. These projects may be ones that can be completed in one evening or they may be projects that the family will complete at home.

CHAPTER II

General Parties

General Parties

A COLOR CARNIVAL

DECORATIONS. Six booths decorated in the six prismatic colors—red, orange, yellow, green, blue, and violet. Or six sections of the room with colored crepe-paper streamers. A rainbow effect at the entrance to the recreation room. Lighting fixtures decorated in rainbow colors.

COSTUMES. Ask all guests to dress as colorfully as possible. Perhaps there could be a welcoming committee of girls in rainbow costumes. Crepe paper could be used over white skirts.

PROGRAM

EYE LOTTO. Give each person a sheet divided into eighteen squares, six down and three across. In the first of the three columns guests are to get autographs of six people with brown eyes. In the second column get autographs of people with blue eyes. In the third column get autographs of persons who have eyes of some color other than brown or blue. Have a list of all names in a hat or box. Draw these out and announce them one at a time. Persons having that name in any of their eighteen squares check it. When a player gets three checks in a row—horizontally, vertically, or diagonally—he yells "Lotto!" Call names until five or six players have lottoed. A stick of candy may be given to those who are successful.

COLOR TOSS. Use a six-hole muffin pan. Color

each hole—red, yellow, blue, etc.—either with enamel paint or by putting colored tabs in front of each hole. Use six checkers or linoleum or wooden disks, each colored in one of the prismatic colors. Players toss the six disks from a distance of six feet or thereabout. Each disk pocketed in one of the holes counts one. If a disk is pocketed in its own color, it scores five points.

COLOR BULLBOARD. With colored chalk mark off a sixteen-inch by twenty-four inch rectangle on the floor and divide it into six squares, eight inches by eight inches, or mark the chart on a long sheet of white paper. Color each square differently. Use linoleum disks three inches in diameter. Color each of these disks to match the squares on the floor. Players toss from a distance of ten feet. Score five for each disk completely within a square of its own color. Disks touching a line do not count.

COLOR CALL. Players are asked to number off by fours or by sixes, as desired. The ones are red, the twos are yellow, the threes are blue, etc. All players except one sit in a circle. He stands at center and calls out colors that are to change seats. In the melee the center player tries to get a seat. The player left out takes center and the game continues.

COLOR QUIZ. 1. What are the colors of the rainbow? Violet, indigo, blue, green, yellow, orange, red. 2. What are the primary pigment colors? Red, blue, yellow. 3. What two colors make green? Blue and yellow. 4. What two colors make orange? Red and yellow. 5. Who was the "goddess of the rainbow" according to the ancient Greeks? Iris. 6. What colors are suggested by the following nations: Russia? Red and white (White Russia). Ireland? Green. United States? Red, white, and blue. 7. What are pastel colors? Pale colors of high brilliance. 8. What are achromatic colors? White, black, gray, and their various shades. 9. What color suggests a social function? Pink tea. 10. What dismal type of song suggests a color? Blues. 11. What are some familiar expressions that use colors to say what they say? "Once in a blue moon," "seeing red," "feeling blue," "dark brown taste," etc. 12. What geographic names suggest colors? Yellowstone Park, Red River, White Mountains, Black Mountain, Blue Ridge, Orangeburg, Green Mountain, Greenville, etc.

COLOR IN SONGS.   Have a good pianist play all or parts of certain songs. Guests are to answer with the titles of the songs and the colors suggested. The following are a few suggestions of possibilities: 1. "Sweetheart of Sigma Chi" (gold, blue). 2. "Red River Valley." 3. "Alice Blue Gown." 4. "When You Wore a Tulip" (yellow, red). 5. "I'm Dreaming of a White Christmas." 6. "Wearin' o' the Green." 7. "Little Gray Home in the West." 8. "Lavender's Blue." 9. "Brown October Ale" from DeKoven's Robin Hood. 10. "Silver Threads Among the Gold." 11. "I Dream of Jeannie" (brown). 12. "Blue Danube Waltz." 13. "Tell Me Why" (blue). 14. "Carolina Moon" (blue). 15. "Red Wing." 16. "Green Grow the Rushes." 17. "Darling Nellie Gray." 18. "Morning Comes Early" (blue, red). 19. "Oh, Dem Golden Slippers." 20. "Red Sails in the Sunset."

COLOR BOOK TITLES.   Give each person or group a few moments to jot down book titles that contain some color in them. Examples: The Blue Bird; Green Light; White Fang; Black Beauty; Green Pastures; The Red Badge of Courage; The White Company; Where the Blue Begins; The Green Roller.

Green Pastures: Read a selection from this play or from Ol' Man Adam an' His Chillun, on which Green Pastures was based.

47

Refreshments: Marshmallow pudding in several colors and colored cookies.

COLOR RACE.   Each contestant is given an armload of balloons, stacked up. Then he tries to get across the room without losing a balloon. If he drops one, he must go back and start over. It will be amazing if any of the contestants arrive at the finish line. Try it!

COLOR TARGET.   Make a target in several colors. Allow each contestant three throws with darts. Give the various colors certain values: red (5), blue (4), green (3), yellow (2), black (1).

COLOR BALLOON TARGETS.   Allow contestants to throw one dart each at toy balloons arranged on a target board.

BOOK FESTIVAL

This party could serve as an introduction to a series of meetings built around books worth reading. Or it could serve as an event connected with the organization of a book club.

BOOK COSTUMES.   Each guest could be asked to come wearing something that represents a book, play, or poem title. An apron made of the front page of a newspaper would easily be recognized as *Front Page.* Other titles that would lend themselves to this method are: *Keys of the Kingdom, The House of the Seven Gables, One Foot in Heaven, The Moon Is Down, Peter Pan, White Fang, The Hoosier Schoolmaster* ("I am a teacher from Indiana"), *Cabbages and Kings, A Tramp Abroad, The Little Minister, Green Light, White Banners, The Four Feathers, The Scarlet Letter, The Blue Bird.*

JUMBLED BOOK TITLES. Pass out mimeographed or typed copies of the following jumbled book titles: 1. Waysermot. 2. Tamhel. 3. Runheb. 4. Siquvado. 5. Etoxuqodin. 6. Marblessilees. 7. Brondraeycegarec. 8. Vistolwiert. 9. Gripesgropsrilms. 10. Witngtheihdoewn.

Answers: 1. *Tom Sawyer.* 2. *Hamlet.* 3. *Ben Hur.* 4. *Quo Vadis.* 5. *Don Quixote.* 6. *Les Misérables.* 7. *Cyrano de Bergerac.* 8. *Oliver Twist.* 9. *Pilgrim's Progress.* 10. *Gone with the Wind.*

Or number sets of letters and pass out single letters, one to each person. All the letters in "Tom Sawyer" would be numbered 1, all in "Hamlet" 2, etc. The holders of these letters would get together in their respective sets and try to figure out the book title represented by the letters.

A LITERARY QUIZ. This could be conducted as a sort of "Battle of the Sexes" with the women pitted against the men. Sample questions follow:

1. What quotation is suggested to you by a violet?

> (It is not raining rain to me,
> It's raining violets.)[1]

2. By a primrose?

> (A primrose by a river's brim
> A yellow primrose was to him,
> And it was nothing more.)

3. By pansies? ("Pansies, that's for thoughts.")
4. By a rose labeled "tulip"?

> (A rose
> By any other name would smell as sweet.)

5. By a bouquet of daisies, violets, and lady's-smocks?

[1] From "April Rain," by Robert Loveman.

(When daisies pied and violets blue
And lady-smocks all silver-white
And cuckoo-buds of yellow hue
Do paint the meadows with delight.)

6. By the picture of a tree and a poem?

(Poems are made by fools like me,
But only God can make a tree.)[2]

7. By the picture or figure of a horse? ("My kingdom for a horse!")

8. A needle and thread and a garment with a rip in it? ("A stitch in time saves nine.")

9. A circle?

(He drew a circle that shut me out—
Heretic, rebel, a thing to flout.)[3]

10. An artist's pallet and brush? ("When earth's last picture is painted and the tubes are twisted and dried.")

AUTHORS YOU KNOW. 1. A very tall companion. 2. To tremble; a sharp, pointed, barbed weapon. 3. A native of Scotland. 4. A maker of barrels. 5. Two of them. 6. An exclamation; to rest on the knees. 7. A number; a joint in the middle part of the leg; a male offspring. 8. To purchase; to move rapidly. 9. A young sheep. 10. Finished; obstruction.

Answers: 1. Longfellow. 2. Shakespeare. 3. Scott. 4. Cooper. 5. Twain. 6. O'Neill. 7. Tennyson (Ten-knee-son). 8. Byron (Buy-run). 9. Lamb. 10. Dunbar.

Other authors that might be used in this fashion are Hawthorne, Dickens, London, Masefield (Maize-field), Morley (Mar-lea), Whitman, Noyes, Milton, Markham, Sandburg, Tarkington, Stowe, Service, Galsworthy, Shaw.

[2] From "Trees," *Trees and Other Poems*, by Joyce Kilmer. Copyright 1914 by Doubleday & Company, Inc.
[3] From "Outwitted," by Edwin Markham. Reprinted by permission.

DRAMATIZING BOOKS. Divide into groups and dramatize book titles, fairy stories, or Mother Goose rhymes. One young adult group did an excellent take-off on "Snow White and the Seven Dwarfs."

MY FAVORITE BOOK. Arrange for a snappy symposium on "My Favorite Book and Why." Be sure to line up a few good folk for this feature of the program.

BOOK REVIEW. Another possibility would be a good, brief review of some excellent book.

BOOK EXHIBIT. It would help if a display of good books could be on hand. If interest in a book club should grow out of this meeting, so much the better.

BOOKLAND PARTY

An adult or youth group can have a lot of fun with a party built around the idea of books.

DECORATIONS. Book covers, books, book nooks (reading lamps, tables with varied display of books). Perhaps a local bookstore or the public library will be glad to co-operate.

AUTHORS. Pin the name of an author on the back of each guest as he arrives. When a guest thinks he knows what name is pinned on his back, he reports to the leader. If he is correct, the name is removed from his back and pinned on his lapel. If wrong, he tries again. Cues as to the author's identity are given by other guests. For instance, someone may greet "Shakespeare" with, "How are things going at Stratford?" That ought to be tip enough. If not, other questions may follow, such as, "When did you have your *Midsummer Night's Dream?*"

NAME A BOOK. In this game players wear the same author's name slips pinned on their lapels. Grand march the group into a circle by partners. After getting them into the two-deep circle, have the inner circle reverse and march in the opposite direction from the other circle. When the music stops, players stop and face persons in the opposite circle. Each reads the name of the author the other is wearing, then tries to beat the other person in the naming of a book written by the author. The music starts and the two circles again move in opposite directions. The stopping and calling of book titles is continued for several rounds.

BOOK-TITLE ARTISTS. Give each person a sheet of paper, a pencil, and a pin. Ask each one to draw on the paper something that suggests the title of any well-known book. When through, they pin the sheet of paper on and mix around. On another sheet of paper they write names of other guests and the book titles they represent. Example: Picture of a hat being blown away by a gust of wind—*Gone with the Wind.* This game would make a good mixer.

BOOK DRAMAGRAMS. Divide the crowd into several groups. Give each group a book title to dramatize. After the dramatization, which may be simple or elaborate, the other groups guess what book title is being presented. Titles like *Midsummer Night's Dream, Treasure Island, Vanity Fair, Hamlet, Tom Sawyer, A Lantern in Her Hand, Gone with the Wind, The Robe, The Big Fisherman, The Taming of the Shrew,* and *The Call of the Wild* would be easy to use in this manner.

LITERARY QUIZ. Keep the same groups intact. Read the questions in the quiz aloud. The first group to have someone give the correct answer scores a point.

1. What great novel has a hero who fights windmills? *Don Quixote.*

2. What famous novel did Lew Wallace write about the early Christians? *Ben Hur.*

3. In what novel does the writer have three men enter into an agreement to stand by one another? *The Three Musketeers.*

4. One of the greatest novels ever written tells the story of an escaped convict. What is the novel? *Les Misérables.*

5. What novel tells the story of a great New Testament character? *The Apostle* by Asch, or *The Big Fisherman* by Douglas.

6. In what poem does John Masefield tell the story of the conversion of Saul Kane, a prize fighter? *The Everlasting Mercy.*

7. In what book does Charles M. Sheldon tell the story of a group of young people who tried to do what they thought Jesus would do? *In His Steps.*

8. What novel by Lloyd Douglas builds its story about a happening at the Crucifixion? *The Robe.*

9. What play attempts to portray the family life of Jesus? *Family Portrait.*

10. What play by Shakespeare is a tragedy about a Moor? *Othello.*

BOOK TITLE ART EXHIBIT. Place around the room numbered exhibits (pictures, articles) representing titles of familiar books. Each guest is given a paper on which he identifies the various book titles. Suggestions:

1. *Penrod.* (A pen, a tiny rod.) 2. *The Scarlet Letter.* (A red letter on a card.) 3. *Kentucky Cardinal.* (Picture of a cardinal and map of Kentucky.) 4. *The Blue Bird.* (Picture of a bluebird.) 5. *Ivanhoe.* (Pictures of an eye, a moving van, a hoe.) 6. *The Raven.* (Picture of a blackbird.) 7. *Moby Dick.* (A whale cut from white paper and mounted on black background. 8. *Looking Backward.* (Picture of a man looking backward.) 9. *Little Women.* (Picture of tall

53

men and tiny women.) 10. *Vanity Fair.* (Picture of compact and entrance to fair grounds.)

Other suggestions: *Black Beauty, White Fang, Red Rock, The House of the Seven Gables,* etc.

Variations. Titles of poems and plays may be included in the exhibit.

BOOKLOVER'S PI. Provide each guest with a piece of paper on which twenty book titles or authors are listed. However, the letters in each title have been jumbled. Opposite each name there should be space for the correct title. Examples: Haws (Shaw), Ginklip (Kipling), Ope (Poe), Now log fell (Longfellow), Their wit (Whittier), Quote do nix (*Don Quixote*), Halt me (*Hamlet*), Dans grub (Sandburg), Warn pink live (*Rip Van Winkle*), King not rat (Tarkington), Aw nit (Twain), Altop (Plato), Wit let lemon (*Little Women*), Doin hob ro (*Robin Hood*), Rob ten (Brontë), Kate club bay (*Black Beauty*), A sheep rakes (Shakespeare), Ye hat rack (Thackeray), Fame is led (Masefield), Gas loud (Douglas).

In selecting books and authors for the various games be sure to use those that are within the interest and knowledge of the group attending the party.

A RODEO PARTY

Here's a party enjoyed by one group; it starts with a whoop, and ends in soft harmonies around a campfire. So shake out a lariat and latch on! Invitations informed everyone it was to be a cowboy roundup, and they were all to come "Western"—that is, dressed in loud shirt, levis, tengallon hats, gay kerchiefs, or whatever they could find. The boys thought of things like toy six-shooters, holsters, beaded belts, and snakeskin hatbands.

DECORATIONS. If you are lucky, decorations

might include an authentic deerskin or bearskin, but a shape cut from a huge sheet of brown wrapping paper will serve as well. If you are in doubt, label it with a sign "Bearskin." This sign idea gives unlimited scope for decorations and will lighten the duties of the cleanup committee when everyone wants to take the signs home for souvenirs! Label one corner "Hoosegow—Free Eats," and put all the "dudes" (those who fail to dress in costume) behind bars until they pay a forfeit. Another sign at the door instructs all who enter to "Park yur shootin' arns here," and a "brandin' stashun" near by provides each cowpoke with a brand, stamped on the back of the hands with a rubber stamp, which may be concocted from little brother's printing set. Other decorations include a corral complete with stick horses, rocking horses, saddles, bridles, and what you can find.

GAMES. "Break the broncos" by having outfits line up for a relay. First one of each line runs some twenty-five feet to a stick three-feet long, places one end of the stick on the floor, puts his hands on the top and his head down on his hands. After running three times around the stick in this position, the player must run back to his line and touch off the next player. Just try it for a dizzy ride!

The old favorite of "Cat and Mouse" can be called "Cowboy and Maverick," and "Jacob and Rachel" can be renamed "Wild Bill and Calamity Jane."

Just to let the townsfolk know you are doing something different, organize teams as posses to look for "varmints" and go outdoors. Each leader of an outfit is given a coin and at each corner he is to flip it—tails, the group must turn right for a block; heads, turn left for a block. At the end of half an hour, all race back to the starting spot. First ones back are winners.

After such a strenuous game with some a mile away at the

55

end of the half hour and others only a few blocks, a quiet table game is in order, followed by refreshments. Fresh milk and gingerbread will go over mighty good. The setting of an open fireplace or an outdoor campfire will inspire the cowhands to tune up with "Home on the Range," "Spring-time in the Rockies," "Red River Valley," and other favor-ites. A big cardboard moon and stars might suggest "Prairie Moon" and "Red Wing." If a few have learned the songs before the party, then try the "Night Herding Song," "Bury Me Not," and "Cowboy's Meditation," ending with friend-ship circle and short prayer. You'll have a good time, so let's round up the gang, and let 'er buck!

—REEVA SCHMIDT, Pendleton, Oregon

A MUSICAL PARTY

> Do mi sol do,
> Come on the run!
> Musical show,
> It will be fun!
> Don't fail to go;
> That would be dumb!
> Come one! Come all!
> Both short and tall!
> Friday at eight;
> Now don't be late.

Have two persons or two groups sing this invitation. The first singer would sing "Do mi sol do." The second singer would come down the scale with "Come on the run." On "Musical show" the first singer would sing up the scale again, raising the pitch one tone. Singer Number Two would come down the scale again. The next two lines would be sung in similar fashion, again raising the pitch one tone.

56

The last four lines would be intoned, the singers holding the pitch of low C, the note on which "dumb" is sung. First singer would intone "Come one!" The second singer would sing "Come all!" And so they would alternate to the end.

COSTUME. Guests may be requested to come in a costume representing some familiar song. For instance, a girl dressed as a Scots lassie 'might be "Annie Laurie." A cowboy could represent "Home on the Range." Other songs that would be appropriate and easy to represent are "Jeannie with the Light Brown Hair," "Trees," "Indian Love Call," "Tramp, Tramp, Tramp" (three hobos together), "Kathleen Mavourneen," "Wearin' o' the Green," "Long, Long Trail" (a dress with a long train), "Jingle Bells," "Old Folks at Home" (couple made up as old people).

MUSICAL MIXER. Each person will go around listing names of persons and songs represented. As persons meet, they greet one another by humming a few bars of the particular song each represents.

SONG SCRAMBLE. Give to each guest the title of some song—"My Old Kentucky Home," "She'll Be Comin' 'Round the Mountain," "Sweetheart," "Down in the Valley," and the like.

There will be anywhere from four to eight people who get the same song. These people get together; and when the leader calls for it, they sing their song. Allow a little time for rehearsing.

RHYTHM RINKY-DINKS. Each group will select a familiar song and, after a bit of rehearsing, will clap out the rhythm of the music. The other groups will try to guess the song being used.

DUMB ARTIST. Divide into two or more groups. Each group decides on three or four song titles, writing the

57

titles down on separate slips of paper, one title to a slip. Two captains are appointed to take charge of the slips. They exchange slips. Now the captain of one of the teams calls up one of the members of his side and presents him with one slip. That player tries to communicate the song title to his team by drawing on a blackboard or on newsprint things that represent the various words. As soon as a player on the side gets the idea, he shouts the title, or the group starts singing the song.

For instance, suppose the song title is "Then You'll Remember Me." The artist would draw a cup of tea and immediately after it the picture of a hen. If this does not get over to the group, he tries the letter *T*, followed by the picture of the hen. If they still don't get it, he draws a very thin person and shakes his head as he points to it, meaning "not *thin*," but (pointing to the *T* and the hen) *then*. By this time someone will likely have gotten it. Then he draws a picture of a huge fireplace with a blazing log and "Merry Christmas" written above on the mantlepiece. It may take some time to get "Yule" out of that. Then he draws a picture of a puzzled person (question marks will indicate puzzled state). Next he draws the same person smiling and a light above his head, indicating "the light has dawned." By this time, perhaps, someone has recognized it, but waits for him to draw a likeness of himself. "Then You'll Remember Me," shouts the guessing side. "Down in the Valley," "The Blue-Tailed Fly," "The Old Oaken Bucket," "School Days," "Shine on, Harvest Moon," "I've Got Shoes," "Ol' Man River," and "My Old Kentucky Home" are some suggested songs.

MUSICAL CHAIRS. Have chairs in a circle facing center. Each chair is occupied. Extra players stand in the center. When the music plays, all players march around the circle, the extras getting into the line of march. When the music stops, players try to get a seat. Those who fail drop out of the game. One chair is removed. If the crowd is large, several chairs may be removed. The music starts again and players march till it stops. Again there is the scramble for seats. This continues until only one player is left seated.

MYSTERY MUSIC. One player retires from the room. The others decide on some action for him to perform when he returns, and the spot where he is to stand. The only clues he gets are furnished by the music. When it is soft, he knows he is wrong. Loud music indicates he is nearing the place where he is to perform. It reaches a climax as he reaches the point. Then he begins to try various actions. Again loud and soft music furnish the clues. For instance, the player may be required to lift a pen from one person's pocket and hand it to another.

MUSICAL FLOP. Players march to music. When the music stops, all players flop to the floor in sitting position. Last person down is out. In a large crowd eliminate the last three or four. Keep this up until only a few remain.

MUSICAL PROGRAM AND SING. Climax the program with a good musical program and a sing in which everyone takes part.

STORYTELLERS' FIESTA

Here is an idea that is suitable for indoors or outdoors. It can be made a very colorful affair. In fact it could easily become an annual feature in the recreation program, since it lends itself to endless variety.

GENERAL HINTS. (1) Select the best storytellers available. (2) Check on all stories to insure variety, appropriateness, and brevity. Ten minutes is the top limit on length of stories. Five minutes is even better. (3) Achieve an atmosphere of informality. A good master of ceremonies will help at this point. (4) Climax the fiesta with some beautiful story such as "The Bell Maker" (Chinese), "The White Flame," or "The Selfish Giant" (abridged). (5) Draw the audience into the program with some such story as "Mother, Mother, May I Go?" "A Terrible Ghost Story," "A Halloween Romance," "Paying the Rent," "The King with a Terrible Temper," "Clappertown," or "The Lion Hunt."

If the fiesta is held outdoors, a campfire should make a good setting. Decorative lanterns hung from the branches of trees will lend color. If possible have the storytellers dress in costume. One group had their storytellers—"strolling minstrels," they called them—come on the scene dramatically in an old covered wagon. As they approached, they were singing "Long, Long Ago."

The master of ceremonies may introduce the various features in rhyme. A few suggestions follow:

INDIAN TALES.

> Wigwam gay and firelight's gleam,
> Braves and squaws and starlit stream;
> Indian legends—what a store!
> Hear them once, you'll want some more.

"How Old Man Made the Races" or some other Indian legend.

PIONEER TALES.

> A covered wagon comes 'round the bend
> With tales of brave pioneers, no end.

FAIRY TALES.

> To fairyland let's take a trip;
> The magic carpet is your ship.

60

> Sit tight and soon your ears will hear
> Of fairy queens and maidens dear,
> Of witches, magic, heroes bold—
> The thrilling tales from ages told.

"The Red Shoes," "Rumplestiltskin," or any good fairy story. See Andersen's, Grimm's, or other collections of such tales.

PLANTATION TALES.

> Cotton fields white and gardens rare,
> Old Southern tales will be your fare.

An Uncle Remus story like "Tar Baby" or a selection from Bradford's *Ol' Man Adam and His Chillun'*, perhaps "Little David." "The Tall Corn" from *Grandfather Tales*, by Richard Chase, would be good.

TALES FROM OTHER LANDS.

> Stories from lands beyond the sea
> Will now intrigue both you and me.
> A story's a story the wide world 'round,
> A story's a story where'er it's found.

"Bunny in the Moon," from Mukerji's *Hindu Fables for Little Children* (India), "The Bell Maker" (China), or any of the tales from Aesop, Andersen, or Grimm. *Folk Tales of All Nations*, by Frank Harold Lee, has a wealth of material in it.

OTHER TALES.
A good ghost story, a stunt story like "The Poor Little Match Girl," catches and brain teasers ("The Ranch Story," "The Animals and the Circus," "How's Your Dog?" etc.), and tall tales offer other possibilities.

One college group had a "Liar's Convention" in which tall stories were featured. A popular collection of such stories is *Yankee Doodle's Cousins*, by Anne Malcolmson. It contains Paul Bunyan stories, "John Darling," "John Henry," "Pecos Bill" and many other tales that amuse and entertain. For a tall-tale evening you would not want to leave out James Whitcomb Riley's "Bear Story."

AN ORIENTAL PARTY

An appropriate party for the beginning of the year would be an Oriental party. The Chinese celebrate their New Year around the end of January. This therefore would be an appropriate month for this party.

INVITATIONS. The invitation could be written on small cards containing Oriental pictures or characters. Posters displaying Japanese lanterns done in colors would be effective in publicizing the party.

DECORATIONS. Dragons, kites, colorful lanterns, cherry blossoms, incense burners, tapestries, scrolls, and wall hangings would lend the proper Oriental atmosphere.

Some of these decorations could be made with paper and crayons.

COSTUMES. Guests may be encouraged to wear colorful Oriental costumes—mandarin coats, bright kimonos, etc. In any case it would be advisable to have members of the reception committee in costume.

PROGRAM

KUNG HI. Begin the party with this mixer. In Japan and China it is the custom for people to dress up and go visiting on New Year's Day. Do a grand march. When the music stops, each person must meet at least five different people, greeting them in Chinese fashion, bowing low, and saying, "Kung Hi! Kung Hi!" ("I humbly wish you joy!") The reply is "Sin Hi! Sin Hi!" ("May joy be yours!") As the music starts up, each one begins marching with the person he is greeting at the time. The pianist stops frequently to allow for greetings until the group has been well mixed.

CAT AND MOUSE. This old game is popular in China. The group forms a circle, holding hands. One person has been chosen as cat and one as mouse. The mouse stands inside the circle while the cat stands outside. The circle revolves around the mouse. The cat bides his time outside the circle. When it stops, he darts in and the mouse darts out. The cat pursues the mouse, but he must follow exactly the path taken by the mouse. Thus they wind in and out until the cat catches the mouse. The cat then becomes the mouse, and a new cat is chosen.

YANETSUKI (Japanese). This game is similar to "battledore and shuttlecock" (badminton). The idea is to keep the shuttlecock in the air as long as possible. Shuttle-

63

cocks may be made of large corks and chicken feathers. Ask guests to bring their tennis or badminton rackets. Divide into two equal groups. Each group forms a circle and is provided with a shuttlecock. At the signal to start, the shuttlecock is batted into the air in each circle. The circle keeping its shuttlecock in the air longest wins a point. The winner of three out of five may be declared champion.

A variation of this game would be to use a large toy balloon. In this case each side may have a balloon and proceed as with the shuttlecock, hitting the balloon with the open hand. Or a row of chairs may divide the two teams and one balloon may be batted back and forth over the barrier. When the balloon touches the floor on one side, a point is scored by their opponents.

YOOT (Korean). This is a popular game in Korea at New Year's time. Divide the crowd into groups of four. Furnish each group with the equipment for "Yoot." This consists of a cardboard or paper diagram and four yoot sticks. A Korean missionary said the sticks were twigs split into two pieces and about one foot in length. Smaller twigs may be used if desired.

The diagram is a circle or square of twenty spots. These may be made by dipping a cork in ink and stamping it on a sheet of paper. The circle is divided into four equal segments by a lightly marked cross. A center spot and two extra spots on each arm of the cross complete the diagram.

Each player has four men with which to play. These

64

are disks which may be made of linoleum or heavy cardboard in colors. Each player would have a set of four in a particular color—four reds, four blues, four yellows, or four greens.

When the sticks are tossed up into the air and land, their meaning is as follows: 1. One flat side up, called "pig," move one spot. 2. Two flat sides up, called "dog," move two spots. 3. Three flat sides up, called "knel," move three spots. 4. Four flat sides up, called "yoot," move five spots and get an extra throw. 5. No flat side up, called "mo," move four spots and get an extra throw.

Players take turns in casting the sticks and move one of the disks to the spot indicated. The object of the game is to get around the board and back to the starting point.

If a player gets a disk exactly on an intersection, he may move down from that intersection, thus making it unnecessary to travel all the way around the board.

If a player lands on a spot occupied by an opponent, he captures the opponent and sends him "back home." The player who gets all four of his men around first wins.

MAN, GUN, TIGER (Korean). This is an adaptation of the Japanese game "Jonkenpon" (stone, paper, scissors). Two sides line up facing each other. Each side decides what it will represent, whether man, gun, or tiger. If man, the players hold their two forefingers up to their lips to represent a flowing mustache. If gun, the players aim, as if shooting, and yell "Bang!" If tiger, hold the hands up, claw-fashion, and snarl, showing teeth. The man beats the gun, because he shoots the gun. The gun beats the tiger. And the tiger beats the man. Score points.

SHADOW SHOW. Shadow puppets are distinctly Oriental in origin. The Chinese have used them for centuries. The puppets can be made of construction paper rubbed with linseed oil to make them translucent. They will show through the screen in colors. Use Waverly window curtain for screen. Stick puppets to show only in black may be made of cardboard. Present some Oriental folk tale in a shadow show of this sort.

FORTUNETELLING.   A favorite "indoor sport" of China is foretunetelling. All sorts of devices are used. One of these popular in the United States is "Chi Chi." Have a fortunetelling booth.

REFRESHMENTS.   Any of the following may be served: Chinese tea, candied apples, preserved ginger, dried coconut, rice or almond cakes, litchi nuts, or almonds.

A WHAT'S YOUR NUMBER PARTY

As each guest arrives, pin a number on him—either one, two, three, or four. Guests wear these numbers throughout the evening.

NUMBER QUARTETS.   When ready to begin, have each person seek out the three other numbers to complete the quartet. Thus a three will look for a one, a two, and a four. Each quartet must render a song. They probably will rend it note from note.

KNOW YOUR NUMBERS.   See Party Games section.

STOCK EXCHANGE.   Give to each person a small envelope containing ten beans. Give each also a number. The numbers will run consecutively from one to whatever number of persons are present. Announce that one of the numbers is the lucky number. When the market is open, players buy and sell numbers, using the beans as money, trying to get the secret lucky number. After a brisk session of bidding, the leader announces the market is closed. He then calls in certain numbers. A player is not out of the game even though his number is called, leaving him with none. As soon as he is ready, the leader opens the market again for bidding. There is spirited buying and selling. The leader closes the market at intervals to call in certain numbers. Finally all numbers are called in except the lucky number. The player with that number and the player having the largest number of beans each receive some sort of prize.

NUMBERED CHAIRS. Players are seated in a circle or semicircle. They number off, beginning with chair Number One. Number One begins the game by calling some other number. That player must answer immediately by calling another number. Players failing to answer immediately by calling another number go to the foot. As players move up, their numbers are changed accordingly. The idea is to catch the top three or four napping and send them to the end of the line.

HUMAN MATH AND HISTORY. Make two sets of numbers from 0 to 9 on large pieces of cardboard. Hang numbers around the necks of players of two sides. Then the leader calls certain problems in mathematics, such as "2 times 2" or "3 plus 6." Or he calls questions about dates in history, such as "In what year did Columbus discover America?" The first team to have the player or players with the proper numbers to stand scores a point.

COUNT TO THIRTY. See Party Games section.

NUMBER QUIZ. Make out a series of questions that can be answered by numbers. A few suggestions:

1. How many red and how many white bars in the American flag? (7 red, 6 white.)

2. What was the number of stars in the original American flag? (13.)

3. What number of players form a regulation team in the following sports: Baseball? (9.) Softball? (9.) Volleyball? (6.) Ice hockey? (6.) Basketball? (5. Girls' rules; 6.)

4. How many months of the year have 31 days? (7.)

5. How many petals has a tulip? (6.)

NUMBER REFRESHMENTS. Give guests a choice of any three of five numbers. The meaning of the numbers is kept secret. "One" may be an empty plate, "two" a piece of cake, "three" a glass of water, "four" a dish of ice cream, and "five" a toothpick. After having some fun with those who ordered the wrong numbers, see that they get some refreshments.

LET'S GO BEAR HUNTING

Select a clear evening when the stars are shining brightly. Ask each person to bring along a blanket and a flashlight. Huh? Hunt bears with a blanket and flashlight? Yup! That's right! You see, we're going to hunt the Great Bear and the Little Bear, for this is to be a "stargazers" party.

Take along some person who knows about stars—their names, where and when they can be found, stories about them. If there can be several such persons in the group, so much the better.

The main objects of the search are the Great Bear and the Little Bear, otherwise known as the Big Dipper and the Little Dipper. Go out to a park or some open space away from all artificial lights. Place blankets on the ground and lie or sit on them as a leader traces out the oldest bears in the world with a flashlight. Discover other constellations also.

Weave in stories and legends of the stars as they are spotted. The early people of Egypt and India invented many interesting stories about them. Read *Field Book of the Skies*, by Olcott and Putnam, for legends, charts, and facts.

It is interesting to note that in India the Big Dipper was known as the Seven Shiners or the Seven Wise Men. In Egypt the people called it the Ear of Osiris. In China it was the Ladle. The Arabs called it the Coffin because of its slow movement around the North Star. The four stars formed the coffin. The three others were the mourners. To the Christian Arabs it was the Grave of Lazarus. To the early Hebrew it was the Bier, to the Syrians, the Wild Boar, and to the Druids, Arthur's Chariot. Other names given this group of stars are David's Chariot, Charles's Wain (wagon), the Plough, and Job's Coffin. But among early peoples the most popular name was the Great Bear.

The Arctic got its name from this constellation. The Greek word for bear is *arktos*. The Great Bear revolves around the North Star. Thus it gave its name to the Arctic region.

Have someone repeat Ps. 19—"The heavens declare. . . ." Sing a stanza of "This Is My Father's World." Benediction and good night.

A MOTHER GOOSE PARTY

Itiskit, Itasket, we knew you would ask it,
Why give grownups a Mother Goose party?
Because they need release from tension;
Because they need more'n we can mention;
A chance for fun and relaxation,
A chance to enjoy the sensation
Of dropping their dignity aside,
And letting their nerves take a ride.

Come dressed as a Mother Goose character.

This is a "kid" party for grownups. Guests will come dressed to represent Little Bopeep; Little Boy Blue; Mary with her little lamb; Tom, Tom, the Piper's Son; Humpty Dumpty; Mary, Mary, Quite Contrary; The Old Woman Who Lived in a Shoe; Mother Hubbard; and other Mother

Goose characters. For those who fail to come in costume, provide paper collars with large crepe-paper bow ties. A fine may be assessed also for such failure. Whatever money is obtained in this way goes in the Christmas fund.

The Program

CONCENTRIC CIRCLE MARCH. Men on the inner circle, women on the other circle. The two circles move in opposite directions to music. When the music stops, as it does at brief intervals, the circles face one another and each person starts quoting the nursery rhyme he represents. Those that are not wearing costumes adopt some rhyme for their own. After several opportunities to meet various ones in this fashion, move on to the next game.

MOTHER GOOSE RHYMES. Divide into two groups. One side starts by singing a nursery rhyme in "Throw It Out the Window" fashion. The tune is "Polly Wolly Doodle." The other side responds with another rhyme. So it continues back and forth until one of the groups is unable to respond.

RHYME DRAMA. Divide into a number of small groups. Give to each group a slip of paper with a Mother Goose rhyme on it. Ask them to arrange a brief dramatization of the rhyme. Insist on brevity. The average group will show great resourcefulness in arranging for costuming and in acting out their rhymes.

PETER, PETER. Have a clever couple prepare an original dramatic version of "Peter, Peter, Pumpkin Eater" or some other rhyme. A couple could present this particular rhyme in two scenes. Scene 1 would be Peter's version of why he couldn't keep her. Scene 2 would be the wife's version.

REVISED RHYMES. Divide into small groups and have each group work out one or more revised up-to-the-minute rhymes to read to the whole crowd. For instance:

Roses are red,
Violets are blue,
Sugar is sweet,
But fattening.

Or "Peter, Peter" might end this way:

Put her in a pumpkin shell
And there she raised all kinds
of vegetables in her garden.

71

REFRESHMENTS. Serve Jack Horner plum pie and milk.

MYSTERY PARTY

Do you want to know what is to be
In the years that are ahead of thee?
Then come to the Party Mystery,
And you shall see what you shall see.

MYSTERY CONVERSATION. March in two concentric circles in opposite directions. When the music stops, the circles stop and face each other. Each person should face a partner. For one minute these partners discuss the subject announced by the leader. The music starts at the end of one minute and the players start marching again in opposite directions. So it goes until the leader announces the end. The first subject announced is "Me," and each person tells his partner about himself—what he likes most, what he dislikes, what his ambitions are, or whatever he wants to say about himself. For the second subject of conversation the leader announces "You," and the players say nice things about each other—recall exploits where the partner played a prominent part, and the like. Then follow, in turn, the following subjects: soldiers, trains, England, Russia, and Yugoslavia. When they have finished this cycle, the leader announces that there has been a mysterious subject interwoven with all the subjects discussed, and asks if anyone has discovered it. If no one is able to answer correctly, the leader may tip them off to the fact that the subjects announced spelled the mysterious subject in acrostic. Thus combining the first letters of each subject will give the answer. The mysterious word is "mystery."

FORTUNETELLING DEVICES. About the room or the house have numerous fortunetelling devices—in-

72

visible ink messages made by writing with lemon juice, fortune spinning wheels, gypsy palmists, dart boards, and various blindfold arrangements, such as the familiar dishes with ashes, flour, sugar, etc. The guests try the various fortunetelling devices.

THE CRYSTAL-GAZER.   Give the crystal-gazer a good build-up. Introduce him as Gunga Din, a Hindu mystic, who can tell the future and read minds unerringly. Have members in the group write questions on slips of

paper provided by ushers. Each person must sign the question with his own name. These slips are then taken up by the ushers. The ushers, unnoticed, pass these slips, or some of them, to confederates at the back of the room. Then they come to the front of the room, pulling the slips (fake ones) out of their pockets. Or better yet, all ushers turn their slips over to one usher and he takes them forward. They really hand him blank slips. The others they keep in another pocket to hand over to the confederate. The usher with the slips puts them into a large urn or pan and touches a match to them with elaborate ceremony. While the slips are burning, the crystal-gazer, ten feet away, appears to be in deep thought. After the slips are reduced to ashes, he begins to come out of his trance. Directly he amazes the group, and particularly the person who wrote the question, by quoting a question, giving the name, and making some sort of answer. Then he calls another, and this is repeated until five or more questions have been called and answered. The secret is this—the crystal-gazer wears a turban. He has

73

earphones connected with wires which contact metal plates on the soles of his shoes. Two small metal plates on the floor just beyond a rug are connected by a wire to a phone in some room in the building. This phone is operated by dry cell batteries. The confederate who has received some or all of the original questions picks out a few of them to read over the phone. The crystal-gazer makes his connections, looks intently into the crystal, receives a question and name over the phone, and proceeds to give his mind-reading demonstration. This stunt should be tried out beforehand to make sure that everything is working perfectly.

After the mind-reading exhibition the crystal-gazer may do some gazing, offering prophecies of things to happen ten years hence. Among the prophecies should be some concerning people in the group.

BLACK MAGIC. Try out a few exhibitions of black magic (see Party Games section). Here is a good one:

TOUCH WHICH? Lay seven or more articles on the floor. A confederate goes out of the room. The group has someone touch a particular article of the seven or more on the floor. When the confederate comes back, the leader touches some of the articles on the floor. When he touches the right one, the confederate indicates it by saying, "That's it." The secret lies in this: The third article counting from the leader's left is the tip-off article. When that is touched, the confederate knows the second one touched after that is it. The leader further confuses the group by occasionally stepping over on the opposite side of the articles. That changes the number three article, for the counting is always begun from the leader's left. If the leader admonishes the confederate that "this one is hard," or "watch carefully," that means that number five, counting from the leader's left, is the tip-off article.

74

FOOTBALL PARTY

Decorate with footballs suspended from doorways, chandeliers, and the like. Use school colors in pennants and streamers.

SCRIMMAGE. Conduct a grand march where players assemble in twos, threes, fours, fives, sixes, and on up to tens as they march, according to the blasts on a whistle. Thus, when the leader blows three blasts, players march by threes; when he blows four, they form in fours, and so on.

TABLE FOOTBALL. Use a ping-pong ball for a football. Players blow this ball across a table, trying to cross the goal line with it. Their opponents, with their mouths on a level with the table, try to blow it back and across the opposite side. After each success the ball is placed back in the center of the table. When the whistle blows, all players start blowing.

BOARD FOOTBALL. Mark off football plays on a large piece of beaverboard. Use darts to indicate plays. Or place hooks on the beaverboard and use Mason jar rings. Or mark off plays on the board and toss disks to make the plays.

BOWL FOOTBALL. Set up ten pop bottles or tenpins at either end of a twenty-foot space. Under each bottle place a card with some play indicated on it, such as "Forward pass—twenty-yard gain," "End run—loss of five yards," "Line buck—five-yard gain," "Touchdown," etc. Players bowl a baseball, softball, or small rubber ball. A team gets four downs to make ten yards. If it succeeds, it continues to "hold the ball." A small football is moved back and forth on the field to indicate the plays. The team on the defensive has the privilege of rearranging the cards

75

at their end after each play, if it desires to do so. Twenty bottles and twenty plays would add interest to the game. Play five-minute quarters.

For refreshments serve hot dogs and pop.

PROGRESSIVE ANAGRAMS PARTY

Anagrams is a game that wears well. Those who do not know it need to be introduced to the joys of the game. Those who already know it will likely be enthusiastic anagram fans.

Play four to a table. Ring a bell to stop play and count scores. The two high-score players at each table progress, except that the winners at table Number One stay put while the losers at that table go to the foot table.

The committee should check to get the necessary number of anagram sets. If they are not available, cheap sets can be found at the ten-cent store.

Players will count their words to determine who progresses. If the bell rings in the midst of a round, the players not having their turn shall be allowed to play until the round is completed.

FUTURAMA

In Edward Bellamy's Looking Backward the main character wakes up in the year 2000. The world is changed. Divide into two or more groups. Give each group fifteen minutes or so to work out a brief skit that portrays the changes in the world in the twenty-first century. Here is a good opportunity to exercise the imagination. Dress, eating habits, travel, and other customs could come in for some good imaginative slants.

CHAPTER III

Autumn Parties

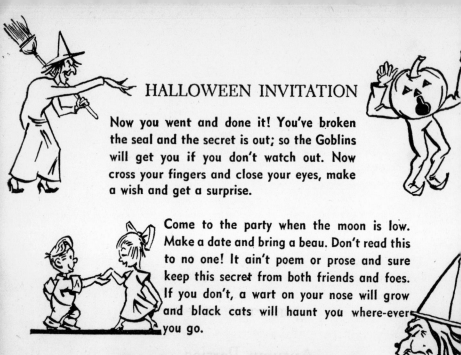

HALLOWEEN INVITATION

Now you went and done it! You've broken the seal and the secret is out; so the Goblins will get you if you don't watch out. Now cross your fingers and close your eyes, make a wish and get a surprise.

Come to the party when the moon is low. Make a date and bring a beau. Don't read this to no one! It ain't poem or prose and sure keep this secret from both friends and foes. If you don't, a wart on your nose will grow and black cats will haunt you where-ever you go.

Now take my advice and write down this date, and be there on time and don't be late. Slip through the back alley and around the block. Sneak up to the door and KNOCK, KNOCK, KNOCK, on the church basement door, just half a square, from the railroad track—be sure and be there! On Friday night, October twenty-nine, Don't dress in your best, old clothes are fine. On that dark night when the clock strikes eight, remember the time—don't be late!

OCTOBER
29

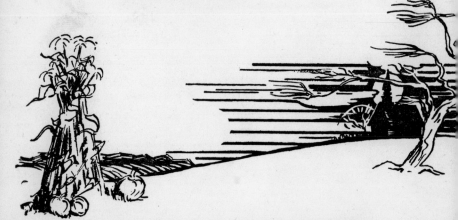

Autumn Parties

SEPTEMBER SHADOW SOCIAL

Shadows are falling
Voices are calling
Come to our party at eight.
Twenty-first of September,
You had better remember,
If you want fun, it's a date!

IN THE SHADE OF THE OLD APPLE TREE. Players march in two concentric circles, the outer circle clockwise and the inner circle counterclockwise. When music stops or whistle blows, circles stop and face each other. Each player must make complimentary remarks about the other, the more extravagant the better. That's the "applesauce" "in the shade of the old apple tree." Continue for several rounds.

SHADOWS OF THE PAST. Work out some shadow shows presenting old-fashioned dress styles (hats, hoop skirts, bustles, etc.), historic events, local happenings, and the like. This would be a good place for the old shadow show stunt, "The Operation." The doctor uses saw, hatchet, big knife, funnel for anesthesia. He takes out various things from the patient's interior—string of wieners, alarm clock (which goes off), book, etc.

Hang a sheet. Place a light about six feet behind it. A flashlight will do. Try out shadow to get proper effects.

SHADOW OF THE FUTURE. Present shadows showing hat styles for the future, prophecies concerning

79

well-known people in the group, and possible coming events.

SHADOW FOLLIES. Put on a brief shadow show skit. Perhaps an original one can be worked out. There are some suggestions in *The Fun Encyclopedia.* Another source is *Funny Shadow Pantomimes,* by Elizabeth Hart (Eldridge Entertainment House, Franklin, Ohio).

REFRESHMENTS. Lemonade ("made in the shade and stirred with a spade") and wafers.

SPOOKS DELUXE SOCIAL

INVITATION

Let no engagement nor any fluke
Keep you from dressing up like a spook
And coming to meet with the SPOOKS DELUXE.

Friday, October 31   8:15 P.M.

COSTUMES. Guests will be requested to dress like spooks. An old sheet and an old pillowcase will answer the purpose. Or large paper sacks with eyes cut in them will do for the heads. Guests are not to unmask until directed to do so by the committee. Much of the fun will come from guessing who is who.

WITCH'S ROLL CALL. As each guest enters, he is given a number and a slip of paper on which is written some trade, profession, or activity, such as sailor, policeman, auto salesman, milliner, lawyer, doctor, preacher, politician, ballplayer (baseball, football, or basketball), golf player, jockey, bus driver, teacher. The witch takes her place on her throne and calls the numbers one at a time. As a player's number is called, he performs in pantomime to represent his particular trade, profession, or activity. The

80

others guess what he is representing. Then they try to guess his name. The player then unmasks and takes his place in the crowd.

GHOST WHISTLE. One guest is blindfolded. He stands in the center of a circle of guests. A whistle is passed around the circle until the blinded player shouts, "Stop!" Whoever has the whistle must blow it and remain standing in the same spot. The one blindfolded tries to pick out the one who blew the whistle and then identify him by touching his face. If he is unable to identify him from this contact, he may require the player to laugh. The laugher may try to disguise his laugh, of course. If the guesser is not successful, he tries again. He is given three guesses. If he is successful, the whistle blower must take his place in the center, and the game continues.

GHOSTS' MEET. This is a relay race, with each team competing in turn. Time is kept to determine the winning team.

The team is divided into two equal lines, standing diagonally opposite each other at opposite ends of the room. At a given signal the two at the head of each line are blindfolded by one of their number. They race to meet each other, shake hands and say, "Glad to meet you!" Then they remove the blindfolds and rush back to their respective lines, where they blindfold the next two to race. This continues until all the members of the team have sallied forth to shake hands and return. The home team gives the racers advice to help them discover each other. Opponents must not give wrong directions.

SPOOKS' CONVENTION

Boo! Boo! Ain't you scared?
Boo! Boo! Come prepared!

81

Better get ready for the Spooks' Convention!
It's an occasion worthy of mention.
Dress to look spookified, both man and maid;
Come for a good time, and don't be afraid.

DECORATIONS

SILHOUETTE LANTERNS. Make lanterns out of cardboard (or parchment or fiberboard) and cellophane. Silhouette pictures cut from black opaque paper and fastened to the cellophane on the inside—witches, black cats, skull and crossbones.

SPOOK LIGHTS. Cut old coffee cans off short. Mount on ends of flashlights. The end of the can should be cut out in various designs—a jack-o'-lantern face, a skull, a cat. Cover the open spaces with cellophane or tissue paper. Flash on and off in dark rooms and passageways.

FLOOR DECORATIONS. Shocks of corn; a caldron and a synthetic campfire; pumpkin jack-o'-lanterns; corn shucks and straw.

WALL DECORATIONS. Black cats; witches; skull and cross-bones; booths made of black and orange crepe paper; crepe-paper fringes and festoons.

LIGHTS AND CEILING. Cover with the silhouette lanterns described above, or with blue cellophane or paper. Make Halloween shades for lights and chandeliers. Festoon or mat the ceiling with black and orange crepe paper. Drop serpentine strips from the crepe paper.

GHOSTS, GOBLINS, WITCHES. These are effective in dark corners and passageways. Detachable cold and clammy hands, noisemaking instruments, ticklers, and the like should be used. A giant ghost stands in one corner. He grows tall and short by turns. This is achieved by the ghost standing under a sheet attached to a broom handle. On the

top is a ghost head. This implement the ghost raises to produce the giant effect.

GENERAL HINTS.   Insist that all guests come dressed as spooks. An old sheet and pillowcase will do the job. Cut a hole in the sheet and drop over the shoulders. Cut eyes, nose, and mouth in the pillowcase, and perhaps make ears.

Have a silent ghost at the door pointing the direction guests are to go. The guests are thus steered into a room where another ghost (or several) shows them to seats. Silence is required.

Announce that the convention begins promptly at 8:17 or 8:31 and begin on time.

THE CONVENTION BEGINS

The spook chairman calls the meeting to order by a tap of the gavel. He then leads the group (or calls on a spook song leader to do so) in the convention song, sung to the tune of "Auld Lang Syne":

> We are the spooks, we are the spooks,
>   We're here for our convention.
> We are the spooks, we are the spooks,
>   Our past you'll please not mention.

COMMITTEE REPORTS. The Committee on Dead Ones will report a list of dead ones that includes names of well-known persons. The list will include, perhaps, "John Doe, who is dead to the wiles of women," "Thomas Tidbit, who is dead to the lure of labor," etc.

83

There could be other committees, such as a Committee on Ghost Complaints, and a Committee on Improvements. All committee reports should be brief.

CONVENTION GAMES

SHADOW GHOSTS. Divide into two sides. One group stands behind a sheet stretched across a doorway. Lights out. One light shines so as to throw on it a shadow of a person who stands between it and the sheet. Players step up, one at a time. The players on the other side try to recognize the player by the shadow and call the person's name. Each side takes its turn behind the screen.

SKELETON NAMES. Each guest prints his own name on a slip of paper, omitting vowels, thus, R-ch-rd Fr-nc-s (for Richard Francis). These are worn. Players write down as many names as they can recognize. Where most of the guests already know one another, the committee may furnish them the names of well-known persons (movie stars, political figures, athletes, fictional or historical characters).

GRAVEYARD GOSSIP. This is played like the old game of gossip. The players sit or stand in a circle or straight line. The head player whispers something to the next, and so on down the line. The last player tells what the message is. The chances are ten to one that it will be different from the original statement. A player whispers his message only once.

GHOSTS OF FICTION OR HISTORY. There are two sides. Each person (or with a large crowd, ten from a side) chooses to be the ghost of some well-known character in fiction or history—Pinocchio, Gulliver, Tom Sawyer, Peter Pan, Ferdinand, Napoleon. He acts out the particular

84

character while the other side tries to guess who the character is.

GHOST'S TOURNAMENT. Divide into three groups. Have each group work out an original poem of not less than four lines, draw a picture of a cat (crayons and paper should be furnished), and present a charade. Offer a simple prize for each. Arbitrarily the judges make the awards so that each group gets a prize.

In presenting the prize for the best poem the donor says:

> The ghost of Shelley bids me write,
> That if you keep this pace tonight,
> You'll make all other poets sad,
> They'll wish they had the skill you had.

In presenting the prize for the best drawing the donor says:

> The ghost of Rembrandt smiles on you,
> He says that you're an artist true,
> He advises you to count your blessings,
> And take a few more drawing lessons.

To the group winning for its charade or skit the donor says:

> The ghost of Hamlet bids me say,
> That if you keep right on this way,
> The drama never will survive
> As long as you are kept alive.

GHOSTLY ADVICE. Unwind a ball of yarn (or cord). Every two feet have a written warning or bit of advice on a piece of paper tied to the yarn. Rewind so that the paper will not show. The leader tosses the ball to one player who unwinds until the first slip is found. He reads this slip aloud to the group and tosses or hands the ball to another player. So it goes until the end of the ball is reached. Suggested bits of advice:

85

1. Don't go near the cloakroom. There's a wrap there for you.

2. If you don't want to get torpedoed and sunk, avoid a ship called courtship.

3. Don't go into the woods. Where there's a bark there's likely to be a bite.

4. Don't ever plan to get married on February 30.

5. Never tell your secrets near cornstalks. They have ears.

6. If you lose your head, buy a cabbage. It will serve you just as well as the one you have.

7. If you sit on a tack, remember that you'll be better off.

8. If you expect to rate in this crowd, please do not expectorate on the floor.

9. Keep away from the clock when it strikes one if you don't want to get hurt.

10. If you go out boating, don't try to show your love of nature by hugging the shore.

11. Don't lie down on the river just because it has a bed, nor take a sheet of water for to cover up your head.

12. If you want to find happiness, look for it in the dictionary.

HUNTING GHOST FORTUNES. Hand each person directions for finding his fortune: "Look in the green book on the table in this room." "Look in the corner near the piano." "Search in the wastebasket." "Look under the back steps." At each place designated will be a fortune written on a slip of paper.

APPLE SPEARING. Instead of ducking for apples, provide players with homemade darts. Each player gets three chances to spear an apple by throwing the darts. Players eat the apples won in this manner. Darts may be made by using a cork, a needle, and some chicken feathers or paper wings.

THE OLD WITCH IS DEAD.   The leader starts by saying to the person to his right, "The old witch is dead." "How did she die?" comes back the question. "With her face awry," answers the leader, twisting his mouth and contorting his face. The second person now turns to the third and says, "The old witch is dead." The same routine is repeated until it goes around to all players. Then the leader repeats the same announcement, only this time the old witch is "waving good-by." The next time he adds, "with her foot up high." Each time the player suits the action to the way the witch died, and continues to hold that pose throughout to the end of the game, when the leader shouts, "The old witch is buried."

In a large crowd whole sections would do the responses simultaneously.

GHOST STORY.   Close the convention with a good ghost story. "Dey Ain't No Ghosts," by Ellis Parks Butler (in *Best Ghost Stories*, Modern Library), *The Legend of Sleepy Hollow* (Ichabod Crane and the headless horseman), by Washington Irving, or "Tam o' Shanter," by Robert Burns, would provide excellent material.

MURDER.   The leader now announces that a "murder" is to be committed on the spot. Each person draws a slip of paper from a box. What is on it is kept secret. Only one slip is marked and it carries the one word "murderer." The lights are turned out and the group mills around in the room until the "murderer" selects his victim. He does this by putting his hands loosely about the throat of some person. That person screams (the more bloodcurdling the better) and falls to the floor. The lights are turned on. The prosecuting attorney, who has been selected previously, requires every person to take the witness stand.

Each person, except the guilty party, must answer truth-

87

fully any question asked by the attorney. When the questioning is finished, everyone votes on who he thinks the "murderer" is. Then the "murderer" confesses. A good prosecuting attorney can make this a most interesting feature.

GHOSTLY REFRESHMENTS. Have ghosts bring in sandwiches and punch. This could be done with an air of mystery.

A WITCHES' CARNIVAL

Right this way, folks! Come right this way!
Hear the barkers! Heed what they say.
A Witches' Carnival! Big stuff!
We're telling you, and it's no bluff.
Witches, owls, and ghosts galore;
We'll be meeting you at the door.
Such a show you've not seen before.
You'll laugh, you'll thrill, and ask for more.

DECORATIONS. Use the usual Halloween decorations in unusual ways—witches, owls, brooms, black cats, spiders, pumpkins, cornstalks. Carnival booths can be made out of shocks of corn and black and orange crepe paper. A floor lamp can be made into an unusual-looking scarecrow.

Booths and Games

WITCHES' MUSEUM. Tables and stands on which objects are displayed, appropriately labeled or numbered. Some suggested articles: Witches' charms (rabbit's foot, wishbone, penny, four-leaf clover, horseshoe); witches' pet (black cat); witches' cooking utensil (caldron); witches' means of transportation (broom); witches' ghosts (pictures of famous persons who have died). These latter may be numbered and the guests be required to guess who they are. Suggestions: 1. George Washington. 2. Abraham Lincoln. 3. Robert E. Lee. 4. Theodore Roosevelt. 5. Thomas Edison. 6. Jenny Lind. 7. William Shakespeare. 8. Ralph Waldo Emerson. 9. Will Rogers. 10. Ignace Jan Paderewski.

WITCHES' CALDRON. A large caldron containing sticks of candy and inexpensive trinkets. The guest fishes with a bent pinhook on a string. He gets what he catches. No person is allowed to get more than one article. The articles have strings or wire so looped that it is easy to catch something.

FORTUNETELLING. Several foretunetelling booths may be arranged. In one is a palmist. In others are various fortunetelling devices such as invisible writing, fortune wheels ("Round and round and round she goes, and where she stops nobody knows"), dishes with flour, water, etc., and blind pointing at numbers or articles.

WITCHES' CATS. Cut wooden cats out of three-ply, paint them black, and set on saw horses. Or use toy cloth cats. Protect the walls by suspending gym mats or blankets back of the saw horses. Mats on the floor will help also. Guests throw tennis balls or ten-cent store baseballs, trying to knock the cats down. Five throws for each guest.

WITCHES' CHAMBER OF HORRORS. A dark room, weird noises such as rattling chains, groans, and the sound of sighing winds. The gruesome story of the death of Mr. Smith or Mr. Brown and the usual passing of the parts of his body—grapes for his eyes, dried peaches for his ears, hard corn for his teeth, a moist sponge for his brain, an oyster for his tongue, etc.

WITCHES' GAME ROOM.   One room may be set aside for games of various sorts:

BOBBING FOR APPLES.

PIN THE TAIL ON THE CAT.

FEED THE WITCH'S CAT.   Cut a hole in large carton. This is the mouth of the cat. Toss beanbags at a distance of ten feet. Five throws to a person.

RING THE WITCH.   Dress up pop bottles to represent witches. Place them in a single row or in tenpin formation. Players toss Mason jar rings and try to ring a witch. Twelve throws. Double score for a person who rings all ten of the bottles.

PUMPKIN SNAP.   Mark a miniature shuffleboard court on a table. Cut quarter-inch thick disks from broom handle and paint half of disks orange and half of them black. Snap disks at the scoreboard with thumb and forefinger. Checkers will do for disks.

PUMPKIN TOSS.   Use broom handle disks. Toss them at a muffin pan in which are paper pumpkins with scores indicated on them. Distance: about six feet.

WITCH'S MARCH.   Players march by couples as music plays. An extra player marches around with a broom. When the music stops, all players change partners. The extra player drops his broom and seeks to get a partner. The player left out picks up the broom and the game continues.

WITCH'S FLOOR SHOW.   Arrange tables and a

platform. Serve doughnuts and sweet cider or milk. Plan a good floor show. This would include some excellent musical numbers, group singing, a quiz (perhaps a "battle of the sexes"), stunts, a dramatic presentation, and probably a good ghost story.

MIDGET WITCHES. For a dramatic stunt try midget witches. Have from three to five or more midget witches. One person sticks his face in a hole in a sheet and his hands and arms through two holes below.

On the hands are stockings and shoes. Another person puts his hands and arms through two holes in the sheet just under the armpits of the person whose face is showing. A witch's costume is pinned or sewed on the sheet, so that the figure looks for all the world like a miniature witch. The witches may dance, sing, carry on a dialogue, crack jokes, etc.

STROLLING MUSICIANS. During the evening strolling musicians may play at intervals—accordions, violins, banjos, guitars, mandolins, or harmonicas would be appropriate.

CATERWAUL CAPERS

Black cat cutout invitations. Come dressed as a cat or a witch. Greeting: "Meow."

CATERWAUL. Hide a toy mouse in plain sight, but camouflage it so it is difficult to see. Guests hunt. When a player finds it, he sits down in the room and begins to meow. This is kept up until all players have found the mouse. When a player starts meowing, he continues until all players have found the mouse.

CATNIP. Players in circle. Leader starts by pinching cheek of player to right and saying, "The cat nips a cheek."

91

Each player in turn follows suit. Next, "The cat nips a chin." Then, "The cat nips a nose." The secret is that one of the players in the circle has his fingers smeared with soot or lipstick. The player next to him gets a decorated face.

CAT-CRIER RACE.   Two sides of not more than ten players each. They line up facing one another. Each player has a number that corresponds to the number of an opponent on the opposite team. The leader calls out some bit of instruction, such as "Touch the piano," "Touch the doorknob," "Bring a man's tie to the leader," etc. Then the cat-crier meows. The number of meows indicates which players are to perform. The first of the two players to do the required stunt scores a point for his side.

CAT CONTEST.   Each of the two sides is given two minutes to write down all the words they can containing the word "cat"—such as catalogue, catalytic, catch, etc. It is not allowable to use the dictionary.

COLLARING THE CAT.   Use a small toy cat and one dozen Mason jar rings. Or use rope rings such as are used in ringtoss. Players try to collar the cat by tossing the rings so that they drop down over the cat's head, ringing his neck.

TAGGING THE CAT'S TAIL.   Divide players into two teams of not more than ten to a team. Teams line up single file. In each line players must keep hands on shoulders of the person in front of them all during the game. The head player in each line tries to tag the last player in the opposing line. Each group, by twisting and turning, tries to prevent this. Every time the "tail" is tagged, the leader of the tagging side goes to the foot of his line. Thus a new player becomes leader. Whenever a line breaks, the rotation is reversed. In this case the player at the foot goes to the head of the line. This rotation con-

92

tinues until one line has its original head man in that position once more. Winner is the team getting its rotation completed first. This is a strenuous game. It is particularly adapted to boys.

In a large crowd three or more teams could operate at the same time. This would speed up the rotation.

BACK FENCE DOINGS. Select three or four contestants. Stretch adding machine tape the length of the room in parallel lines (one for each contestant). The "cats" must walk backwards on all fours, meowing and keeping the feet and hands on the "back fence" all the way.

TOMMY CAT. The leader stands in front of the group with fists clenched and thumbs up. All players follow suit. The leader calls, "Tommy, Tommy, Tommy, Meow; Tommy, Tommy, Thumbs Up!" Or he may call, "Thumbs Down!" All players must obey immediately the command of the leader by putting thumbs up or thumbs down. The leader may cross them up by doing just the opposite to his order. However, players must follow the leader's order and not his action. Players who make mistakes drop out.

GOBLIN DOIN'S

The goblins 'll get you ef you don't watch out,
Better come to the party to see what it's about.
GOBLIN DOIN'S
    GOBLIN DOIN'S
        GOBLIN DOIN'S great!
Put your goblin clothes on and don't be late!

DECORATIONS. Lights softened by the use of cardboard lanterns or crepe paper. Gray crepe-paper moss. Ghosts and witches appear in unexpected places in dark halls and corners. Jack-o'-lanterns.

93

GOBLIN CHORUS.   Each guest is given a slip of paper with a single vowel written on it. He then searches for the others who have that vowel. When the five groups have formed, they go to different parts of the room and all together they say their letter. Effort is made to vary the sounds—shrill "*e's,*" painful "*o's,*" mournful "*u's,*" high-pitched "*i's,* and distressful "*a's.*" Each group may shout in turn, and then all together.

GOBLIN NUMBERS.   Players may be seated in a straight row or in a circle. Each player has a number from 1 on up, according to where he is sitting. Number 1 begins the fun by calling any number. The player whose number is called must immediately call another number. If a player does not respond immediately, or if he calls his own number, he must go to the foot and the players below him move up one, thus changing their numbers. Effort, of course, is made to get top-numbered players down by catching them napping.

GOBLIN WILLS.   Each goblin has a part in making his own will. Slips of paper are handed out. In each of three columns across the paper appear the numbers 1, 2, 3, 4, 5. At the top of the paper is written: "The last will of ———." Each guest writes his own name in the blank space provided for it. Then in the first column he writes the names of five of his most precious possessions. He folds the column under so it cannot be seen. The paper is passed three persons to the right. This person now writes the names of five people to whom the five possessions are to be left. Again the column is turned under and passed three persons to the right. The third person to handle the paper now writes in his column the uses to which each person will put what was left him in the will. The wills are passed again, unfolded, and read aloud.

94

GOBLIN'S BROOM. Players form a circle about the goblin, who stands in center with his index finger on top of the broomstick, which is perpendicular to the floor. Players are numbered. The goblin lifts his finger off the broomstick, at the same time calling the number of some player. That player must catch the broom before it falls to the floor. If he fails, he takes the place of the player at the center. If there are more than thirty guests, form two or more circles.

GOBLIN GAMBOLS. Do some folk game that features the grand right and left, such as "Bingo," "O Susanna," "Sandy Land," or "Old Dan Tucker." An extra player stands at center with a broom. On the grand right and left he drops the broom and seeks to get a partner. The player left out picks up the broom.

OTHER GOBLIN DOIN'S. The usual Halloween games and stunts may be introduced, such as bobbing for apples, telling fortunes, and ghost stories.

A HALLOWEEN CARNIVAL

Get both the carnival and the Halloween atmosphere in your decorations—booths, side shows, barkers, pumpkin heads, black cats, witches, cornstalks, owls, broomsticks, caldrons, spiders, skulls, ghosts, bones, skeletons, and other things appropriate for Halloween.

Immediately at the announced hour barkers begin to spiel for their particular shows and exhibits. "Right this way, folks! Try your skill!" "Have your palm read!" "Try your fortune!" "See the great House of Horrors!"

GAME BOOTHS. Here are some game booths that are always good fun:

PUMPKIN BEANBAG BOARD. (Make of beaverboard and paint orange color.)

PUMPKIN TOSS IN. (Toss bottle tops into a pumpkin at a distance of six to eight feet.)

WITCHES' BROOMSTICK TOSS. (Make a ring toss game by driving five pieces of broomstick six inches in length into a board one foot square. Make rope rings three or four inches in diameter, or use teething rings.)

TUMBLE BONE. (Toy tenpins and small wooden ball.)

APPLE DUCKING.

WORD FINDING. (Players are given five minutes to find as many words as they can in the letters in the word "Halloween." This may be done as soon as players arrive. They sign their lists and drop them in a box at the Word-Finding Booth.)

FORTUNETELLING BOOTHS. These are always very popular and here are a few types to use:

PALMISTS.

FORTUNE WHEELS.

INVISIBLE INK FORTUNES. (Use lemon juice; when held over a lighted candle, the message becomes visible.)

DART FORTUNES. (Heart-shaped targets with fortunes written on them.)

TOP FORTUNES. (Make hexagon-shaped tops with a fortune indicated on each of the six sides; player spins top with fingers, and side landing up indicates fate.)

BLINDFOLD FORTUNES. (The possibilities are limitless here.)

SIDE SHOWS. These shows will also fit well into the fun of the party:

HOUSE OF HORRORS. A dark or darkened room with all of the usual and maybe some unusual Halloween thrills. Spooks, skeletons, rattling chains, groans, soft objects and springs on which guests must walk, clammy hands to shake, buzzers set off when guests step on certain spots, damp streamers that are blown into the faces of guests, squawkers, feather dusters that brush surprised faces.

If it hasn't been overworked, you might use the old stunt of passing around the parts of a dead man while someone tells a gruesome story—hulled grapes for eyes, hard corn for teeth, moist sponge for brain, empty spools strung together for spinal column, etc.

MUSEUM OF THE DEAD. Arrange an exhibit, numbering each article. Guests are to fill in the proper numbers on cards handed them as they enter the museum. A few suggestions for the exhibit: 1. Eve's Leaves (some tree leaves). 2. Nero's Zero (report card with zero in "hot music"). Adam Had 'em (picture of boy with measle-marked face). Noah's Boa (toy snake). 5. William Tell's Apple (an apple). Ben's Pen (a quill pen marked "Property of Benjamin Franklin"). 7. George's Charges (George Washington, debtor: Powder, $1.00; ham, 20c). 8. Rip's Slips (two pillow slips marked "Property of Rip Van Winkle"). 9. Caesar's Tweezers (a pair of pliers marked "Property of J. C.").

THE HALLOWEEN STROLLERS' PARTY

Instead of having the Halloween party at one location, why not visit four different places during the evening's fun?

Here is a suggested invitation: "Join the Halloween Strollers and visit PUMPKIN HEAD INN (picture of a jack-o'-lantern), HAUNTED HOUSE (picture of ghost), WITCH'S CAVERN (picture of a witch), and HIDE-OUT (picture of a pirate or a skull and crossbones). Come masked."

PUMPKIN HEAD INN. A jack-o'-lantern or two just outside the door of the first home where the masked strollers meet. After the fun of guessing who is who, play a game or two. One of these games should be "The Ghost Test." In this, members of the group are required to eat four crackers and then whistle. The first successful whistler is rewarded with a lollypop. Have each guest make a guess as to the number of dried pumpkin seeds in a glass jar. Have a pumpkin a third full of pumpkin seeds mixed with beans. Each player ladles out a spoonful. The person or couple with the largest number of pumpkin seeds wins.

HAUNTED HOUSE. If a barn can be used for this place, it will be of advantage. The place is dark. The leader knocks on a door. Simulate the noise of a squeaking door as the door opens. Lock step to a dimly lighted room or corner of the barn. Have someone tell a good ghost story. Provide apples to eat.

WITCH'S CAVERN. This can be a stroller's house. Guests are greeted by a witch. Caldron full of cookies and fortunes. Fortunetelling games: darts, blindfold choosing, invisible ink, etc. A good palmist would help.

HIDEOUT. This stop can be another house. Set the group to work hunting hidden peanuts. If time permits, play a few games. "Shoe Scramble" would be a good one.

A folk game may be in order. Then do a little harmonizing and bring the evening to a close.

A FOUR-POINT HALLOWEEN

Use different rooms in a house or club. Name and decorate the rooms appropriately: Goblins' Garden, Witch's Den, Spooks' Cavern, Tombstone Alley.

GOBLINS' GARDEN.   Apple ducking, nut hunting, beanbag boards, flower fortune. In this last game a blindfolded player points a wand at some flower, real or artificial, on the table. Violet means "romance coming your way"; daisy, "a big secret will be entrusted to you"; bachelor's-button, "prospects of marriage slim"; goldenrod or golden glow, "riches"; ragged robin, "tough luck"; orange blossom, "wedding bells"; rose, "promotion."

WITCH'S DEN.   All sorts of fortunetelling devices:

> Double, double toil and trouble;
> Fire burn and cauldron bubble.

SPOOKS' CAVERN. Almost complete darkness. Guests follow a stout rope trail. Damp threads hang down and brush their faces. An occasional suspended damp sponge. Suspended fur coat that suggests a hairy monster. Tin cans rolling on floor. A prop man who makes weird noises with a whistle, a siren, rattling tin that sounds like thunder, a vacuum cleaner, groaning ghosts on chairs with white slip covers on them. An occasional pillow on the floor gives the effect of stepping on a body. Ghosts with detachable hands.

TOMBSTONE ALLEY.   Tell ghost stories, such as "A Terrible Ghost Story" (page 109), and "A Halloween Romance" (page 111).

THE GHOST WALKS

How about building a Halloween party around "The Ghost Walks" idea? Ask each guest to come dressed as a ghost.

GUESS WHO?   Number each ghost by pinning a numbered slip on his back. Each person lists all of the persons he can identify. When the listing is finished, or when a sufficient amount of time has been given to it, call the numbers in order and have each person unmask. Guests correct their own lists.

SPEARING APPLES. Ducking for apples may be a bit damp for adults. So have guests throw darts at the apples in a tub. Each guest gets three throws. Apples speared may be kept. Darts may be made out of needles, corks, and papers or feathers.

THE GHOST TALKS. Divide into two or more groups. Read the questions suggested here. The first side to have someone answer correctly scores a point. All the answers are words that are appropriate for a graveyard.

If you lived in a graveyard: 1. With what would you open the gate? (With a skeleton key.) 2. What would you do if you get a bad cold which settles in your throat? (Start coffin.) 3. How would you identify in three letters a plaintive poem? (L-E-G; elegy.) 4. What kind of jewels would you wear? (Tombstones.) 5. Where would you keep them? (In a casket.) 6. How would you get money? (Urn it.) 7. What would you eat? (Pyre cake or buries.) 8. How would you move things about? (By carrion them.) 9. What would protect you from the sun? (The shades.) 10. What would you do getting ready for a play? (Re-hearse.) 11. Supposing a woman told you she was going to call? (You would specter.) 12. What would be your disposition? (Grave.)

GHOST SHADOWS. Hang up a sheet with a light behind it for shadow pictures. Three different types of things may be done: (a) Some of the guests may walk or stand behind the screen while the rest try to guess who makes the shadow. (b) Groups may pantomime episodes or dramatic skits—the dentist's chair, the operation, Washington cutting the cherry tree, etc. (c) Objects may be strung on a rope and hung behind the screen. Guests try to identify the objects (an apple, a screw driver, a cup, a peanut, a horseshoe.)

GHOST STORIES. Plan for one or more good ghost stories. One of the best is "Dey Ain't No Ghosts," by Ellis Parks Butler, from Best Ghost Stories (Modern Library). Others are: "Tam o' Shanter," by Robert Burns; The Legend of Sleepy Hollow, by Washington Irving (famous story of Ichabod Crane and the headless horseman); "The Canterville Ghost," by Oscar Wilde, in Novels and Fairy Tales; "The Black Cat," by Edgar Allan Poe.

A NEIGHBORHOOD HALLOWEEN PARTY FOR BOYS

A city Y.M.C.A., desiring to do something positive to combat Halloween activities of a destructive nature, put on a big Halloween party for two hundred boys. The program outline was as follows:

1. Welcome
    Tagging in groups
2. Program in Big Gym
    Group singing
    Races
    Group games
3. Program in Small Gym
    Pillow fighting
    Tug of war
    Hog-tying
    Apple ducking

101

Fortunetelling

Doughnut grabbing

4. Trail of Terror

Dark passageway of terrors from gym into boys' lobby

5. Refreshments

Caramel apples and two doughnuts as boys file out

HALLOWEEN BANQUET

This unusual banquet plan was used by Centenary Methodist Church, Chattanooga, Tennessee, when Rabun Calhoun was director of religious education. The program can be adapted for use without the banquet idea.

INVITATIONS.

Ghosts and goblins summon you
To sup with us on witch's brew.
Heed this summons—or beware—
The goblins'll getcha if you're not there!

DECORATIONS. Typically Halloween—black and orange pumpkin heads, caldrons for flowers, skull, etc.

Program Outline

Orange-colored paper, shaped like a pumpkin; program on second page, menu on third, new officers' names on back cover.

1. Invocation
2. Witch Queen gives command and welcomes all this spirit band.
3. Opening Toast (see below).
4. Witch:

102

Ghosts and goblins—solemn throng—
Join the witch's doleful song!

(Group singing: "The more we get together the
gloomier we'll be.")

5. Witch:

'Tis time now for each one of you
To have your share of witch's brew!

(Eats)

6. Speech. (Toastmaster with aid of senior counselor
and young people's counselor pulled the gag in *The
Fun Encyclopedia*, pages 100-101.)

7. Witch:

To entertain this mournful host—
Music for the dance of ghosts.

(Violin music—ghost dance—dirgelike music.)

8. Ghost story. (Without announcement from behind
curtain, weird noises.)

9. Witch:

Now we look the future o'er
To see what Fate can have in store.

(Inspirational talk by leader on plans for the new
year.)

MENU.

Goblins' Feast
WITCH'S BREW

GHOST OF CHICKEN   SPOOKS DELIGHT IN HOLLOW SHELLS
(Creamed chicken)   (*Sweet potatoes and marshmallows in
                             orange peels*)

SALAD OF BUTCHERED VEGETABLES

OLIVE GREEN EYES   CELERY RIBS

SPIRITS OF COFFEE
ALL-HALLOWS MIX FAIRY FLUFF
(Gingerbread and whipped cream)

OPENING TOAST.   (This was given by the youth president in a dirgelike tone.)

Double, double toil and trouble;
Fire burn and cauldron bubble.

Spirits all, we welcome you
To watch us make our witch's brew.

Into it goes some part of all
Who now have Burns instead of Hall (young people's and senior counselors).

As seniors they have "passed away"
And come to haunt with us for aye.

Some epitaphs for them we've writ
We'll hear them now, if you see fit;

"Tat" Anderson's life went on the blink
When he drank a bottle of printer's ink" (Tat was working for one of the newspapers).

Peggy Osborne ceased to be—
She strangled when she hit high "C" (Obviously Peggy sings).

Don Chandler, we all know quite well,
He came here instead of going to ——— (Name some rival school or town).

Jean Bishop's last days were very bad
For in a fight were all the suitors she'd ever had.

It's a sad sad tale about Charlie White
He had to listen to a violin every night (his girl friend plays).

What other spirits have we here?
Their epitaphs will make it clear—

104

Poor John Carriger lost his mind
When that 700 average he could not find (Sunday-school
  superintendent).

The fate of Dorothea Reid was sad:
She lost her speech. It made her mad (talkative person).

And poor Bess Wigs met her sad fate (Teacher of girls'
  class)
Trying to keep Clift and Bandy straight.
And when she went, Jack went too— (Her husband)
Can't say I blame him much, do you?

Death came to our counselors in a brawl
Over whose group was best—Burns' or Hall.
And then they missed the pearly gate
By waiting too long for those who were late.

But the saddest life was that of Jimmy— (Preacher)
He always gave when his wife said, "Gimme"—
But wicked Fate his actions did mock
For Huldah, poor soul, died from the shock.

But whate'er the fate of this woeful group,
We'll never let our spirits droop.
And though in grief we're gathered here,
Come, let our sorrow disappear,
And in this solemn company
We'll be as happy as ghosts can be!

FAMILY HALLOWEEN FUN

Halloween ideas in this book may be adapted for use in
the family group. Where the children are very young,
Halloween festivities can be planned for the early evening.
Halloween table decorations, Halloween cookies, and even
a Halloween salad may be created. Ample Halloween games
may be planned. A Halloween puppet show is possible,
using white sock puppets.

Where the children are older, they may have their own

plans for the evening. In this case confine the Halloween celebration in the family to the dinner hour.

A COMMUNITY HALLOWEEN CELEBRATION

Perhaps the adults can sponsor a community Halloween celebration of some sort, working in co-operation with other agencies in the community. Such celebrations have been successfully promoted by many communities, and have attracted large numbers of children, young people, and adults. They have been the means of eliminating much vandalism. An organized community Halloween program would mean co-operation on the part of all community interests—schools, churches, clubs, etc. Usually a street block is roped off and in some cases an auditorium is used. There would be a parade of marchers in costume before a judges' stand, floats (witch's caldron, for instance), a home talent performance of dramatics, music, etc., an outdoor bonfire, strolling musicians, and the like. The permission and aid of the police department will be necessary.

OTHER HALLOWEEN SUGGESTIONS

HALLOWEEN TENPINS. Ten corncobs mounted on cardboard bases are set up in tenpin formation. Players bowl with an apple or orange. Bowling distance: ten to fifteen feet.

GET A PUMPKIN. Divide the group into couples. Give each couple seven small pumpkins cut out of paper. On each pumpkin is a letter that appears in the word "pumpkin." By trading, couples try to get the necessary letters to spell "p-u-m-p-k-i-n." The trading continues until one couple is successful.

106

I HEAR A GHOST. Divide the players into two groups of equal numbers. Each group appoints a witch. This person is blindfolded. The two witches stand at center, side by side. The opposing teams line up at opposite sides of the room. Players attempt to steal across to the opposite side. Those from one side walk to the right of the witches. Those from the other walk to the left. This continues until all players are across or out.

If a witch thinks she hears a player from the opposite side going across, she cries, "I hear a ghost." If she is right, the player must drop out. If she is wrong, a player from her own side must drop out.

NUT TOSS. Place a baking dish inside a dishpan. Inside the baking dish place a tin cup. Standing at a distance of eight to ten feet, players try their skill in tossing nuts (peanuts, hickory nuts, or any nuts available). Five throws are allowed each player. A nut falling in the cup counts five points, in the baking dish, three points, in the dishpan, one point.

NUTS TO CRACK. What are the following nuts?
1. A holder of treasure. 2. To make full and a boy's name. 3. A girl's name. 4. The side of a building. 5. A vegetable. 6. A dairy product. 7. An instrument of correction. 8. A letter of the alphabet and a tin container. 9. A South American country. 10. A sandy stretch at the seaside. 11. Ready money and to cut. 12. A beverage.

Answers: 1. Chestnut. 2. Filbert. 3. Hazelnut. 4. Walnut. 5. Peanut. 6. Butternut. 7. Hickory nut. 8. Pecan. 9. Brazil nut. 10. Beechnut. 11. Cashew. 12. Coconut.

FOOD FORTUNES. Place articles of food on a table. Blindfold each person, in turn, and have him point with a wand at some article of food after he has been turned around three times. If he points to the pork, he'll be a politician; the ham, a stage career; the hot dog, an animal trainer; cereal, a radio writer; bread, a church worker ("bread of life"); salt, a seaman; beans, a school-teacher ("use of the old bean"); liver, a physician; candy, a dentist.

Or make a chart containing pictures of these items. The player points to the chart.

FORTUNE HUNTERS. Hide a ring, a purse, and a button about the room. The person who finds the ring will be happily married. The finder of the purse will be wealthy. The one who finds the button will not have wedding bells ring for him.

BOWL FORTUNE. Five bowls are required for this game. One bowl contains water, another milk, another vinegar, another sugar, and the fifty is empty. Blindfold each person in turn. Whatever bowl he touches indicates his fortune. Water means clear sailing and much travel; milk, a successful career; vinegar, a sour and unhappy experience; sugar, a happy life; and the empty bowl, unwedded bliss.

A Halloween Story

Mrs. Jones and her neighbor, Mrs. Smith were discussing how some people commit suicide by hanging. They decided they'd like to know how it feels to hang by a rope. Mrs. Jones was to try it first; then Mrs. Smith.

Mrs. Jones stood on a chair, the noose was put about her neck, and the chair removed. When she wanted the chair put back so that she could get down, she was to wiggle her feet.

However, just after the chair was removed, the phone rang and Mrs. Smith ran downstairs to answer it. When she came back she was horror-stricken. Mrs. Jones was dead.

Because she was afraid she would be accused of murder,

she let Mrs. Jones down and took her downstairs. Then she seated her in an armchair by the window and went home.

Mr. Jones came home from work. He waved his hand to his wife and called out a greeting. Since she did not answer, he tossed a pebble at the open window. It hit Mrs. Jones in the head and she toppled from the chair.

The husband was panic-stricken when he found she was dead. For fear that he would be accused of her murder, he bundled her into their old jalopy, making her look as natural as possible. Then he drove away, hoping to have a wreck. Thus it would appear that she was killed in the wreck.

As he careened around a corner, she was thrown out of the car and through a basement window, where an old shoemaker was at work. He was punching holes in some leather soles with an—oh, what is it you call it? [Someone shouts "awl."] "Yes, that's all."

A Terrible Ghost Story

This story may be used either as a dramatic skit, rehearsed by a picked cast and produced in costume, or it may be done by assigning the parts to different groups in the audience. They give the proper response when their cue is given. (From Bruce Tom.)

Character	Sound Effect	Character	Sound Effect
Timid Young Girl	(Sob)	Yellow Dog	(Howl)
Old, Old Woman	(High cracked laugh)	Big Black Crow	(Caw, caw)
		Four Black Bats	(Squeak)
Large Black Cat	(Meow)	Bogeyman	(Boo)

109

Long Black Snake	(Hiss)	Terrible Ghost	One or more confeder-ates scream at the mention of "A Terrible Ghost")
Tall Man	(Groan)		

It was a stormy night in October. A stagecoach rumbled along a country road. A *timid young girl* bounced up and down on the hard cushions and gazed frightened into the darkness. Suddenly the coach stopped. In stepped an *old, old woman*. From under one arm peered a *large black cat*, and around the other twined a *long black snake*.

"Hoity! toity! a *timid young girl* traveling alone tonight?" she exclaimed with a hideous grin. "Let me tell your fortune, my pretty dear."

Toward the *timid young girl* the *old, old woman* stretched a bony arm. The *large black cat* arched his back and growled. The *long black snake* watched with beady eyes.

"No, no," cried the *timid young girl*, shrinking into a corner with her pretty hands behind her back.

At that moment the door was thrown violently open. In rushed a *tall man* in a long raincoat. His face was hidden by a drooping hat. His voice was low and pleasant. He said, "Allow me," and gently pushed between the *timid young girl* and the *old, old woman*.

"Allow me," said the *old, old woman*, and three times pointed her finger at the *tall man*. A *yellow dog* howled from under the seat. The *large black cat* growled again. The *long black snake* hissed.

On the window sill a *big black crow* lighted and croaked most dismally. Into the coach flew *four black bats* and beat their wings in the face of the *timid young girl*. Through each window peered the grotesque face of a pumpkin

110

bogeyman. Nearer to the *old, old woman* bent the *tall man*. He fixed on the *old, old woman* two startling eyes and pushed back his hat. With a terrified shriek the *old, old woman* sprang to the door, followed by her *large black cat*, howling *yellow dog*, *long black snake*, *four black bats*, and the *big black crow*. In the coach the *timid young girl* had fainted, for under the hat of the *tall man* was the ghastly countenance of a *Terrible Ghost*.

A HALLOWEEN ROMANCE

The following story can be used in either of two ways. Select a cast and present the story as a skit, with costuming and setting. Or divide the crowd into eight groups. Assign each group a character. Have it give the proper response when the character is mentioned.

CHARACTERS	SOUND EFFECT
Sweet Young Thing	("A-a-a-ah")
Great Big He-man	("You are my sunshine"—sung)
Cruel Papa	("Naw-w-w-w"—out of side of mouth)
Clammy Ghost	("O-o-o-oh"—low and ghostly)
Cat	("Meow")
Polly Parrot	("Polly wants a cracker")
Cold, Windy Night	("Hoo-oo-oo-oo"—whistling wind)
Lonesome Hound-dog	("Ow-oo-oo-oo"—head up, howling in mournful doglike fashion)

Once there was a *sweet young thing* who fell in love with a *great big he-man*. However, she had a *cruel papa*. He didn't like the *great big he-man*. So the *cruel papa* said, "No!"

On Halloween night the *sweet young thing* was sitting at home with the *cat* and the *polly parrot*. The wind whistled down the chimney for it was a *cold, windy night*. Outside a *lonesome hound-dog* howled.

111

The *sweet young thing* went out and brought the *lonesome hound-dog* inside.

"Oh, no you don't," shouted the *cruel papa*. Whereupon, he kicked the *lonesome hound-dog* out.

Just then the *great big he-man* entered. Said the *great big he-man* to the *sweet young thing*, "I've come to marry you."

"Oh, no you won't," shouted the *cruel papa*.

A *clammy ghost* came down the chimney just at that moment.

"Oh, yes he will," said the *clammy ghost* as he pushed the *cruel papa* back in his chair.

So the *sweet young thing* fell in the arms of the *great big he-man* and sighed, "Ain't this peachy?"

And the *sweet young thing*, the *great big he-man*, the *clammy ghost*, the *cat*, the *polly parrot*, the *lonesome hound-dog* and even the *cruel papa*, just laughed and laughed (Everybody laughs).

And all this happened on a *cold, windy night*.

A POLITICAL PARTY

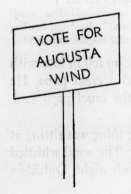

This is one of those parties where the sky is the limit as far as originality and spontaneity are concerned. Encourage both in developing the plan.

DECORATIONS. Have signs about the room, such as "Vote for Augusta Wind," "Gabriel Hornblower—Our Candidate," "Senator Claghorn Says, 'Vote for *Dixie Dugan*—Dixie, that Is!' "

112

POLITICAL WHO'S WHO. Have tacked up on the walls, or laid on tables or mantels around the room, pictures of well-known figures, each picture being numbered, but nameless. Pictures may be obtained from magazines and newspapers. The pictures may include American historical heroes such as Washington and Lincoln, government officials, past and present, and other well-known individuals. On entering, the guests are given cards with corresponding numbers, opposite which they may write their guesses as to the names of the persons in the portraits. The guests will move around the room to examine the pictures and enter the names on the cards. This is one method of avoiding the stiffness that ensues sometimes when guests become apparently glued to their chairs.

An interesting variation of this game consists in having the heads of prominent people pasted on bodies which do not belong to them. The head of a man, for example, may be pasted on the body of a woman, or vice versa. Some ludicrous effects may be produced and this makes it much more difficult to identify the individual. A party at which pictures of well-known local citizens are used may be made most enjoyable.

POLITICAL QUIZ. Work out an interesting political quiz. Introduce some questions with local color. Divide the crowd into two groups and select representatives for the quiz session. The leader should alternate sides in asking questions. The following are some suggestions:

1. What great political figure was known as "The Rail Splitter"?

2. What father and son and what grandfather and grandson were presidents of the United States?

3. What president later became chief justice of the Supreme Court?

113

4. What famous statesman said, "I'd rather be right than president"?

5. What president had a wife named "Dolly"?

6. What president was defeated for re-election, but later was elected for a second term?

Answers: 1. Abraham Lincoln. 2. John Adams and his son John Quincy Adams. William H. Harrison and his grandson Benjamin Harrison. 3. William Howard Taft. 4. Henry Clay. 5. James Madison. 6. Grover Cleveland. (See *The Fun Encyclopedia,* p. 280, for other suggestions.)

IMPROMPTU DEBATE. Subject: "Resolved, That a woman would make a good president of the United States." Select two teams, one to present the affirmative and the other to present the negative. Each team should be composed of one man and one woman. Limit the entire time for the debate to ten minutes. If desired, debaters could be notified ahead of time so they may prepare their arguments.

ELECTION. At this point the chairman announces that an important statement is to be made to the group following the singing of a few songs. After two songs the speaker begins his speech. At intervals there are appropriate (?) sounds, as indicated. The people who are to provide these noises should be carefully instructed so that the sounds will be properly timed. Most of the noisemakers should be hidden from view and each noise should be made with enthusiasm. The speech should be given with oratorical flourish. Here is a typical speech:

"Friends and Fellow Citizens: In the stillness of this hour (clash and clatter of falling pots and pans), in this time of crisis (someone off stage blows a loud toot on a horn) we are to have an election (loud cries of 'Aye! Aye!'). We are alarmed (ringing of an alarm clock) and rightly so. Around the world there is the shuffle, shuffle, shuffle, shuffle

114

of men's feet (shuffling of feet). Babies are crying (loud wail of a baby). Justice seems to be asleep (loud snores). But a new day is dawning (bugle plays a few bars of reveille, or rooster crows, or a group breaks out singing 'O What a Beautiful Morning,' or all three). Go on with the election" (shouts of "Hurrah!").

Then the crowd is divided into two groups. These could be the same group used earlier in the evening. Each group holds a caucus in which it selects a campaign manager, a candidate for president of the United States (one of their own group), campaign speaker or speakers. Members of the group also draw some banners (paper and crayon are provided), and arrange some campaign entertainment features (songs, special music, parade, hill-billy band, etc.).

The two parties might be named the Publicrats and the Redemicans, or any other names the groups desire. The time given each party for its part of the program should be limited to fifteen minutes. This, of course, does not include the time spent in the caucus session. In some cases it may be possible to allow each group thirty minutes for its presentation before the entire crowd. This would include platform, speeches, and entertainment.

Ballots are cast. It would be fun if the election committee should decide that the election is a draw, and that therefore there will be two presidents who will serve on alternate days.

Now let the group get back to normal and serve refreshments.

"Good night, ladies!"

AMERICA SINGS

Drama, music, color, a chance for everyone to sing! Join the happy crowd to enjoy this unusual musical program.

SUGGESTIONS TO THE COMMITTEE. 1. Begin preparation for this program in plenty of time to do it justice. 2. Get the best musical talent available in the community for special numbers. 3. Use a large number of people on the program—choruses, quartets, duets, solos. 4. Provide opportunities in the program for participation of the audience—group singing, quizzes, memory tests. 5. Dramatize some of the special numbers. 6. Note that as the program develops it becomes a sort of musical pageant. 7. Invite the entire membership of a club or a church to enjoy this program with you. Or better, make it a community affair.

PROGRAM. This will be arranged in six sections: 1. American Indian Music. 2. Music of Pioneer Days. 3. Cowboy Songs. 4. Old Favorites. 5. Modern Favorites. 6. Negro Spirituals. Selections of numbers would be made of the following and others suggested by them:

Begin with everyone singing "The Star Spangled Banner" or "America, the Beautiful."

1. AMERICAN INDIAN MUSIC

Setting: Campfire scene. Indian wigwam. Indians seated in semicircle about the fire.

Selections from the following:

Solo: "From the Land of the Sky-Blue Water," Cadman.

Piano: "Love Song" (from "Indian Suite, No. 2"), MacDowell; "From an Indian Lodge," MacDowell.

Chorus and Dance: Zuni, "Sunrise Call," in *The Brown Book* (C. C. Birchard & Co.); "Sun Worshiper's Dance."

Solo: "By the Waters of Minnetonka," Lieurance.

Duet: "Indian Love Call," Friml.

116

Solo: "By the Weeping Waters" (Chippewa Indian mourning song), Lieurance.

Dramatic action should be introduced. An Indian lookout in the background. A chief who presides. Dramatic presentations of "Indian Love Call," "By the Waters of Minnetonka" (see story), Zuni, "Sunrise Call," and other songs in the list.

2. MUSIC OF PIONEER DAYS

Setting: Campfire scene. Outdoor setting. Covered wagon in background.

Community Sing: "O Susanna."

Solo and Chorus: "Shuckin' of the Corn."

Dramatic Duet: "The Old Man in the Wood."

Chorus: "Red River Valley."

The latter three songs all appear in *Singing America* (C. C. Birchard & Co.).

3. COWBOY SONGS

Setting: Same as for music of pioneer days.

Community Sing: "Home on the Range."

Solo (with banjo accompaniment): "I Can't Play an Accordeen" (see *The Fun Encyclopedia,* p. 466).

Chorus: "Night Herding Song" (in *Singing America*).

Solo: "Good By Old Paint."

Men's Chorus: "Big Choral" (in *Singing America*); "When the Curtains of Night" (see *The Fun Encyclopedia,* p. 468); "Old Chisholm Trail" (in *Singing America*).

Solo: "The Last Roundup."

4. OLD FAVORITES

Setting: Sitting room.

Community Sing: "Swanee River" (in *Singing America*).

117

Solo: "Jeanie with the Light Brown Hair" (in *Singing America*).

Chorus: "Old Uncle Ned" (in *Singing America*).

Male Quartet: "Soldier's Farewell"; "The Bulldog on the Bank"; "The Old Oaken Bucket."

Girls' Trio: "Grandfather's Clock."

Other possibilities are "Silver Threads Among the Gold," "When You and I Were Young, Maggie."

5. Modern Favorites

Setting: Sitting room.

Piano: "To a Wild Rose," MacDowell.

Chorus: "Sylvia," Speaks.

Baritone Solo: "Ol' Man River," Kern.

Duet: "Will You Remember?" Romberg.

Other numbers that might be used are "L'Amour, Toujours, L'Amour," Friml; "Ah, Sweet Mystery of Life," Herbert; "Night and Day," Porter.

6. Negro Spirituals

Setting: Cotton field.

Community Sing: "Swing Low, Sweet Chariot."

Solo: "Deep River."

Male Quartet: "Standin' in the Need of Prayer"; "Listen to the Lambs"; "Lord, I Want to Be a Christian."

Community Sing: "Trampin' "; "Jacob's Ladder."

Memory Test

Work out a short story with a sequence of songs which the pianist plays while the group tries to guess the song titles.

It was ("Way Down upon the Swanee River") where our story began. Her name was ("Rose Marie"), while his

118

was ("Danny Boy"). ("Night and Day") they longed for each other. Many a night did he ("Serenade") her. Often they walked ("Down by the Old Mill Stream"). It was ("A Merry Life") until he had to go ("Over There"). He promised to send her a ("Souvenir") from Tokio or Berlin. She longed for peace to come so he could come back to ("America, the Beautiful").

Musical Quiz

1. An American composer wrote the music for "Narcissus," "The Rosary," and "Mighty Lak a Rose." Was his name George M. Cohan, Edward MacDowell, or Ethelbert Nevin? *Answer:* Ethelbert Nevin.

2. What famous American bandmaster wrote the marches "Semper Fidelis" and "Stars and Stripes Forever"? *Answer:* John Philip Sousa.

3. Name at least one musical number written by Edward MacDowell. *Answer:* "To a Wild Rose," "To a Water Lily."

4. What famous violinist and musician, born in Austria, makes his home in the United States? *Answer:* Fritz Kreisler.

5. What American composer wrote *The King's Henchman*, an opera performed by the Metropolitan Opera Company? *Answer:* Deems Taylor.

6. In what musical show was "Ol' Man River" first sung and who wrote it? *Answer: Show Boat*; Jerome Kern.

7. Who wrote "Dixie," and for what purpose did he write it? *Answer:* Dan D. Emmett; for use in a minstrel show.

8. "Carry Me Back to Old Virginny" was written by whom? *Answer:* James A. Bland, a Negro song writer.

9. "The March of the Toys" is played in *Babes in Toy-*

land; "Gypsy Love Song" is sung in *The Fortune Teller*; "Ah, Sweet Mystery of Life" and "I'm Falling in Love" are sung in *Naughty Marietta*; "Kiss Me Again" is sung in *Mademoiselle Modiste*. Who wrote these popular light operas? *Answer:* Victor Herbert.

10. What famous writer of gospel hymns was blind? *Answer:* Fanny Crosby.

A MASQUERADE PARTY FOR NOVEMBER

> Make up and dress up,
> Come to our party
> Be a maid six or a dame forty,
> Cowboy, Indian,
> Drama star, or what,
> Just be somebody that you are not.

MAKE-UP. People are requested to come made up to represent some type of character: an aged person, a child, a snob, a clown, a gypsy, a farmer, a tough, a tramp; or some particular person: a fairy story character like Hansel or Gretel, a Mother Goose herself.

Some groups might find it practical to have a theatrical make-up kit at the place of the party. This could be used by those who desire to put some finishing touches on their make-up. It could also be used to make-up guests who neglected to conform to the request of the committee. Perhaps a make-up committee should be on hand to manage this feature.

GRAND MARCH. After all guests are ready, stage a grand march bringing the group finally into a double circle. Then do a mixer with the two circles marching in opposite directions until the music stops, when they face partners and converse a moment. Music intervals and stops should

120

be brief so as to allow guests to meet a number of different persons.

NOVEMBER FOOTBALL DRAMA. Have a pantomime football game. Stage a brief burlesque football game with girls calling time out to powder their noses. An amazing forward pass scores the winning touchdown. The ball is an imaginary one and there is no physical contact whatever between players.

CHARADES. Divide into two or more groups and present appropriate November words in charades. Some suggested words are "Thanksgiving," "pilgrim," "turkey," and "Plymouth Rock."

DRAMATIC STUNTS. These should be rehearsed stunts. Suggestions: *Wild Nell, Pet of the Plains* (Walter H. Baker & Co., 178 Tremont Street, Boston). *Pokyhuntus* (Lynn Rohrbough, *Handy I*). *Precious Priscilla* (*The Fun Encyclopedia*, p. 570), *Othello* (p. 311).

A REHEARSED PLAY OR PLAY READING. Top off the evening's program with a well-prepared play. If time for rehearsals is limited, do a good job of play reading or try a walking rehearsal.

Try *The Courtship of Miles Standish*, by E. W. Presbrey (Samuel French, New York), two men, two women; forty minutes. If other games are desired as substitutes for any of the suggestions offered, try impromptu dramatizations (fairy stories, Mother Goose rhymes, or original creations). Social games and folk games could also be used.

Try finding words in the letters in "masquerade."

A NOVEMBER PARADE OF TIME PARTY

DECORATIONS. Footballs hanging from chandeliers. Thanksgiving decorations. Flags. Stacked muskets or rifles.

INVITATION:

We'll celebrate the Parade of Time
All through November days
Football, turkey, armistice
We like November ways.

Come to the November Parade of Time Party.
Friday, November 15, 8 P.M.

WORDMAKING. As the guests arrive, put them to work on making as many words as they can out of the letters of the word "November." If desired, they might make several sets of words, using the letters in Thanksgiving," "football," "armistice," etc.

PING-PONG FOOTBALL. The ping-pong ball is placed in the center of the table. Two teams of players (as many as can be accommodated) gather around the table, with chins up to the edge of the table. Players must hold this position. If a player gets his face over into the field, that is, over the table, an off side is called and the opposing side gets a free blow. When the ball goes outside, the referee blows his whistle as he retrieves it. He places it in the middle of the table out from the point where it went outside. He

122

then blows his whistle as a signal for players to start blowing. When the ball crosses the goal line, a touchdown is scored.

After a touchdown the ball is placed back at center. Players do not start blowing until the referee's whistle is blown. Play five-minute quarters. Change sides for each quarter.

For a variation, put up miniature goal posts and allow players one at a time to try to blow the ball from center through the opponent's goal. Only one continuous blow is allowed to a player. Sides alternate in blowing.

A FOOTBALL QUIZ.　1. What football player was known as "The Galloping Ghost"?

2. What Indian football player achieved fame as one of the greatest backs of all time?

3. What school had a backfield that was nicknamed "The Four Horsemen"?

4. What annual football classics are played at the following places: (a) Pasadena, California, (b) New Orleans, Louisiana, (c) Miami, Florida, and (d) Dallas, Texas?

5. What college football teams bear the following nicknames?

Southern: (a) Commodores. (b) Crimson Tide. (c) Wildcats. (d) Volunteers.

Eastern: (a) Old Elis. (b) Tigers. (c) Middies. (d) Crimson. (e) Violets. (f) Crusaders. (g) Owls. (h) Tartans.

Big Ten: (a) Wildcats. (b) Gophers. (c) Wolverines. (d) Hoosiers. (e) Buckeyes. (f) Badgers.

Big Six: (a) Sooners. (b) Corn-huskers. (c) Tigers. (d) Jayhawkers.

Southwest: (a) Mustangs. (b) Longhorns. (c) Bears. (d) Aggies. (e) Razorbacks.

West: (a) Trojans. (b) Golden Bears. (c) Indians. (d) Huskies. (e) Uclans.

123

6. What famous football coach was killed in an airplane accident?

7. What celebrated football coach is called "Pop"?

8. What are the dimensions of a football field?

9. What is the difference between a punt, a drop kick, and a field goal?

Answers: 1. Red Grange. 2. Jim Thorpe. 3. Notre Dame. 4. (a) Rose Bowl. (b) Sugar Bowl. (c) Orange Bowl. (d) Cotton Bowl. 5. *Southern:* (a) Vanderbilt. (b) Alabama. (c) Kentucky. (d) Tennessee. *Eastern:* (a) Yale. (b) Princeton. (c) Navy. (d) Harvard. (e) New York University. (f) Holy Cross (g) Temple (h) Carnegie Tech. *Big Ten:* (a) Northwestern. (b) Minnesota. (c) Michigan. (d) Indiana. (e) Ohio State. (f) Wisconsin. *Big Six:* (a) Oklahoma. (b) Nebraska. (c) Missouri. (d) Kansas. *Southwest:* (a) Southern Methodist. (b) Texas. (c) Baylor. (d) Texas A. and M. (e) Arkansas. *West:* (a) Southern California. (b) California. (c) Stanford. (d) Washington. (e) University of California at Los Angeles. 6. Knute Rockne. 7. "Pop" Warner. 8. It is 160 feet wide by 360 feet long. Twenty yards of the length is taken up with two end zones. 9. A player punts when he drops the ball and kicks it before it touches the ground. In a drop kick he drops the ball and kicks it the moment it touches the ground. In a field goal one player holds the ball to the ground while another player kicks it.

THANKSGIVING PANTOMIMES. Divide into groups and have each group prepare a pantomime on "Things for which to be thankful." The possibilities are limitless. For instance, the group pantomimes a dinner party, or a song fest, or a religious meeting. It pantomimes some games. It pantomimes some books. The rest guess what is being presented.

The groups may be asked to pantomime something for

124

which we are not thankful. Such subjects as war, funny-looking hats, swing music, etc., might be portrayed.

ARMISTICE DAY. Climax the party by one of several methods. (a) Present in full or in part some good play on peace. (b) Have a reading-rehearsal of a portion of a play on peace, such as *Pawns*, by Percival Wilde.(c) Have someone read portions of some play such as *The Enemy*, by Channing Pollock. (d) Sing songs of various lands.

A NOVEMBER PARTY

INVITATION:

> You'll remember this November
> If you attend our November party.

DECORATIONS. Autumn leaves, turkey cutouts and miniatures, footballs, pennants, corn stalks, pumpkins, corn on the cob, cornucopias with fruit.

FINDING TURKEYS. Hide small turkey and football cut-outs about the room. Divide into squads, each with a leader. When anyone discovers a turkey, that person starts a "gobble-gobble" imitation of a turkey as a signal for the leader to come and pick up the turkey. When a football is discovered, the finder continues to shout "Rah! Rah! Rah!" until the leader comes. At the end of three minutes a whistle is blown to end the hunt. Each group announces its count of turkeys and footballs.

GOBBLE-GOBBLE. The leader stands before the group and makes a short Thanksgiving speech. Each time he uses the words "Thanksgiving," or "pilgrim," or "turkey," or "football," he raises either the right or left hand, or both, in gestures. Each guest has been given the name of some animal. For a large crowd the names can be given to groups of players. If the leader raises the right hand, all of the crowd must "gobble-gobble" until the hand is lowered. If the left hand is raised, each person or group imitates the cry of the given animal. If both hands are raised, then the players must alternate the "gobble-gobble" calls with imitations of the animals. Anyone who makes a mistake must get up and stand with the leader.

TURKEY CONUNDRUMS.   Use either paper and pencil or have the crowd divided into two groups, and award points to the group in which someone first calls the correct answer.

1. What part of a turkey does my lady uses in dressing? Comb.

2. What part of a turkey opens the locked door? Key.

3. What part of a turkey is part of a sentence? Claws.

4. What part of a turkey concerns the farmer? Crop.

5. What part of a turkey is in Ankara? Turk.

6. What part of a turkey comes the first of the month? Bill.

7. What part of a turkey does the army flying cadet desire? Wings.

8. Why is a big eater like a turkey? Both are gobblers.

9. In what country is a turkey cooked? Greece.

10. What part of the turkey appears in the band or orchestra? Drumstick.

11. Why should we feel a bit embarrassed at the Thanksgiving dinner? Because we see the turkey dressing.

TABLE FOOTBALL.   Cover long tables with shelf or wrapping paper. Mark off as a football field. Use empty eggshell footballs. Players try to blow the football over the goal line.

THANKSGIVING COUPLETS.   Have each individual compose a couplet using the word "thanks" as the

126

ast word in either the first or second line. In large crowds
divide into groups and have each group work out several
couplets. Banks, cranks, flanks, planks, ranks, and tanks
suggest some rhyming possibilities.

A *SHIP QUIZ.* There is fun guessing what kind of
'ship" applies in each of the following:

1. A ship for the lovelorn.
2. A ship for comrades.
3. A ship that directs and sets the pace.
4. The pride of the navy.
5. A ship useful in the theater.
6. A ship for church.
7. A learner's ship.
8. A very speedy ship.
9. A good ship for athletes.
10. A ship that takes sides.

Answers: 1. Courtship. 2. Friendship. 3. Leadership. 4.
Battleship. 5. Showmanship. 6. Worship. 7. Apprenticeship.
8. Airship. 9. Sportsmanship. 10. Partisanship.

CHAPTER IV

Winter Parties

Winter Parties

A CAROL FESTIVAL

Make this an outstanding feature of the Christmas season. Spend much time in preparation. Advertise by posters and announcements to assure a good crowd. Arrange for rehearsals of dramatic episodes and special musical numbers.

The master of ceremonies can be an important factor in the success of the program. He should familiarize himself with the history of carols, stories of particular carols, and incidents connected with some of the songs. Any general encyclopedia will furnish facts about the history of carols. There is a general belief that carols owe their origin to Francis of Assisi, who, early in the thirteenth century, used them to tell the Christmas story simply and effectively. However, the earlist carols were festive in nature, and this would indicate an earlier and different origin. In the early days of their beginnings they were used as themes for revels, masques, carnivals, and processions.

GENERAL SINGING. Give everyone a chance to sing some of the more familiar hymns and carols: "Joy to the World," "O Come, All Ye Faithful," "O Little Town of Bethlehem," "Hark! the Herald Angels Sing," "It Came upon the Midnight Clear," "While Shepherds Watched Their Flocks by Night," and that universal favorite, "Silent Night." A story now and then about the song to be sung will help.

A CAROL QUIZ. Quiz questions can be interspersed in the program, or the quiz may be conducted without interruption until finished. The answers may be shouted from the audience, or special people may be called to the platform. When they cannot answer, the audience is given a chance. Here are enough questions to indicate possibilities. Work out a longer list if desired.

1. What carol is about a Bohemian king of the tenth century? *Answer:* "Good King Wenceslas."

2. What carol is featured in Dickens' *Christmas Carol?* *Answer:* "God Rest You Merry, Gentlemen."

3. What carol was written by a German priest, with the music composed by a German schoolmaster? It was first sung as a duet by these two. *Answer:* "Silent Night."

4. What carol was translated from a Latin hymn of the eighteenth century and is sometimes known by the title *Adeste fideles? Answer:* "O Come, All Ye Faithful."

5. What French carol mentions a torch? *Answer:* "Bring a Torch, Jeanette, Isabella."

CAROL DRAMATIZATIONS. "Good King Wenceslas," "We Three Kings of Orient Are," and "God Rest You Merry, Gentlemen," easily lend themselves to dramatization. For instance, "Good King Wenceslas" tells the story of aid the good king gave to a poor peasant. All you have to do is follow the story as told in the carol.

A modern touch could be introduced by having a camp scene, with one of the soldiers singing "I'm Dreaming of a White Christmas."

TABLEAUX. Some lovely tableaux can be worked out for special musical numbers. If done behind a net to give depth, they will be particularly effective. Suggestions for tableaux may be found in *The Nativity*, by Rosamond Kimball. It contains a series of tableaux with music.

CHRISTMAS CAROL. Present a portion of Dickens' *Christmas Carol*. A good dramatization of this famous story is issued by Walter H. Baker & Co., 569 Boylston, Boston.

SPECIAL MUSIC. Intersperse the program with special musical numbers, both instrumental and vocal. Good solo numbers: "Holy Night" (Adam), "The Birthday of a King" (Neidlinger), "Jesu Bambino" (Yon), "Sweet Little Jesus Child" (Guion). A choir director will be able to suggest other numbers for quartet and chorus use.

A GOOD CLOSING. A good closing is suggested by the story of the funeral of Mme Schumann-Heink. One of her favorite songs was "Silent Night." At the close of her funeral service the clear bugle notes of "Taps" sounded. Then followed the soft strains of a harp and cello playing "Silent Night." Perhaps this story can be preceded with the use of a record of "Silent Night" as sung by Schumann-Heink. Tell the story, have "Taps" played, and close with hidden musicians softly playing or singing the song.

A STAR PARTY

INVITATION:

Star light, star bright,
Come to our Star Party Friday night.

133

DECORATIONS. Paper gilt stars decorating walls and hanging from chandeliers.

WHAT STAR AM I? As guests arrive, pin on their backs name of stars or constellations, without letting them know what the particular star or constellation is. Questions and remarks dropped by others should give them leads to their identity. For instance, "How are your six sisters?" would be a dead giveaway. Immediately the person is likely to know that he represents the Pleiades. When a person guesses what star he represents, he reports to the chairman of the evening and, if he is correct, the name is pinned on the coat lapel or dress front. Several guests may carry the same name. Some suggested names: Vega, Cassiopeia, Orion, Ursa Major, Ursa Minor, Sirius, Venus, Saturn, Mars, and Scorpio.

If desired, the committee may also use names of movie stars, star athletes, etc.

PROGRESSIVE STAR CHECKERS. Play Chinese or Star Checkers progressively. Winning boy and girl at each table progress. Do not allow this feature to consume more than thirty minutes.

STAR QUIZ. Make out a list of questions about stars of various kinds. Call out certain people in the group for each question. If they cannot answer, throw the question out to the crowd. Here are some sample questions:

1. What group of stars reminds you of a kitchen utensil? *Answer:* The Big Dipper.

2. What star is used by mariners? *Answer:* The Polar Star.

3. What group of stars reminds you of a large family of girls? *Answer:* The Seven Sisters (Pleiades).

4. What star retired from professional baseball because of paralysis? *Answer:* Lou Gehrig.

134

5. What athletic star was known as "The Galloping Ghost"? *Answer:* Red Grange.

6. What pugilistic star was known as "Gentleman Jim"? *Answer:* James J. Corbett.

7. What pugilistic star was nicknamed "The Manassa Mauler"? *Answer:* Jack Dempsey.

8. What famous movie star usually played tramp parts and excelled in pantomime? *Answer:* Charlie Chaplin.

9. What famous stage star's brothers made considerable reputation in the movies? *Answer:* Ethel Barrymore.

10. What famous French actress was called "The Divine Sarah"? *Answer:* Sarah Bernhardt.

STAR SONGS. For special music have someone play Wagner's "Evening Star" on the piano. Or get a good record of this famous number and play it on a phonograph. "Stars of the Summer Night" would make a good male quartet number, or the entire crowd could sing it. "Evening Star Up Yonder," a Danish song, would make a good number for group singing. "Stardust" is another song that might be used.

STAR LEGENDS. Have someone prepared to tell briefly some interesting bit of star lore. *Field Book of the Skies*, by Olcott and Putnam, has a wealth of material for such a feature.

A STAR STORY. An abridged telling of Henry van Dyke's *Story of the Other Wise Man* would be appropriate. Perhaps just a synopsis would be enough.

FOLLOWING THE STAR. A tableau or shadow picture of the three wise men following the star would be a fitting climax. Take pains to see that it is well done. If done in tableau, then there should be beauty and color in it. If done as a shadow show on a screen or sheet, practice it to get the desired effect. As a special musical number for this feature have three men sing "We Three Kings of Orient Are," or have this song sung as a solo.

CLOSING WORSHIP MOMENTS. Read Ps. 19, "The heavens declare," and the story of the birth of Christ in Luke 2:1-20. Follow these readings with a moment of meditation on the meaning of the Christmas star. Benediction.

SEEING STARS. If it proves practical, go outside to look at the stars through a telescope or binoculars. Have someone who can tell the group about various December constellations.

REFRESHMENTS. Star-shaped cookies and punch. If a salad is desired, star-shaped pineapple is obtainable. Star-shaped sandwiches are also appropriate.

A CHRISTMAS TREE PARTY

INVITATION:

A
Christmas
party for large
and small; A Christ-
mas party for short
and tall; A Christmas
party, come one, come all!
F
R
I
D
A
Y
December 19

Mimeograph the invitations on Christmas tree cutouts. Also use posters with sprigs of fir, pine, or spruce for borders.

136

Tannenbaum

O Christmas Tree! O Christmas Tree!
Thy leaves are so unchanging;
Not only green when summer's here,
But also when 'tis cold and drear;
O Christmas Tree! O Christmas Tree!
Thy leaves are so unchanging.

Use the familiar song "Tannenbaum" ("O Christmas Tree") as a mixer. The movement is as follows:

Formation. Double circle by couples, man with his partner to his right.

Action. 1. Couples move counterclockwise around the circle four steps and repeat, with a brief pause at the end of each four steps.

2. The man bows and the woman curtsies to partner.

3, 4. On "O Tannenbaum" or "O Christmas Tree" the above action is repeated.

5. Couples take right hands and circle around one another eight steps and back to place.

6. Couples take left hands and circle around one another eight steps and back to place.

7, 8. Couples repeat action in 1 and 2, except that at the end each person bows to a new partner to the left.

Repeat entire routine as often as desired. Use a walking step throughout.

If the group is not well acquainted, stop each time to allow time for new partners to become acquainted.

CHRISTMAS TREE ART. Furnish each couple with a piece of cardboard or paper, pencils, and colored crayons. By cutting crayons into small pieces a few boxes will serve a large crowd. Each couple will draw a decorated Christmas tree and sign their names to the artistic result. These creations will then be put on display.

137

HUMAN CHRISTMAS TREES. Divide the crowd into two or more groups. Provide each group with Christmas tree decorations (crepe-paper streamers, popcorn strings, etc.), and have them each decorate one person in the group as a human Christmas tree.

CHRISTMAS TREE TOYS. Each person has been requested to bring some toy or plaything from home. Discarded dolls, outgrown scooters and bikes, toy automobiles, and the like, should be part of the lot. These are placed under a large Christmas tree as people arrive.

The toys are to be delivered to the homes of children who may otherwise not have much in the way of Christmas joy. At this time the toys are assembled and assorted. Those that need repairing are turned over to a repairing committee. Perhaps a scooter needs repairing, or a doll needs new clothes. It may be that other meetings will need to be held to get all the toys in shape for delivery Christmas Eve.

THE FIRST CHRISTMAS TREE. Have someone tell the story of *The First Christmas Tree,* by Eugene Field. As a second choice take Hans Christian Andersen's story by the same title. Perhaps this feature should precede the assorting of toys.

The story can be prefaced by the story of the meaning of the Christmas tree. The legend goes that on the day of the birth of Christ the trees bloomed and bore fruit, though all about it was cold and barren. Thus early Christians on Christmas Day began the practice of decorating trees with fruits and lights.

A WHITE ELEPHANT PARTY

An appropriate party for the Christmas season could be built about the above theme. Ask the guests to bring something they have that they do not want—a last year's Christmas present or something of the sort. These presents may be wrapped any way the donor desires. Some will, no doubt, try to disguise their articles by some unusual wrapping.

Packages are numbered. Each guest draws a number and is entitled to the package bearing the same number.

After examining the "white elephant" he has drawn, a guest may rewrap it, and then try to trade it, sight unseen, for the package another guest has drawn. This trading may continue until the leader closes the market.

Preceding the drawing for packages, give the group an opportunity to play some games. Let them have a few minutes to try their hands at finding words in the letters in "white elephant." Examples: whit, whet, while, whelp, tent, help, etc.

Perhaps the group would like to try "A Trip to the Zoo." Divide the elephants, the lions, the tigers, the bears.

Sing some animal songs such as "I Went to the Animal Fair." End with singing some Christmas carols.

A CHRISTMAS SWAPPING PARTY

Each person brings a present, not to cost over a quarter. The present should be carefully wrapped so as to conceal its identity. In one such party one person brought a very large package. It proved to be a series of boxes, one inside the other. In the last tiny box was the present.

As guests arrive, they place their packages on a table or under a Christmas tree. The group sings carols to start the program.

Grand march the group into a circle formation. Then stop and hand each person a package. While the music plays, packages are passed to the right. When the music stops, each person keeps the package he has. He opens it, discovers what it is, and then rewraps it and tries to trade it to someone else in the room. This swapping goes on for five or ten minutes. When the leader announces, "All swapping stop," each person keeps the present he has at that time.

Have someone tell a Christmas story such as can be found in any good collection. In one such party Roark Bradford's *How Come Christmas?* was used.

End the party with more carols. "Silent Night" would make a good closing number.

TOYLAND PARTY

Here's a "kid" party for grownups—a "kid" party with a purpose! The purpose is to provide Christmas toys for needy children. Each person who comes to the party is asked to bring some toys to be distributed. Discarded toys will be welcomed—wagons, scooters, rocking horses, dolls, toy automobiles, doll furniture, etc.

INVITATION.

Said Ima Dumbunny to Ivan O'Branes,
"There'll be lots of fun Friday nite."
Said Ivan to Ima, "There'll be nothing finer;
That Toyland Party sounds just right."

Toyland Party—Friday, December 19, 8 p.m.
Come Dressed in Kid Clothes—Bring Some Toys

TOY SHOP. Give each man a slip of paper with the name of some toy on it. Give duplicates to the women. At the signal of the leader, each man starts imitating his toy and continues doing so until his "owner" discovers him. The "scooter" will imitate a boy using one. The "mamma doll" will cry "mamma." The horn will do a good job of tooting. And thus it will go until all "toys" are claimed.

MARCH OF TOYS. The couples will now participate in a grand march to the music of "The March of the Toys" from *Babes in Toyland.*

TOYLAND GAMES. Kiddie Car Race: Have two adults race across the room on kiddie cars. *Balloon Burst:* Blow up balloons until they burst. *Balloon Flight:* Blow up toy sausage balloons and turn them loose to see how far they can go.

Play other children's games, as desired.

TOY WORKSHOP. Assort toys. Paint and repair them for distribution. This will mean that a committee in charge of this feature will have made special preparations. Necessary materials and plans of organization will have to be arranged. Most of the party time will be given to this feature.

A CIRCLE PARTY

INVITATION. Be square with yourself and come round to the circle party.

DECORATIONS. All decorations should be done in circles. Cut out circles of cardboard or construction paper of various colors. Hang some from chandeliers, place on

141

walls, tables, etc. Also hang about the room automobile inner tubes covered with crepe paper of various colors, and use toy colored balloons.

PROGRAM. Play circle games such as "Revolving Circle," "Three Deep," "Toe Ball," "Who's the Leader?" "Sandy Land," "Chebogah," "Ach Ja," etc.

CONCENTRIC CIRCLES. Begin the party with concentric circles. Boys on the inside and girls on the outside. Let them march in opposite directions to music. When the music stops, stop and face a partner. As they meet new partners, they can do any number of things suggested by the leader, such as discussing a subject that is announced, getting acquainted, swapping jokes or conundrums. Typewritten slips of the last two things may be given them on arrival by the committee.

TEN LITTLE INDIANS.

> One little, two little, three little Indians,
> Four little, five little, six little Indians,
> Seven little, eight little, nine little Indians,
> Ten little Indian boys.

> Ten little, nine little, eight little Indians,
> Seven little, six little, five little Indians,
> Four little, three little, two little Indians,
> One little Indian boy.

The concentric circles sing this song. As they sing it, the men in the inner circle move counterclockwise, the women standing still. Each man steps up one woman as each number is sung, taking her hand. On "three little Indians," "six little Indians," and "nine little Indians" they take hands four counts, pumping up and down in rhythm. On "ten little Indian boys" they take that partner with both hands and march around the circle, singing the sec-

142

ond part of the song, "Ten little, nine little, eight little Indians," etc.

CIRCLE OF THE MONTHS. Divide the crowd into groups according to the month of each person's birth and have each group present some pantomime or dramatic skit appropriate to the particular month.

CIRCLE OF THE YEARS. Play games representing the various steps of life: babyhood, childhood, youth, and adulthood. For babyhood the game might be "Ten Little Squirrels" or "Three Blue Pigeons." For childhood, "Peas Porridge Hot," "Pussy Wants a Corner," or "Looby Loo." For youth, any of the familiar games the group likes to do. For adulthood try a quiz.

CIRCLE OF PROGRESS. Put on a shadow show showing the progress in the field of transportation. This can easily be done by stretching a piece of Waverly window curtain on a frame, having a light behind the curtain while figures on sticks are held up against it, as is done in Chinese shadow shows. Have somebody read up on the history of transportation and cut out cardboard figures to represent the various stages of progress. For instance, transportation by land would picture the sledge, then the crude, rough-wheeled vehicle, with the wheels made out of heavy logs, then the wagon, the stagecoach, the locomotive, the automobile, and the airplane. Transportation by water could picture a man riding on a log, then a crude canoe, then the rowboat, the sailboat, the steamboat, the giant ocean liner, and the hydroplane. If desired, these could be worked out in colors by cutting the figures out of pyralin (a Du Pont product).

Or present an episode on growth in courting. The first scene would show courting in grandmother's day; the second would depict courting today.

143

REFRESHMENTS. There is a variety of things that might be done in the way of refreshments. The following are suggested: apples, doughnuts, pineapple salad, jelly roll, Life Savers, and round cookies.

A TRIPLE-H PARTY

Have a heart! Use your head! And then give a hand!
You'll be smart if you're led to this party grand!

HANDSHAKING. Use some handshaking plans such as the following: (a) As guests arrive, tie paper sacks on their right hands. Each person is to continue shaking hands until he wears out the sack. (b) Secret handshakers are provided with pennies. The thirteenth person to shake hands with a secret handshaker gets a penny. (c) Spiral handshake (see *The Fun Encyclopedia*, p. 254).

TRIPLE-H CHAMPS. Divide into groups of three each. Each group is to list as many words as possible containing the words "hand," "head," and "heart." Suggest that each member of a team be assigned one of the three words. When a player reaches a stopping point, he consults with his teammates so that the group's total list represents the thinking of all three. At the end of five minutes call time. Have each group count what it has. Let the group with the largest total read its list. They are declared "Triple-H Champs" and may be decorated with cardboard medals attesting the fact. Suggested words: handsome, handy, handball, handle, heady, headfirst, headpiece, hearty, heartache, heartsick, heart-warming.

USE YOUR HEAD. A quiz or guessing game. Or play "Categories," using the letters H-E-A-D for the headline. The leader will call the category and players write all the articles or words they can under each of the letters. Food, clothes, furnishings, animals, birds, and other categories may be called.

HANDCRAFTS. One of the purposes of this party is to introduce the guests to the joys of handcrafts. If plans can be made to follow up with some opportunities for learning and practicing some of these crafts, so much the better. Have on exhibit a display of hobbies and crafts. Scour the community for interesting specimens of carving, leatherwork, puppets, painting, sketching, linoleum block printing, and other results of someone's creative hobby. Arrange demonstrations. Provide opportunities for guests to try their hands at a few simple hobbies such as soap carving, spatter printing, and finger painting.

STAGEHANDS. Divide into two or three groups. Have each group list as many situations as they can where the hand tells a story. Then have them take turns acting out the proposed situations. Examples: a traffic cop at a busy corner, a baseball umpire calling out a base runner, a baseball pitcher, an outfielder catching a fly, a hitchhiker, "thumbs down," disgust, "come to me," "I don't care."

HEARTTHROBS. Do a romantic shadow show. Scene 1: The heroine darns a sweater for her sweetheart. Scene 2: The villain sneaks up behind her and claps his hand over her mouth to prevent an outcry. Scene 3: The hero returns in time to take care of the villain. Scene 4: The hero and heroine gaze soulfully into each other's eyes. Practice this shadow show at least once to get proper effects.

HEART SONGS. Close the party with group singing of romantic songs: "Love's Old Sweet Song," "Let Me Call You Sweetheart," "White Wings," "Sing Your Way Home," and the like.

HANDOUT. Refreshments.

145

VALENTINE DRAMATIC FESTIVAL

VALENTINE DRAMATIC FESTIVAL
(Date and Hour)

All the world's a stage,
And all is romance in it;
Cupid is the star,
In fact, he doth begin it.
So rustle up your drama togs,
Be Pan, Bopeep, or Legree,
Be Robin Hood or Juliet,
Or just what strikes your fancy.

COME DRESSED
AS SOME CHARACTER
IN DRAMA

DECORATIONS. Hearts, red-and-white crepe streamers, and the traditional masks that symbolize drama would be appropriate decorations.

PROGRAM. Urge everyone to come dressed to represent some character in drama, ancient or modern.

SILHOUETTES. Tack large sheets of paper (newsprint) upon the wall. Arrange a strong light for projecting shadow. Pose each guest, as he arrives, so that the shadow of his profile will fall upon the paper. Let someone quickly trace the outline with black crayon. These outlines are numbered and later put on display. Each person fills out a "who's who" list in which he tries to identify each silhouette.

DUMMY LINE. March the guests in two concentric circles, the men inside moving counterclockwise, and the women outside moving clockwise. When the music stops, both circles stop and face each other. Then the players discuss in pantomime such subjects as the leader announces. No spoken word is permitted. Sample subjects: What kind of valentine do you like best? Best book I've read. The songs I like best. For men: What do you think of women's hats? For women: Who is the boss in every family and why?

ETERNAL TRIANGLE. Divide into two sides. Each side decides whether it will represent a maiden, her lover, or the minister. If the maiden, players assume a coy expression, finger under the chin; if her lover, one hand is placed over the heart, with the other extended in pleading; if the minister, the right hand is held up in blessing. If desired, "the demon chaperone" may be substituted for the minister. In this case each player would fold his arms over his chest and glower. At "One-two-three" both sides assume the chosen pose. The maiden beats the lover. The lover beats the minister. The minister beats the maiden. Score one point for each win. Continue until one side scores three points. This is an adaptation of "Jonkenpon" (stone-paper-scissors).

IMPROMPTU PANTOMIMES. Keep the same two sides. Have each side make out a list of half a dozen situations to be acted out in pantomime by the other group. These lists are exchanged, and then each side takes turns having persons from its group act them out one at a time.

147

Suggestions: (a) The first date. (b) The lovers' quarrel. (c) Three's a crowd. (d) The first wedding anniversary and the twenty-first. (e) Posing for the family portrait. (f) Husband meets wife; she's thirty minutes late. (g) How to propose marriage three different ways. (h) At the picture show together. (i) The rejected suitor (melodrama). (j) Making the touch as painless as possible—the wife wants a new fur coat.

SHADOW SHOWS. Have each side prepare a shadow show of a romantic nature. If these can be planned for ahead of time, and better, if they can be rehearsed, it will be advantageous. Put up a sheet on the platform or in the doorway, with a strong light behind it so as to throw the shadows upon the sheet.

A brief take off on *Snow White and the Seven Dwarfs* could be presented. Scene 1: The Seven Dwarfs Go to Work. Scene 2: The Evil Witch Gets in Her Dirty Work. Scene 3: The Dwarfs Mourn the Loss of Snow White. Scene 4: The Handsome Prince Brings Snow White to Life.

Or a "mellerdrammer" could feature the evening. (a) Jack Dalton abducts the heroine. (b) The hero comes to the rescue. "Curses!" says Jack Dalton. (c) "We'll live happily ever after."

A MUSICAL VALENTINE. An excellent musical feature could be worked out by building a large frame and fitting it up like an old-fashioned valentine. Within this frame two singers could sing a duet—"Bendemeer's Stream" or "Will You Remember?"

CUPID'S QUEST PARTY

Hey, hey, diddle—luma—dey
Cupid's coming 'long this way
He's looking for you,

148

He's looking for me,
He'd like to have our company,
As he searches high,
And he searches low,
For victims of his trusty bow.
So lock up your house
There'll be plenty of fun
At Cupid's Quest Party
There'll be thrills by the ton.

CUPID'S COBWEB. Make a cobweb of strings in one corner of the room. Some of these strings, at least one for each guest, extend from the cobweb to various parts of the room or building. They loop around chair legs; they cross with other strings; they move along the floor or wall. Each player takes hold of an end of string at the center of the web. The girls select white strings and the boys red. Then each guest follows his string to the end, unwinding, pulling it through a staple, untangling from the strings of other players. When he gets to the end he finds an envelope attached containing some such message as this: "You are a member of Group Two. Wait here until your partner arrives. Her (his) string is attached to yours. When both of you have arrived report to the leader." The white strings and red strings are tied together at the ends. The messages are sealed or clipped over the string. Guests should not break their strings.

QUESTING. Guests report to the leader according to instructions. The leader then sends them to various parts of the room or building. Group One reports in one corner, Group Two in another, and Group Three in another.

Each corner is fitted up appropriately. Group One is to discover the best love song. A book of love songs and other song collections should be on a table in this corner. The members of Group One discuss famous love songs and come to some agreement, after suggestions and discussion.

149

They are instructed that they must sing the song of their choice when called upon to do so. If there is difficulty in deciding on one song, they may sing two or three, letting the other groups help them in deciding.

Group Two is to quest for the best love poem. Volumes of poetry are on hand. They use much the same method as Group One. They may also be requested to compose an original love poem.

Group Three is to decide on the world's best love story. Lists of stories of romance are provided and possibly some books. When they have decided on their story, they must arrange a very brief dramatization of at least part of it. In this dramatization they may be allowed to introduce such variations in the story as they may desire.

Written instructions should be provided to each group as to what is expected of them. The various groups perform as directed.

CUPID'S MIXTURE. At this point mix your crowd with a grand march. Perhaps you might play some game such as "Sent My Brown Jug Downtown."

BROWN JUG

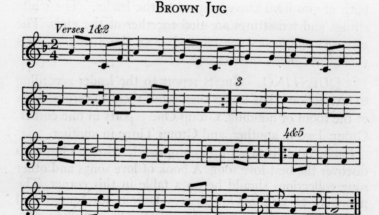

I. 1. Sent my brown jug downtown
   2. Sent my brown jug downtown
   3. Sent my brown jug downtown
   4. So early in the morning.

II. 1. It came back with a waltz around
   2. It came back with a waltz around
   3. It came back with a waltz around
   4. So early in the morning.

III. 1. Railroad, steamboat, river and canoe,
     Lost my true love, don't know what to do.

IV. 1. Oh, she's gone, gone, gone; oh, she's gone, gone, gone.
   2. Oh, she's gone on that raging canoe.

V. 1. Let her go, go, go! Let her go, go, go!
   2. Let her go on that raging canoe!

Formation: Single circle of partners, holding hands. The girl stands on her partner's right.

I. 1-4. Holding hands around the circle walk left.

II. 1-4. Continue holding hands and walk right.

III. 1. Partners face each other, take right hands and walk around one another.

   2. Take left hand of opposite (this will be the girl who held the man's left hand in the big circle) and walk around and back to partner (allemande right).

IV. 1. Partners face, men with backs to center of circle. Catch both hands and slide four slow steps to man's left.

   2. Swing partner once around and move immediately to new partner, each taking the one he swung in III-2.

V. 1. Repeat IV-1 with new partner.

   2. Swing the new partner once, finishing with the girl on the man's right.

151

GREAT LOVERS' QUEST. Give to each couple a typewritten list of initials of famous lovers. They are to discover the names of these lovers and list them correctly. After allowing a suitable time, the leader reads the correct list.

1. R. and J. 2. T. and I. 3. R. and B. 4. A. and C. 5. J. A. and P. 6. H. and M. 7. R. B. and E. B. 8. G. and E. 9. O. and D. 10. H. and O. 11. S. and D. 12. J. and R. 13. F. and M. 14. F. and J.

Answers: 1. Romeo and Juliet. 2. Tristan and Isolde. 3. Ruth and Boaz. 4. Anthony and Cleopatra. 5. John Alden and Priscilla. 6. Hiawatha and Minnehaha. 7. Robert Browning and Elizabeth Barrett. 8. Gabriel and Evangeline. 9. Othello and Desdemona. 10. Hamlet and Ophelia. 11. Samson and Delilah. 12. Jacob and Rachel. 13. Faust and Margaret. 14. Frankie and Johnnie.

I'M LOOKING FOR A WIFE. The men sit in a circle. The women are onlookers. One man turns to his neighbor to his right and says, "I'm looking for a wife who is amiable" (or any descriptive word beginning with the letter a). The next man then says, "I'm looking for a wife who is amiable and beautiful." The next one says, "I'm looking for a wife who is amiable, beautiful, and cute." The next one may add "dumb." So it goes until the men have completed the alphabet. If a player is unable to think of a word beginning with the letter he gets, or if he makes a mistake in repeating the attributes already mentioned, it is scored against the men.

Then the women go looking for a husband in the same fashion.

The side finishing the alphabet with the fewest mistakes wins.

152

A VALENTINE CRUISE

INVITATION. "Sail on the good ship Valentine on the Sea of Good Fellowship. Leaves dock at 8 P.M. (Date and place.)"

DECORATIONS. Lifesavers on walls about the room. Festoons of hearts.

COMMITTEE. Committee members should be dressed as seamen, even if they do no more than wear a sailor's cap.

PASSPORTS. Each guest on arrival is given a comic valentine pasted on a piece of cardboard. These are strung so they can be hung about the neck. Each guest must wear his valentine throughout the evening. These will serve as icebreakers when people meet.

CRUISING FOR HEARTS. Hide paper hearts about the room where they can easily be found, one heart for each guest present. These hearts are numbered 1, 2, and 3. Each player hunts until he finds one heart. When each player has a heart, announce that all of the One's are to get together, and the Two's and Three's are to do likewise.

HEARTWALK. Have each group select a team of from five to ten players. Supply each team with two large cardboard hearts. Teams gather their players at either side of the room for a shuttle relay. At the signal to start, the first player on each team walks across the room stepping only on the two hearts, that is, he puts down a heart, steps on it; puts down the other heart, steps on it. Then lifting the hind foot, he picks up the heart on which it rested, and moves it forward to step on it again. At no time must either foot touch the floor. When he reaches the opposite side

153

of the room, he hands the two hearts to a teammate, who repeats the performance. This continues until all teammates have completed the course.

CONVOYED. There are five players on a team. One sits in a chair. At the starting signal the other four players pick up the chair and carry the seated player across the room. On reaching the goal line, the seated player gets up. He becomes a carrier while another teammate sits down and is carried back across the room. This continues until each player has been convoyed across the room.

MY SWEETHEART. Seat all the guests but one in a circle. The extra player goes to someone of the opposite sex and kneels before that player, saying, "I love you." The person thus addressed must then stroke the head of the kneeling one and solemnly say "My sweetheart" without smiling or laughing. If he laughs or smiles, he must take the place of the kneeler, finding someone else before whom to kneel and declare his love. If he does not smile, the kneeler repeats the statement a second and third time, requiring an answer and a pat on the head each time. Failure to elicit a smile in three trials means the kneeler must try again on someone else in the circle. The kneeler may get as dramatic as he desires in his efforts to bring a smile. This ought not to be difficult since the rest of the crowd will probably be convulsed with laughter. Several persons may be chosen to be kneelers if the group is a very large one.

HEART SHUFFLEBOARD. Draw a heart shuffleboard diagram on the floor with chalk. The hearts should be arranged in triangular formation with the point of each heart facing the "shover." At the apex there should be one heart about twelve inches wide at its widest part. This

154

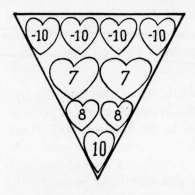

heart counts 10. In the second row there are two hearts, each eighteen inches wide. These hearts count 8 points each. In the third row are two hearts twenty-four inches wide. These count 7 points each. The fourth row has four hearts, each about thirteen inches wide. Each of these counts 10 off. Use regulation shuffleboard equipment or make your own cues and disks. Disks should be circular, four inches in diameter, and three-eighths of an inch to one inch thick. Four disks should be red and four black. The cues should not be longer than six feet, three inches. Play the game as regular shuffleboard.

HEART QUOITS. Paint a red heart on a block of wood. At the center drive a long spike. Spikes may also be driven at the tips and sides. Use teething rings or rope rings for quoits. Players toss five rings, scoring five points for ringing the center spike and two points for each of the others.

CLOSING. Sing such songs as "Anchors Aweigh," "Sailing, Sailing," "When All My Little Ships," and other ship songs.

HEART HOODOO PARTY

This Heart Party will be a smart party,
    A Hoodoo Party—yes, sir!
You'll be sorry if you're not present
    When the fun begins to stir.

155

DECORATIONS. Black cats, horseshoes covered with crepe paper, cardboard horseshoes. Large number thirteens about the room. Large paper four-leaf clovers. Black and red hearts.

LUCKY HANDSHAKER. Start the party by having everyone shake hands with as many persons as possible. As each person shakes hands, he greets people with "Luck to you," or "Happy landing," or some similar good wish. Each of several persons in the group has been given secretly a lucky penny. He must give that lucky penny to the thirteenth person who shakes hands with him. After receiving the penny, the possessor must give it to the thirteenth person who shakes hands with him, counting from the time the penny came into his possession. The whereabouts of the pennies must be kept secret throughout. After a few minutes the leader blows his whistle to end handshaking. Persons having possession of the pennies at that time keep them.

THE ORDER OF THE BLACK HEART. The group stands or sits in a circle, the players with hands behind their backs. The leader walks around outside the circle. He pretends to slip some small object into the hands of each person. In reality he hands to some one person a small black heart. One could easily be cut out of wood and painted for the occasion. In a large crowd several black hearts may be distributed.

After the leader has been around, he notifies the players that they may bring their closed fists around in front of them.

The object of the holder of the heart is to pass it on to his neighbor. This he can do only by presenting both closed fists and having the neighbor tap one as a signal that he desires its contents, if any.

156

Players number off all around the circle. When ready to begin, the leader calls for the odds to present their fists to the neighbors to the right. When the choice is made, the chooser holds both hands together and open enough to receive whatever is coming. Whether he has anything or not, the other player pretends to drop something in the other's hands. Then the evens turn to the neighbors to their right and go through the same process. Players must make their choices of hands immediately.

The skill lies in judging the contents of an opponent's hands and in concealing the contents of one's own.

Music should be played while the heart is being passed. When it stops, the player in possession of it is decorated with a black paper heart. He then deposits the heart with some player. In doing this he goes through the motions of giving the heart to three different players, depositing it with one of them. Then he resumes his place in the circle.

Continue until a half dozen or so have been decorated with the Order of the Black Heart. Then require these persons to perform some stunt as a group.

HOODOO HEART HORSESHOES. Paint red hearts on a piece of board at least twelve inches square. Place curtain pole hooks or nails in the center of the hearts. The center hook is the "Hoodoo." Paint that heart black. Make fine wire hearts four inches wide for each board, using heavy wire and covering it with white cotton and with tape. Or use Mason jar rubber rings. Set the boards up at a slant. Each hook is numbered except the center, the "Hoodoo." Divide into sides and give each player five trials at a distance of six feet. Ringing the "Hoodoo" subtracts ten points. For a large crowd have several games going simultaneously.

HOODOOS. Ask each group to list all the bad omens they can recall. After three minutes ask each group

157

in turn to act out one bad omen it has listed. The other groups try to guess what omen or ill-fortune is being presented. A few suggested hoodoos: break a mirror, seven years' bad luck; sing before breakfast, cry before supper; black cat across the path, bad luck; walk under a ladder, bad luck; if you spill salt, throw some over the shoulder; number thirteen; take the last biscuit and you'll be an old maid; bad luck to open an umbrella in the house; giving a knife for a present without collecting a penny cuts friendship; when a dog howls someone is going to die;

> See a pin and pick it up,
> All that day you'll have good luck.
> See a pin and leave it lay,
> Bad luck you'll have all that day.

> A whistling girl and a crowing hen
> Will never come to any good end.

HOODOO VOODOO. If a girl wanted to put the hoodoo sign on a Scot, with designs toward marriage, she would wear *plaid* to attract his eye. What would she wear to hoodoo each of the following?

Barber—mohair; dairyman—cheesecloth; confectioner—taffeta; artist—canvas; banker—checks; gardener—lawn; milkman—jersey; musician—organdie; editor—prints; financier—cashmere; hunter—duck; baseball player—batiste; prisoner—stripes; undertaker—crepe; fisherman—net.

HOODOO ART AUCTION. The auctioneer and the leader, perhaps, should be the only persons in the know on these "sells." The works of art are identified by name and number only. The contents of each package should be a secret. Much of the fun will come from the element of surprise as the packages are opened. They are opened only when the last package has been sold. Then all packages are opened at once. Players bid with imaginary money. The auctioneer may be arbitrary in designating to whom the articles are knocked down, arranging it so that each person gets a package. The auctioneer can add much to the fun of the occasion. Packages are done up in a variety of ways. It would be appropriate for each package to be decorated with a valentine. Some suggested "art" objects: (1) "Sweethearts," by Gum (two candy hearts with a stick of chewing gum); (2) "The Sower," by Dresser (a needle); (3) "Who's Who," by Knight (a picture of an owl); (4) "Horse Fair," by Hay (a bit of hay and oats or corn); (5) "The Tutor," by Horn (a toy trumpet); (6) "A Study in Greece," by A. Jarr (a vaseline jar); (7) "The Fortune-teller," by A. Medium (a daisy); (8) "The Lost Chord," by Hamm (a piece of string; you're "hamstrung" by this one); (9) "Black Beauty," by A. Miner (a piece of coal); (10) "The Tie That Binds," by Knott (a cravat); (11) "Downfall of China," by Disch (a broken teacup or saucer); (12) "The Fairy Spinner," by Webb (a toy spider); (13) "A Drive Through the Wood," by Knox (nail driven through wood); (14 "View of Castile," by Kleenor (cake of castile soap); (15) "Author of Our National Anthem," by Knote (a key); (16) "Spring, Beautiful Spring," by Weyer (an old spring); (17) "Wayworn Traveler," by Treadway (an old shoe); (18) "The Lamplighter," by Wood (a match); (19) "Maid of Orleans," by Cook (molasses candy); (20) "Skyscraper," by High (a toy airplane). Mimeographed copies of the list of articles to be sold may be distributed.

VALENTINE PARADE

INVITATION:

Hey, come along, ho, come along, hi, come along, hey!
The Valentine Parade is coming along this way

159

You come along, we'll come along, I'll come along, say!
You will never forget it if you join in our play.

Begin with a grand march, the couples coming down by twos, then forming a double circle, man inside with his partner to his right.

Then do "Glow Worm" (music by Lincke). The action is as follows:

1. Partners forward four steps around the circle.

2. Partners back away from one another four short steps.

3. Players point to a new partner to the left and walk four steps to meet one another taking hold of both hands. Thus, each man gets for a new partner the woman who was immediately in front of his former partner.

4. New partners now circle four steps. These four figures are repeated as often as desired. Where the group is not well acquainted, allow a few moments every now and then for partners to talk with one another.

WHERE IS MY HEART? The players are seated in a circle. In a large crowd have several circles. One player begins the game by saying to the player to his right, "Where is your heart?" That player answers, perhaps, by saying, "My heart is on the ocean blue." The first player must now add a line that rhymes, such as, "My, my, that's awful if it's true." The second player now turns to his neighbor and repeats the question. That player may answer, "My heart is in the tallest tree," whereupon the second player says, perhaps, "Well, that is certainly all right with me." And so it goes around the circle. If a player cannot think immediately of an answer that rhymes (and the best will be in that fix at times) move on to the next player, perhaps collecting a forfeit from the losing player. Insist on persons speaking loud enough so as to be heard by everyone playing.

160

HEART COVER. The music now begins and players get up and start marching around the room single file. Paper hearts have been pinned to the walls about the room within easy reach. When the music stops, all players rush to the walls and cover one heart with either the right or left hand. There is at least one less heart than the number of marchers. In a large crowd there may be several less so as to eliminate players in quicker time. Players who fail to cover a heart drop out of the game. One heart is removed each time and the game continues until only one player is left.

SPECIAL DELIVERY. At this point in the program two girls dressed to represent postmen appear on the scene. Each of them has a large heart-shaped pouch out of which they draw half hearts which they deliver to the guests, one serving the women and the other the men. Each half heart carries one or two valentine lines that rhyme with lines on the other half of the heart. The hearts may be cut different shapes. Players match hearts and read their rhymes.

HEART-HUNT PARADE. Couples now march around the room as the music plays. When it stops, each couple holding hands must hunt about the room for hidden hearts. They must not break hands as they hunt. Whenever the music starts up, the heart-hunters must cease hunting and start marching. Two sticks of candy may be given to the couple finding the largest number of hearts.

AIR MAIL. Two girls dressed as aviators interrupt proceedings by blowing whistles. One of them asks the men to gather around her at one side of the room, while the other invites the women to the other side. Out of heart-shaped pouches they take valentine post cards and deliver them, one to a person. The cards in the two pouches are

161

duplicates. It is not necessary to address the cards. Players now look for persons who hold the duplicates and they pair off in couples. Be sure that there are just enough cards for the crowd. If the matter of expense is a considerable item, cards may be cut into two pieces for matching.

BLIND FLYING. String a wire across the room about six feet from the floor. Suspend paper hearts from the wire at different heights. The leader announces that a feature of the Valentine Parade will be some blind flying. Each girl in turn is to be a "clipper," and to make an effort to clip a heart from the air. The girl is blindfolded and is turned around three times. In one hand she holds a pair of scissors (her airplane); and in the other she holds the end of a string about two feet in length. Her partner holds the other end of the string. He tries to guide her to a heart by pulling the string. Three clipping attempts is all that a player is allowed. In a large room several "clippers" may operate at the same time.

LOVE LETTERS. Each couple receives a paper sack containing the letters of the alphabet written on white hearts. When the signal is given, the partners open their bag and take out two letters at a time. The first couple to spell the word "love" wins. The letters may be put back in the sack for another try. This time the first couple to spell "valentine parade" wins. In this latter case it will be necessary to have extra "a's," "n's" and "e's" in each set.

VALENTINE QUARTETS. Cut a number of comic valentines into four parts each. Hide these parts about the room. Each person hunts until he finds one part. Then he seeks out the other three people who have the remaining three parts.

VALENTINE COUPLETS. Each quartet is now asked to write a valentine couplet such as

For you, dear, my heart doth pine.
Won't you be my valentine?

These are to be read to the crowd.

GOOD NIGHT QUARTETS. Have a grand march to get the quartets in a circle, four deep. Now have the quartets number off all around, such as Quartet Number One, Number Two, etc. Then have the even numbers turn and face the quartet immediately behind them. If there is an extra quartet don't despair. It will proceed as if it actually had a quartet facing it. The piano strikes up "Good Night Ladies" and the players sing. The following action takes place.

1. On the first "Good Night Ladies" partners shake right hands.

2. On the second "Good Night Ladies" men shake hands with the women opposite.

3. On the third "Good Night Ladies" partners shake hands again.

4. On "We're going to leave you now" all persons in the set take hold of hands around the ring and raise hands together and lower them in rhythm. This would make a ring of eight people.

5. On the chorus all players holding hands circle left with a walking step until they reach "O'er the deep blue sea."

6. On "O'er the deep blue sea" players should be back in place, the quartets facing. They now drop hands and walk through, passing right shoulders to persons opposite. Thus they face a new quartet.

REFRESHMENT STAND. Decorate a refreshment stand and have the guests march past.

163

A WASHINGTON-LINCOLN PARTY

February is a month of red-letter days. Washington's Birthday, Lincoln's Birthday, and St. Valentine's Day. Combining the two birthdays in one party is often appropriate. If you want to combine all three of these special days and call it a Red-Letter Day Party, that can also be done.

Perhaps the decorations can include an exhibit of antiques. This can be made quite an interesting feature in many communities. An old-time spinning wheel would help to give the proper atmosphere. Red, white, and blue crepe-paper streamers will also help.

A CATCH USED IN COLONIAL TIMES. This catch dates back to Washington's time. Much depends on the leader. He must encourage the group to shout immediately, full volume, each "So am I." Rehearse a couple of times on the first response until the desired effect is obtained. Explain that each time the leader speaks, the group is to respond by shouting "So am I." After the rehearsal on the first item, he repeats the four statements rapidly, not giving the group time to think through on what is being said. Here are the statements and responses:

Leader: "I am a gold lock."

Crowd: "So am I!"

Leader: "I am a silver lock."

Crowd: "So am I!"

Leader: "I am a monk lock."

Crowd: "So am I!"

Leader: "I am a monk key."

Crowd: "So am I!"

With so many "monkeys" present there ought to be a good time. It is barely possible that an alert crowd will turn it back on the leader by shouting "So are you!" on the last line. In that case he should be able to take it.

WASHINGTON CURTSY. Three men are placed ten feet apart, forming a triangle. A tricornered hat is placed on one of the men. He represents Washington. A girl is placed in the center of the triangle, blindfolded, turned around three times, and told to advance eight steps and curtsy to Washington. Try several of the women at this. One of them may succeed.

CHERRY-TREE DRAMA. Select three or four persons. Have them repeat in turn the words: "Father, I cannot tell a lie. I did it with my little hatchet." This is to be done thirteen times, each time emphasizing a different word and striking a different dramatic pose.

WHAT CAN BE FOUND ON A LINCOLN PENNY? Each person should have a penny to examine as the questions are called. The questions may be mimeographed and each person asked to fill in the answers. Sample questions and answers:

1. Name a song ("America"). 2. A privilege (liberty). 3. Part of a hill (brow). 4. A tropical fruit (date). 5. A beverage (T). 6. A religious edifice (temple).

SONGS OF THE SIXTIES. For special numbers and for group singing try some of the old-timers: "Tenting Tonight," "Darling Nellie Gray," "Battle Hymn of the Republic," "Dixie," "O Susanna," and others.

PENNY PASS. Line up two teams of ten people each. They sit facing one another. At the feet of the head player on each team is a row of ten pennies. At the signal to start this player picks up the pennies one at a time and passes them to the next player in the line, again one at a time. The last player in line must place the pennies in a row at his feet. As soon as he has all ten he starts them back, so that finally the starting player has them all placed in a row in their original position. The first team to finish wins.

CHAPTER V

Spring Parties

Spring Parties

A SHAMROCK PARTY

INVITATION. Have a small group sing the invitation to the tune "There'll Be a Hot Time in the Old Town":

One, two, three! We're inviting all of ye!
Four, five, six! We'll show you some new tricks!
Seven, eight, nine! You'll have a grand good time!
At the party—Shamrock Party—Tuesday night.

DECORATIONS. Green crepe-paper streamers. Large shamrocks on walls and hanging from chandeliers. "Shamrock" comes from the Irish word *seamróg*, meaning trefoil, and is applied to various trifoliolate plants native to Ireland. It was used on St. Patrick's Day because legend has it that St. Patrick used it as a symbol to illustrate the Trinity. It has come to be regarded as the national emblem of Ireland.

SHAMROCK HUNT. Hide paper shamrock cutouts about the room. Mark half of them with the letter "A" and the other half with the letter "B." Pin a shamrock on the one who finds the most. Have each player count those shamrocks he has marked "A" and those "B." If the "A's" predominate, he goes to the "A's" side for the next game; if "B's" to the "B" side.

AN IRISH QUIZ. Call the questions and score a point for the side on which someone first answers correctly.
1. What is a shillelagh? *Answer:* A cudgel or club.

169

2. What is the meaning of mavourneen? *Answer:* My darling.

3. What is a colleen? *Answer:* A girl.

4. What is a colleen bawn? *Answer:* A blonde maiden.

5. What is a hooligan? *Answer:* A ruffian.

6. What is the meaning of machree? *Answer:* My heart (a term of endearment).

7. What is a spalpeen (accent the *peen*)? *Answer:* A rascal or scamp.

8. What is blarney? *Answer:* Flattery.

9. What is a garsun? *Answer:* A boy.

10. What is a pratey? *Answer:* A potato.

11. What is shenanigan? *Answer:* Trickery.

12. What is a Hibernian? *Answer:* An Irishman.

13. What is a caibin? *Answer:* A hat.

14. Fill in the missing word of the following songs:

"The rose of ———." *Answer:* Tralee.

"Where the river ——— flows." *Answer:* Shannon.

"Come back to ———, Mavourneen." *Answer:* Erin.

"It's a long way to ———." *Answer:* Tipperary.

"There's a bower of roses by ——— stream." *Answer:* Bendemeer's.

SHAMROCK ANAGRAMS. Have the same two sides make as many words as they can out of the letters in the word "shamrock." Five minutes. Have the side with the largest number of words read the list it has.

SHAMROCK BEANBAG. Get a large corrugated box. Paint a large shamrock on it and cut a four-inch hole in each wing of the shamrock. Use three-inch beanbags covered with green cloth. Give each player three tosses. Count one point for each beanbag that goes through one of the three holes. Let the players of two sides alternate.

PINNING THE SHAMROCK. Make a map of Ireland and pin it on the wall. Blindfold players in turn and have them see how near they can come to pinning the shamrock on Ireland.

A SHAMROCK GRAND MARCH. All the boys line up on one side of the room and all the girls on the other. The lines march around the room to meet one another. As they do, they pair off and come down the middle by twos. Put them through various marching figures, ending by bringing them up in lines of eight couples each.

IRISH WASHERWOMAN. To the music of "The Irish Washerwoman" do some marching. End with two concentric circles, men inside and women outside. Then have men march one direction and women the other. When music stops, marchers stop, face, and shout "Top o' the mornin'!" When music starts, leave partner, start marching again, shouting "Top o' the mornin'!" as each leaves.

IRISH SCULPTURE. Provide each person with a stick of chewing gum and a card. Each one will chew the gum and then use it to mold an Irish hat, a pipe, or a shamrock on the card.

If it is possible to get a supply of modeling clay, the guests might try their hands at some real modeling. In this case have on hand some pocket or paring knives and some meat sticks for making lines. Modeling is appropriate because March is the birth month of Michelangelo.

SHAMROCK FINDINGS. Ask players to find in the letters in the word "shamrock" the following things: (1) A writer of one of the Gospels (Mark). (2) What aviators strive to avoid (crash). (3) Hypocrisy (sham). (4) What students do before examination (cram). (5) A kind of coffee (Mocha). (6) What they call a poor actor (ham). (7) What soldiers sometimes have to do (march).

(8) A male sheep (ram). (9) Swampy land (marsh). (10) A member of the body (arm). (11) A well-known uncle (Sam). (12) The god of war (Mars). (13) An Irish city (Cork). (14) A pesky insect (roach). (15) Used as a means of disguise (mask).

Allow the players to add to this list. Then when each one has checked his list of fifteen answers, have those who have thought of other words propound their questions to the crowd. There are many others, such as hack, hock, smack, rock, shock, car, etc.

DOWN WITH THE SHILLELAGHS. A shillelagh is an Irish cudgel. Play five-point bowling. If Indian clubs or tenpins are available, well and good. If not, use pop bottles—four at the points of a square and one at the center. Bowl with a softball. Each player gets five chances. Ten extra points for knocking down all five pins.

Since the shamrock was used by St. Patrick as a symbol of the Trinity, threesome games would be appropriate if additional material is needed. Suggestions: "Squirrel in a Tree," "Three Deep," "Pop Goes the Weasel."

SHAMROCK SONGS. The story of the land of the shamrock is indelibly linked with her music. Who has not thrilled to the beauty of some lilting Irish tune? Pass out mimeographed sheets with familiar phrases from well-known Irish songs. The players are to guess the titles of these songs. Suggestions:

1. "That bow'r and its music I'll never forget"—"Bendemeer's Stream."

2. "Left blooming all alone"—"The Last Rose of Summer."

3. "Sure, they're like a morn in spring"—"When Irish Eyes Are Smiling."

4. "They're hangin' men and women"—"Wearin' o' the Green."

5. "Like fairy gifts, fading away"—"Believe Me, If All Those Endearing Young Charms."

6. "The soul of music shed"—The Harp That Once Through Tara's Halls."

7. "It may be for years, and it may be forever"—"Kathleen Mavourneen."

8. "The old rusty mill is still"—"When You and I Were Young, Maggie."

9. "And his wild harp slung behind him"—"The Minstrel Boy."

10. "Loudly he can play or low"—"Galway Piper."

11. "There's a place in my mem'ry, my life, that you fill"—"Mother Machree."

12. "She was lovely and fair"—"The Rose of Tralee."

13. "The sweetest flower that grows"—"My Wild Irish Rose."

14. "Where the three-leafed Shamrock grows"—"Where the River Shannon Flows."

15. "And when the fields are fresh and green"—"I'll Take You Home Again, Kathleen."

SHAMROCK MELODIES. The crowd should be in a mood now to sing some of those lovely Irish songs. Have a pianist ready to play them, and send the group home with shamrock melodies ringing in their hearts.

A GREEN PARTY

DECORATIONS. Naturally, green will be the color scheme in decorations. Potted plants, green crepe-paper streamers, green lamp shades. As soon as the first guests arrive put them to work making bows out of green crepe paper. Use two shades of green, light and dark, and divide them evenly among girls and men. The girls wear them in their hair. The men pin them to their coat lapels.

173

The Wearin' o' the Green

Oh, Paddy dear! an' did ye hear the news that's goin' round?
The shamrock is by law forbid to grow on Irish ground!
No more St. Patrick's Day we'll keep, his color can't be seen,
For there's a cruel law agin the wearin' o' the green!
I met wid Napper Tandy, and he took me by the hand,
And he said, "How's poor Ould Ireland, and how does she stand?"
She's the most disthressful country that iver yet was seen,
For they're hangin' men and women there for wearin' o' the green.

Form a double circle by couples, the man with his partner to the right. Hold hands, skating position. Couples move counterclockwise with walking steps.

On "I met with Napper Tandy" and through the next line, ending "how does she stand?" partners face one another shaking right hands, pump handle fashion in rhythm.

On "She's the most disthressful country" start the grand right and left. On "wearin' o' the green" stop grand right and left and keep the partner whose hand is held at that time.

New partners greet each other with the name of something that is green. For instance, the boy calls "spinach," while the girl calls "pickles." Other green things that may be called: grass, water cress, turnip greens, weeds, trees, traffic lights, cucumbers, gourds, freshmen. The game continues for several more rounds.

A GREEN QUIZ. The green bows made earlier in the evening were made of two shades of green for a purpose. At this point let the Lights and Darks get together on either side of the room in preparation for the quiz.

The quiz may be conducted in either of two ways: (a) Line up the contestants and ask the questions of an individual on first one side and then the other. A correct answer scores a point. (*b*) Call the questions. The side on which someone first answers correctly scores a point.

1. What fruit is red when it is green? *Answer:* Blackberry.

2. What green is used for legal tender? *Answer:* Greenback.

3. What green is an arm of Lake Michigan? *Answer:* Green Bay.

4. What green is the home of DePauw University? *Answer:* Greencastle, Indiana.

5. Who was a prominent Revolutionary War green? *Answer:* General Nathanael Greene.

6. What is amphibian green? *Answer:* Green frog.

7. What is florist's green? *Answer:* Greenhouse.

8. What is an Arctic green? *Answer:* Greenland.

9. What green was in a name given to the soldiers of Vermont in Revolutionary War days? *Answer:* Green Mountain boys.

10. What is a green that says "Go ahead"? *Answer:* Green light.

11. What is a theatrical green? *Answer:* Greenroom.

12. What is an edible green? *Answer:* Turnip greens.

13. What is an old English ballad green? *Answer:* "Green Sleeves."

14. What is a prickly green? *Answer:* Greenbrier.

15. What is a green fruit? *Answer:* Greengage plum.

16. What is a jealous green? *Answer:* Green-eyed.

17. What is an inexperienced green? *Answer:* Greenhorn.

18. What is a forest green? *Answer:* Greenwood.

19. What is a green that is a popular game? *Answer:* Bowling on the green.

SHAMROCK STUNTS. Make some large shamrocks of green construction paper. Write some stunt to be

175

done on each leaf. Persons pull leaves and perform according to instructions. In a small group each individual may draw. In a larger crowd pick out persons to perform.

Suggested stunts: 1. Greet ten people in turn with "Top o' the mornin' to you." 2. Dance an Irish jig. 3. Give three reasons why you think green is a good color. 4. Tell the story of "Goldilocks and the Three Bears" by whistling and pantomime. 5. Recite "Mary Had a Little Lamb" by whistling and pantomime. 6. Imitate a girl, "green" about football, at the game with her escort. 7. Imitate a boy who is "green" asking a girl for a date. 8. Tell in pantomime why you would rather live in Greencastle, Indiana, than in Greenland.

GRASS SNAP.   Provide each person with two blades of grass. Players pair off and try their hands at grass snap. One player holds a piece of grass with the ends in either hand. The other player slips his piece through and holds both ends. The two players pull. The one whose blade breaks hands the two broken pieces to the winner and moves on to another player to try out his other blade. When the two blades have been broken, the player drops out of the game. Players continue to play as long as they have a whole blade left. At the end all players count their pieces.

BOWLING ON THE GREEN.   Use the idea of "Square five bowling." Set five regulation pins up on a two-foot square with one pin at center. Allow each bowler three chances with a croquet ball. One point may be allowed for each pin knocked down. If regulation pins cannot be obtained, use pop bottles.

GREEN SLEEVES.   This game was played in the days of Shakespeare. The name suggests a possible connection with Robin Hood and his merry men and their Lincoln Green. If the original music is not available,

176

the game can be played to the tune of "She'll Be Comin' 'Round the Mountain."

The players stand in a double circle by couples, the woman to the man's right. A skip or walking step is used.

Figure One: All move forward around the circle sixteen counts. The head should be thrown back, and the players swing their clasped hands back and forth in rhythm.

Figure Two: Without pause, the players, in sets of four, join right hands across (thus each takes the right hand of the opposite partner) and walk around in a circle eight counts. They then turn in place, join left hands, and circle eight counts back to place.

Figure Three: Without pause, players drop hands, all facing forward, holding partner's hand. The head couple of each set bend heads and skip backward four steps under the joined hands of Couple Two, who skip forward four steps at the same time. Without pause, the action is repeated back to place with Couple Two bending and coming back under the arch provided by Couple One. This takes eight counts. The figure is repeated for eight more counts.

Repeat the entire game three times.

SONGS TO SING. "Green Grow the Rushes," "Wearing o' the Green," "Over the Meadow Green and Wide," "And the Green Grass Grew All Around" ("All in a Wood"), "Little Grove, All in Green."

REFRESHMENTS. Pistachio or mint ice with green icing cake.

IRISH SHENANIGAN PARTY

Listen to me, Mike Flanagan, me hearty,
There'll be lots of fun at the Shenanigan Party.

177

And the Murphys, O'Briens, and O'Tooles will be there
So you come along, some laughter to share.

The shenanigan starts as soon as the guests begin to arrive. Each guest is given an Irish name which he pins on himself. This name he bears throughout the evening. There will be the aforesaid Mike Flanagan, Bridget O'Toole, Shamus O'Brien, Pat Murphy, Nora O'Brien, Maggie Murphy, and the like. These names should be printed on cards or heavy paper before the party.

TOP O' THE MORNIN'! Furnish each guest with a card or sheet of paper marked off into twenty-five squares. For a small group sixteen squares will do. Each person must get an autograph in each of the squares. Guests will sign the Irish names they bear for the evening. The greeting will be "Top o' the mornin'! May I have your autograph?" The response may be, "Sure! Top o' the mornin' to yourself! And scribble your name on my card." This continues until each person has a name in each space.

The leader has duplicate names in a box. He begins to draw these one at a time, calling them. When a person has a called name on his card, he checks it. When he gets five in a row, either across, down, or diagonally, he calls "Bingo!" The first three players to bingo each get a stick of candy. If only sixteen squares are used, four in a row bingoes. Players stand for a brief moment when their names are called.

If desired, and space permits, a grand march may be used to pair off guests. Then march two concentric circles in opposite directions. When the music stops, the players stop marching, face one another, and exchange greetings and autographs.

SHENANIGAN JOKES. Only four families are represented in this party—the Flanagans, the O'Tooles, the

178

O'Briens, and the Murphys. At this point these family groups gather in the four corners of the room and organize, with Pa, Ma, Aunt, Uncle, etc.

Each family group begins swapping Irish jokes within its own group with a view to selecting the best joke for retelling to all the other groups. They also select a story-teller.

Each representative in turn tells the chosen joke to the whole company. The other three families receive the story in silence, looking bored and unconcerned. There is to be no razzing or wisecracks, however. The storyteller's own family laughs uproariously, however. It will be considered a triumph if they make any of the members of the other three families even smile.

SHENANIGAN HIT PARADE. Ask each family to list as many Irish songs as they can recall. "My Wild Irish Rose," "When Irish Eyes Are Smiling," "Mother Machree," "Galway Piper," "Rose of Tralee," "Wearin' o' the Green," "Bendemeer's Stream," and others will probably be suggested. Allow about five minutes for list-ing and then ask each group to report the number of songs it has. Have the group with the longest list read the titles of its songs. Then have the other groups add such songs as have not already been called.

Following this, have each family group select its favorite Irish song, with perhaps a second and third choice indi-cated. Allow a song three points for first choice, two points for second, and one point for third. Have the entire group sing the three songs receiving the highest number of points.

SHENANIGAN GOLF. Arrange an indoor golf course of an unusual nature after either of the following fashions:

(1) Hole Number One, a wastebasket; Hole Number

179

Two, a green cardboard St. Patrick's hat; Hole Number Three, a bucket; Hole Number Four, a small basket; Hole Number Five, a shoe box. The game is played with a small green beanbag. Starting at Hole Number One, each player tries to "hole" the beanbag from one to the other of the "holes," in turn. If a player misses, he tosses from the point where the beanbag rests after the miss. Each toss counts a stroke. The family with the smallest score wins.

(2) The second golf game approximates a golf course with traps and obstacles. An old stovepipe, a piece of hollow tile, a hoop decorated with green crepe paper, two green-covered box tops propped together tent fashion, an old piece of tin gutter, a piece of muslin with a hole in the center tacked across a doorway, and other such obstacles should be arranged.

For golf balls use wooden balls or regular golf balls. Small round potatoes could be used. Wooden spoons can serve as sticks.

Green paper pennants numbered and stuck in large potatoes would mark the course.

Score cards, decorated with shamrocks, are furnished the players.

IRISH WAKE SHENANIGANS. The group is seated in a large circle, or if preferred, it may be seated by family groups in four circles. The leader of each group in the latter case would be furnished with a potato or beanbag. At the signal to start, the potato or beanbag is passed to the right. Each person, after he receives it, holds it straight out in front of him, looks at it and says, "Ha ha!" Then he passes it to the person to the right. An alarm clock has been set to go off in one minute, or a minute and a half, or in thirty seconds. If a person has possession of the photo or beanbag when the alarm sounds, he must perform whatever stunt the neighbor to his left requires of him. Continue

180

until five or six have performed. If the group is seated in one circle, use one or more beanbags, according to the size of the crowd.

FOLK GAMES. If a folk game is desired, use "Waves of Tory" or "The Irish Washerwoman."

A DUBLIN PARTY

It's a rocky road to Dublin, so they say;
But come along with us St. Patrick's day.
    You'll find the fun is merry,
    And the crowd is bright and airy;
Oh, the Dublin Party'll be an evening gay.

DECORATIONS. Green streamers and other St. Patrick decorations.

DOUBLE UP. Pass out two sets of numbered paper shamrocks, one to the girls and the other to the boys. Boys and girls match numbers to find partners.

ON THE DOUBLE. With the partners found by matching, do some grand marching figures—under, over and under, zigzag, arch, etc.

COMPLETE THE DOUBLE. Each couple is given a sheet on which has been written a list of words which suggest certain Bible characters. Couples write by the side of each word the name suggested. Read the correct list after allowing three to five minutes to fill in the answers. Couples check their own papers. A suggested list: 1. Bulrushes (Moses). 2. Ark (Noah). 3. Lion's den (Daniel). 4. Slingshot (David). 5. Hanging by hair (Absalom). 6. Whale (Jonah). 7. Salt (Lot's wife). 8. Jawbone (Samson). 9. Plagues (Pharaoh). 10. Mantle (Elijah). 11. Pottage (Esau). 12. Golden calf (Aaron). 13. Ladder (Jacob).

GAY PARTIES FOR ALL OCCASIONS

14. Star (Wise men). 15. Prison (Paul). For several of these more than one name may be suggested. For instance, "plagues" may suggest Moses; "mantle" may also suggest Elisha. Count answers correct if they may properly be associated with the word or idea.

DOUBLE YOUR SCORE. (a) *Bowlem Ball.* Bowl softball or croquet ball at tenpins or soft drink bottles. On each bottle tie a bow of a different color—red, blue, yellow, green, white. Before each tenpin indicate a score— 5, 6, 7, 8, 9, 10. Before the player bowls he calls the color at which he is aiming. If he knocks it down, he doubles the score. If he knocks down a pin other than the color he named, he gets the score indicated for that pin. (b) *Muffin Pan Toss.* Toss checkers or disks (wooden or linoleum) trying to hole them in the pockets of a muffin pan. Indicate score in bottom of each pocket. Paste a strip of colored paper in front of each pocket. Color the disks to match. Players toss the disks, as many as there are pockets. If a disk lands in the pocket of its color, it doubles the score for that pocket.

DOUBLE GAMES. Three types of double games are possible.

GAMES FOR TWO PEOPLE. Use "Salvo," "Hangman," "Ticktacktoe."

PARTNER GAMES. Use anagrams or games such as "Bug" or "Cootie." If desired, much of the time of the party may be given to one or the other of these games, the couples progressing at the end of each set.

COUPLE GAMES. "Hook-on Tag," and "Two Deep." Or folk games could be played.

DOUBLIN'. Ask selected persons to double for certain prominent people by impersonating them. Local celebrities, movie and stage stars, radio personalities, and

182

people of state, national, and world prominence would furnish an adequate list.

DOUBLE RATIONS. Serve a plate on which are two cookies, two peanuts, and two pieces of ice cream.

A BIT O' BLARNEY PARTY

Replenish your applesauce larder,
Oil up the old tongue to a *T*,
Stock up with a good bit o' blarney,
Then what a party this will be.

A Bit o' Blarney Party. March 17, 8 P.M.

A FAIRY WISHING WELL. On arrival guests are invited to go to the wishing well and test their fortune. Green strings are drawn by the women, and white strings by the men. All fortunes are good, containing a bit o' blarney. Examples:

"You've latent powers more than you know,
They'll bring you fame wherever you go."

"You're not afraid to get out and dig;
For you there's no job that is too big."

"You're good at anything you do,
You're humble, kind, and always true."

"There'll never be a time for you
When your mate regrets he said, 'I do.'"

KISS THE BLARNEY STONE. Pin a piece of white muslin on the wall, at center draw a gray stone. Require each guest in turn to stand about two feet away from the wall, bend forward from the waistline, with hands on

183

hips, and try to kiss the "Blarney stone." If anyone thinks this is easy, let him try it. It's a good plan to have strong-armed men stand ready to catch those who lose their balance.

BLARNEY. Seat the group in a circle, alternating men and women. Each man is given one minute (thirty seconds may be better) to say all the nice things he can to the woman on his right. The leader taps a gong as a signal for the men to move to a new partner. This continues until each man has been around to each woman. Each time he displays his best line of blarney. The interesting thing, of course, is that as one tries to think of nice things to say, he inevitably finds good points in the person to whom he is talking. At the end, the women cast a secret ballot on the best blarney exponent. A green tie may be given to the winner.

As a variation the women may respond to each partner with flattering remarks. In this case the men could cast a secret ballot on the best blarney exponent among the women. A green bow or predominantly green handkerchief could be given to the winner.

A BLARNEY MARCH. The women form an outer circle, the men an inner one. As the piano plays, they march in opposite directions. When the music stops, they stop and face partners. The leader calls out a letter of the alphabet, such as "B," for instance. Partners must immediately change compliments using some blarney adjective beginning with the letter called, such as "You have beautiful eyes," or "You have a bonny disposition," or "I like your becoming manner." Other "B's": beneficent, benevolent, blessed, blithe, bountiful, bright, buoyant. The music starts up again as soon as there has been time for greeting, and the players start marching again. Each time there is a stop the leader calls a new letter for use.

A variation is to write letters of the alphabet on paper shamrocks, and place face down on table. The leader picks one, turns it over and calls the letter. The player whose turn it is must respond in a reasonable time with a complimentary adjective to the person to his right.

THE BLARNEY LAW. In the beginning of the evening it should be explained that there is a law that only complimentary remarks may be made all evening long. Secret detectives should keep their ears open for any remarks that by any stretch of the imagination can be construed as breaking the law. At this time in the party they should report the offending parties. An alert detective force with a sense of humor can add much to the fun of the evening. If secret recordings of some choice remarks could be made and reproduced for the crowd, it would help.

Offenders should be required to stand before the crowd, and to repeat together six times the following: "We have had a good time." Each time they must emphasize a different word in the sentence, beginning with emphasizing the first word.

AN IRISH QUIZ. Give out a list of Irish words and ask the guests or contestants to define them as accurately as possible. Suggested words:

1. Shillelagh: oak stick or cudgel.
2. Mavourneen: my darling.
3. Colleen: an Irish lass.
4. Hooligan: a ruffian.
5. Machree: my heart (term of endearment).
6. Spalpeen: scamp, rascal.
7. Blarney: flattery.
8. Pratey: potato.
9. Shenanigan: trickery.
10. Hibernian: Irishman.

Many of the cities, lakes, and historical scenes in Ireland have been mentioned in song and story. Thus they are well known. Give out a list of familiar places and ask for a phrase or song title containing each of them.

1. Blarney: "The _____ stone."
2. Kilkenny: "The cats of _____."
3. Tara: "The halls of _____."
4. Tralee: "The rose of _____."
5. Shannon: "Where the river _____ flows."
6. Dublin: "The rocky road to _____."
7. Killarney: "The lakes of _____."
8. Erin: "Come back to _____."
9. Tipperary: "It's a long way to _____."

Another way to use this quiz would be to call the phrase and ask the players to fill in the name of the place.

BARREL O' FUN RIDE. Use a child's wheelbarrow. Fill it with blown-up balloons. Cut out large shamrocks and place them in a line across the floor, about ten inches apart. Contestants steer the wheelbarrow in and out between the shamrocks to the end of the course. If a shamrock is touched, or if a balloon falls off the wheelbarrow, the contestant may be required to pay a forfeit or he may be declared out of the game. The winner is the player who manipulates the course with the fewest mishaps.

ST. PATRICK RELAY. Two teams of nine players each. At the opposite end of the room place a basket for each team. In each of these baskets is a collection of articles —soap or string, toothpick or tablet, pencil or pan, apple or airplane (toy), tie or tissue, rock or rag, infant (picture) or Indian (picture), can or candy, knot or knob. Note that the initial letters of these articles spell "St. Patrick."

At the signal to go, the first player on each team must run to the basket belonging to his team, pick out an article beginning with the letter "S," and return to touch off his next teammate. The second player picks an article beginning with the letter "T." Thus it goes until the team has spelled out St. Patrick with the articles brought back.

KING APRIL ENTERTAINS

Put on your rubbers,
  Go get your raincoat out;
Come all you lubbers,
  Let's make this thing a rout.
Good old King April
  Will hold his royal court.
Sail the ship of Good Times
  Into the royal port.

Bring along *some trick or practical* joke.

DECORATIONS. Tiny umbrellas. Green and white crepe-paper fringes around the lights. Large open umbrellas with thin crepe-paper streamers hanging down from them. A throne for King April.

KING APRIL. Wears galoshes or rubber boots. Holds an umbrella as a scepter. A red raincoat will serve as a royal cape. A crown made of oilcloth or cellophane. The king opens the festivities of the evening.

187

King April

AS GUESTS ARRIVE. Each guest is asked to get a name tag or card as he arrives. These are arranged on a table near the entrance. Where it is known beforehand who will attend, have names written on each card. Otherwise ask guests to pick up a card and write their names. The joke lies in the fact that the backs of the cards are lampblacked. The name business is just a come-on.

THE ROYAL COURT ASSEMBLES. At the time for the party to begin, a herald appears and toots a horn three times or simulates the usual trumpet call. "Hear ye! Hear ye! The royal court of the kingdom of Tomfoolery is about to assemble. Make way for the king!" There is a beating of tin pans and the royal personage enters and seats himself on the throne. He may be accompanied by a jester and one attendant dressed in raincoat and galoshes and carrying a sprinkling can. A jester's cap would be all the special costuming that person would need. The king and the jester share in introducing the events of the evening.

THE ROYAL MESSAGE. The king arises, holds

his umbrella-scepter up and speaks: "My loyal subjects of the kingdom of Tomfoolery, we are here for fun and frolic. The royal jester will take charge. Let joy abound!"

DIPSY DOODADDLES. The jester takes charge, announcing "The first event on the program is Dipsy Doodaddles. We will do a grand march. When I shout 'Dipsy Doodaddles,' everyone will begin mixing around trying to trick, fool, or mystify someone else. When the music starts, all persons must drop into the line of march again."

Guests have been asked to come prepared for this event. The sleight of hand artist will be in his glory. Practical jokers will have a chance to shine. Hand buzzers and mechanical tricks of all sorts, available at novelty stores, will provide lots of fun. Stunts like that of calling the victim's attention to something supposedly on his tie and then flipping him under the nose as he looks down, ought to get a good workout. The old stunt of having a thread on the garment, which some unwary person tries to pick off, will likely be used by someone. The thread has been threaded through by a needle and is attached to a spool of thread in a pocket.

ROYAL SURPRISES. Various sorts of April fool traps may be set for the guests—handkerchiefs tacked to the floor, good candy labeled "Take One," chocolate-covered cardboard candy labeled the same way, metal banisters charged with electricity.

ROYAL GAMES. Bowling games of various sorts, golf-putting games, and skill games of various kinds could be arranged.

ROYAL MAGIC. If some amateur magician can be secured, a short program of magic would be appropriate.

ROYAL DRAMA. Dramatize incidents connected

189

with historical events and names connected with the month of April. Have the group guess what the incident or name is. For instance, a rider on a hobbyhorse shouting, "The British are coming!" is easy. Paul Revere made his famous ride April 18, 1775. Other events that could be dramatized: The discovery of the North Pole by Peary, April 6, 1909, Arbor Day (in some states). Famous April birthdays: Shakespeare, April 23, 1564, Thomas Jefferson, April 13, 1743, Washington Irving, April 3, 1783, and John Burroughs, April 3, 1837.

A PAUL REVERE PARTY

The details of the following party were sent by the Rev. C. W. Hutchens. He said the seed thought for it came from the Paul Revere colonial party in *The Fun Encyclopedia* (p. 662). However, as all good party planners should, he changed it considerably to fit a special situation. The party was given for the students and faculty of Asbury Theological Seminary.

Guests were asked to assemble at the seminary. From there they were to move in a body to the place of the party. The destination was kept secret. Everyone was told to wait for Paul Revere to come along and show them the way, which he did on "a very unwilling nag." Promptly the "Spirit of '76" band marched out and followed behind Paul Revere. All of the rest fell in behind them.

The destination turned out to be the ball park. Under the lights grand marching was done to "The Stars and Stripes Forever." Then the crowd was divided by birthdays into four seasonal groups. Each group chose a name, a yell, and put on a patriotic charade for the rest to guess.

Relays were then done. Two of them that provided lots of fun were "Dizzy Izzy" and "Three Men on a Horse." In the first the runner puts his hands and head down on a stick or cane, turns around five times in this position, and then runs to a goal and back. In the other, three men straddled a broomstick. In this position they ran a designated course.

Following the relays came a skit and a shoe scramble for lunch partners.

A CAMOUFLAGE SCAVENGER HUNT

This idea comes from the Rev. Al Maberry, of Shenandoah, Iowa.

The party may be held indoors, or it may be a combination of indoors and outdoors. Articles are hidden about in plain sight but cleverly camouflaged. Guests are given lists of the hidden articles and are to hunt until all are discovered. They may hunt either individually or in pairs. In no case is a person or couple to tell others where to look. After finding an article, they leave it untouched and simply check it off their list. This checking may be done after getting away from the spot where the article is hidden. A few suggested articles will give the idea:

A needle stuck in the corner of a mirror.

A red button placed on a red background of some sort, such as a table scarf.

A woman's stocking wrapped tightly around a sitting room chair leg.

A thread placed carefully on a cloth cover, drape, or book of the same color.

A phonograph needle resting on a silver card tray or cake plate.

A dog's hair on someone's suit, sweater, or dress.

A blond hair on a background of yellow.

A black hair on a black background.

191

A tack in a thick carpet or rug where its head is difficult to detect.

A pin in a bookcase window.

A scrap of cloth on a crazy quilt.

Others can be added. Endeavor to get a good camouflage effect on each article. Make a rule that the hunters are not to touch or disarrange any article.

The list given to the guest will simply indicate the articles to be detected—a needle, a loose button, a stocking, a thread, etc.

For refreshments try "camouflage pudding"—marshmallow pudding in colored layers.

A PREPROMOTION PARTY

The plans for this event were sent by Miss Marian Stephens Stengel, director of religious education at Monument Methodist Church, Richmond, Virginia.

Here's a party suggestion that will help to do away with the losing of members in promotion from one Sunday-school department to another. The senior department at Monument Church decided one year to make the third-year intermediates feel "at home" among them instead of waiting until promotion day in the fall. So they had a "Business Party." Personal invitations to the intermediates read as follows:

DEAR BETTY:

The seniors are having a party this Tuesday night on the "roof garden" (third floor) and we want you to be one of our special guests.

Since you will be promoted to our department soon, we think this will be a fine time for us to get to know each other better. All the third-year intermediates have been

192

invited. A full evening of fun for all has been planned, and we will be looking for you!

> Sincerely,
> MARYLOU MASSIE, President

Notices to members of the senior department read as follows:

DEAR EMPLOYEE:
You are requested to attend the staff meeting of Senior Department & Co., of which you are an accredited member and stockholder. This gathering will be held on the "roof garden" of our Monument Church Branch Office, Tuesday at 8 P.M.

No white tie and tails necessary. Come prepared for FUN!

> Yours truly,
> MARYLOU MASSIE, President

The receptionist's office was arranged in typical style, with magazines to keep the applicants occupied until their turn. The inner offices included desks at which the officers of the department were seated. Each desk was arrayed with "Out to Lunch," "In Conference," and other signs. The applicant made a tour of the desks, filling out an application blank (see below). Finally he was interviewed by the president and given his "Antisocial Insecurity Number," and then was asked to join the group across the room engaged in recreation.

Naturally the success of this first part would depend largely on the personalities of the officers and their ability to put it across.

After everyone was interviewed, there followed a period of directed recreation, planned to suit the occasion. Next in order was a snappy business session during which the president officially welcomed the applicants to Senior Department & Co.; and the other officers gave brief glimpses of "things to come" in the fall and winter program. Although in a serious vein, this session had just enough humor in it to hold interest at a high level.

Then light refreshments were served, there was singing around the piano, and the meeting closed with a friendship circle. The party stimulated within the prospective new members just the right kind of interest in the department. The result was to make them look forward to becoming seniors, instead of fearing it, because they had got acquainted in a humorous way.

SENIOR DEPARTMENT & CO.

"We Never Fail"

Application Blank
(Form 000 ¾)

Name _____
  Last   First   Middle   Any other

Address _____
  Street and number   City   State

Where Were You Last Born?_____Male____Female____

by Personnel Manager, WILLIAM MALLARD, XYZ

. . . .

PHYSICAL EXAMINATION
WILLIAM MILLER, Phd. pdq. nut

Size of Shoe _____   Condition of Feet _____
                              flat otherwise

Number of Teeth Missing ___ Can You Wiggle Your Ears?___

Pulse Rate _____

Physician's comment as to general condition _____

. . . .

MENTAL TEST

DR. LAWSON CROWE, Psychologist Excellente

1. Why did Washington cross the Potomac? _____

2. How many three-cent stamps in a dozen? _____

3. Identify the following:

   (a) Fearless Fosdick   (c) F. D. Roosevelt

   (b) Mr. T   (d) Elizabeth Gladding

. . . .

APTITUDES

(This information is recorded for future reference)

1. Do you play a musical instrument? _____

2. Would you like to help on programs? _____

3. Could you help prepare the evening meal some Sunday?___

4. Would you like to help with recreation? _____

5. Would you like to usher in our department on Sundays? _____

   Antisocial Insecurity Number _____

Signature of person

MARYLOU MASSIE, President

195

Pulse Rate _____

Physician's comment as to general condition _____

MENTAL TEST

DR. LAWSON CROWE, Psychologist Excellente

1. Why did Washington cross the Delaware? _____
2. How many tries sent stamps in a dozen? _____
3. Identify the following:
   (a) Fearless Fosdick   (c) F. D. Roosevelt
   (b) Mr. T   (d) Elizabeth Glidding

APTITUDES

(This information is recorded for future reference)

1. Do you play a musical instrument? _____
2. Would you like to help on programs? _____
3. Could you help prepare the evening meal some Sunday? _____
4. Would you like to help with recreation? _____
5. Would you like to usher in our department on Sun. days? _____

Antisocial Insecurity Number _____

_____
Signature of person

MARYLOU MASSIE, President
195___

CHAPTER VI

Summer Parties

Summer Parties

THE SCHOOL OF BLISSFUL IGNORANCE

This party was given in honor of graduating high-school seniors. Sophomores, juniors, and seniors were invited as guests. The idea came from Mrs. Henry W. Blackburn of Florida.

Motto: "Where ignorance is bliss, 'tis folly to be wise."
School Song:

> Oh, I ain't gonna work no more, no more,
> I ain't gonna work no more.
> I worked last year and the year before,
> But I ain't gonna work no more.

School Colors: Green and greener.

Pledge of Allegiance: I pledge allegiance to this school in the state of Blissful Ignorance, and to the principles for which it stands: One purpose, no study, with fun and good times for us all.

REGISTRATION CARD. On arrival each guest was required to fill out a registration card that called for the following information: Name, address, mental age, year you wish you had been born, and why (answer in not more than ten words), color of left eye, color of hair at birth, favorite sport, vocal velocity per minute, vocal veracity per minute, pet hate, hours per week spent daydreaming, sleeping hours, including history and English, record for dining-room dash, weight before dinner, weight after dinner, vocational ambition.

199

SCHEDULE OF CLASSES. Each student got a card with a schedule of classes—period, subject, room number, teacher, and a column for remarks. The classes listed were music, postgraduate work, business course, geography, elementary subjects, mathematics, and history. There were also listed the following: lunch hour, conference period, and assembly.

MUSIC. When the bell rang for the beginning of the first period, the entire group assembled in the auditorium for a musical program and sing, which ended with the school pledge and the alma mater song," I Ain't Gonna Work No More."

Elementary Subjects

SPELLING. Students were required to spell aloud the words "receive," "believe," and "wrong." After the word "believe" was spelled, the teacher shook her head and said "wrong." The wise student spelled "w-r-o-n-g." But the others wanted to argue or looked confused.

Try spelling your own complete name in pig Latin. Also use dumb spelling where vowels and other letters are indicated by signs.

READING. Pupils were required to read tongue twisters, such as "Slick, strong Stephen Stringer snared six slick, sickly, silky snakes"; "She thinks three thick, sick throats are a threat to the three sleek sheiks. She seeks sudden Schick tests"; "Ten tremendous tomtits twittering on the tops of three tall trees."

Have you heard about our dittle log difo?
I bought him when he pas a wup,
He can stand upon his lind hegs,
If you hold his lont fregs up.

200

A say bird jitting on a lickory himb;
Me hinked at he and I hinked at wim.

ARITHMETIC. Here some number games were played, such as "Buzz," trick problems, and the like. One of the problems was this one: "Take the number a stitch in time saves; multiply it by the number of heads that are better than one; divide by the number that makes a crowd; add the number of strings on a violin; and multiply by the number of toes on your right foot." Believe it or not the the answer is fifty.

HISTORY. A list of fifteen historical characters was given and the problem was to rearrange them in chronological order. The correct answer: 1. Abraham. 2. Moses. 3. Solomon. 4. Socrates. 5. Julius Caesar. 6. Paul. 7. Mahomet. 8. Joan of Arc. 9. Columbus. 10. Luther. 11. Shakespeare. 12. Washington. 13. Napoleon. 14. Lincoln. 15. Wilson.

Students were asked to identify the historical characters whose pictures hung in the room: Washington, Lincoln, Napoleon, Lee, Martha Washington, Andrew Jackson, Grover Cleveland, William Howard Taft, Lafayette, Theodore Roosevelt.

Pupils answered orally the names of characters in history and literature suggested by certain objects: Gunpowder (Roger Bacon), muddy cloak (Sir Walter Raleigh), hatchet (Washington), spider (Robert Bruce), apple (William Tell), kite (Benjamin Franklin), cotton gin (Eli Whitney), airplane (Wright brothers), slingshot (David), coat of many colors (Joseph), mess of pottage (Esau), pillar of salt (Lot's wife), whale (Jonah), rainbow (Noah), lamp (Aladdin), glass slipper (Cinderella), wolf (Red Riding Hood).

GEOGRAPHY. Scrambled states. Letters in the names of states were jumbled. The students untangled them. Example: Ningawshot (Washington).

201

State abbreviations answered the next questions. Examples: "What state is a father?" (Pa.) "What is used in a flood?" (Ark.) "What is found in mines?" (Ore.)

Alphabetical geography. One player calls the name of a country, state, or city. The next player must call a country, state, or city beginning with the last letter of the name just called.

Modes of travel in Japan, Egypt, Venice, China, Greenland, Palestine in the time of Christ. Answers: jinrikisha, camel, gondola, junk, sled, donkey.

Students filled in the blanks of this rhyme with abbreviations of states:

—— Smith is ——, my —— told ——
And ——, it's sad as sad can be;
A ton of —— in one huge ——
Fell down upon her ——, alas!

Answers: Miss., Ill., Md. Me., O., Ore., Mass., Wash.

BUSINESS COURSE. Some brain teasers like "Y Y U R" ("too wise you are"), meaning of abbreviations such as A.W.O.L., O.K., R.S.V.P., C.O.D., etc.

POSTGRADUATE COURSE

ART: In the dark draw a horse, a dog, a man, a hatbox, and sign name. Drop five grains of rice on a piece of white paper. Make dots where the rice lies. Draw a picture connecting the dots.

CHEMISTRY: Smell unlabeled bottles and identify the odor. Suggestions: Vanilla, vinegar, ammonia, perfume, etc. See "Ten Scent Game."

PHYSIOLOGY: "What part of the human body is
202

something used to build a house?" (Nails.) "What part is filled with treasure?" (Chest), etc.

CONFERENCE HOUR. Class groups repaired to their own classrooms—seniors to one room, juniors to another, sophomores to still another. Here they made plans for the graduation exercises.

ASSEMBLY AND GRADUATION. The lower classmen assembled in the auditorium first, and stood in "respectful" silence as the more or less dignified seniors filed in and took their places in the front rows. The seniors were clad in gowns of classic black. The boys carried arm bouquets and the girls wore boutonnieres.

The dean presided.

A sophomore read the "Prophecy for the Seniors." A junior read the "will" which the junior class thought the seniors should make, with the juniors as chief beneficiaries.

Then followed the "Failedictory Address" by one of the seniors. The diplomas were presented by the chairman of the "Bored of Education." These diplomas were printed on pale green paper and conferred on the recipient the degree of "Master of Nonessential Information." Special honors were conferred, such as "Cum Louder," "Magna Cum Laughter," and "Sub Pedum de la Classe."

A JULY LAWN PARTY

On the ——— of July
The fun lid we will pry,
And that's the reason why
    This invitation.
The time for this fun spree
Is 8 P.M. you see
——— lawn will be
    The right location.

203

PATRIOTIC SINGING BEE. Each person has the name of a familiar patriotic song pinned on him—"Columbia, the Gem of the Ocean," "America, the Beautiful," "Tramp, Tramp, Tramp," "Over There," "God Bless America," etc. Each is also supplied with ten slips of paper. Players mill around. As they meet, the first one to sing several bars of the other person's song collects a slip of paper. At the end of five or ten minutes of this riotous singing each person counts the number of slips he has. The same person may be greeted more than once.

Skill Games

Spot skill games of all sorts about the lawn—beanbag boards, dart baseball, dart target, ringtoss, bowling games. The following homemade games could be arranged:

BOUNCE BALL. A chair, a wastebasket (weighted with a brick), a large rubber ball. The player tries to bounce the ball over the chair and into the basket. Five to ten tries.

EGG CRATE BOWLING. Mark scores in the egg crate pockets. Use a piece of cardboard for an incline. At a distance of four to six feet roll a small ball (golf ball size), trying to land in one of the pockets. Six to ten tries.

CLOTHESPIN DROP. Dropping a clothespin from chin height into a quart milk bottle. Ten trials. One point for each success.

POTATO PUTTING. Mark concentric circles on the lawn with lime or salt. Center circle, six inches (fifteen points), second circle, twelve inches (ten points), and outer circle, eighteen inches (five points). Player tries putting a potato from a distance of six feet, using a cane for a golf stick. If the potato rests on a line, the score is the sum of the two circles divided by two.

BASEBALL BOWLING. Bowl a baseball at tenpins (toy or regular) or use pop bottles.

WIRE HOOP BOWLING. Place a wire hoop, eighteen to twenty-four inches in diameter, on the ground. At a distance of six to ten feet players bowl three balls of different sizes, trying to rest them within the bounds of the hoop. Only those that stay inside the hoop count. Use a baseball or volleyball, a tennis ball, and a ping-pong ball.

MILK BOTTLE TOP TOSS. Players try to toss milk bottle tops into a vase or urn. The urn should have an opening of about six to eight inches in diameter. Ten trials.

TENNIS BALL BOUNCE. Place a wastebasket on the seat of a chair. The player tries to bounce a tennis ball into the basket. Ten trials.

FOURTH OF JULY SOCIAL

Invite both old and young to this party.

NAMING THE PRESIDENTS. Hang on the wall a map on which the pictures of all the presidents are pinned. With a piece of white paper cover the name of each. Armed with paper and pencil, guests are to identify as many pictures as possible. The prize may be a little flag.

MUSICAL CONTEST. Make a list of twelve well-known tunes, such as "America," "Star-Spangled Banner," "Home on the Range," etc.

Give to each person a paper on which are written as many numbers as you have musical selections. Have someone (it will take a good pianist) play just one or two, perhaps one-

and-a-half, measures of the first song as it is announced, and let each write the name or first words of the song on his paper. Continue this throughout the list. Numbers may be repeated once on request. When list is completed, papers are exchanged and the correct list read. The one with the largest number of correct answers may require a solo or stunt from any other person as the next number on the program.

CHARADES. Divide the guests as equally as possible. One side may act out the names of states, and the other the presidents.

OUR COUNTRY. This is a good geography game. Cut a map of the United States on the state lines, and use the states so cut out for patterns to cut a new set of states from white paper. Mount them individually on red cardboard or cambric, or mount several widely separated states on the same strip of cambric, not touching but in the correct position as to north, south, east, and west. Number the states in any order, making the number large and distinct. Pass paper and pencils as for the musical contest. Let the class guess the state from its size and shape and write the name opposite the corresponding number. Winner is the one guessing the largest number correctly.

HISTORICAL PICNIC

The fourth of July would be a good time for such an event but any other date would be appropriate. Suggest that picnickers wear red, white, and blue, if at all possible.

In addition to games usually played on picnic occasions try the following:

WORD FINDING. Divide into two or more groups. Give each group two minutes to discover as many words as they can in the letters of the word "patriot." Samples: riot, trip, iota, etc.

HISTORICAL QUIZ. Have each group select representatives for this quiz. The following are suggested samples of types of questions that may be used:

1. Who was it who said, "I only regret that I have but one life to lose for my country"? *Answer:* Nathan Hale.

2. Who was it who said, "We have met the enemy, and they are ours"? *Answer:* Commodore Oliver Hazard Perry.

3. Who said, "Why don't you speak for yourself, John?" *Answer:* Priscilla Mullens to John Alden.

4. What was the name of the Indian girl who saved the life of Captain John Smith? *Answer:* Pocahontas. What was her father's name? *Answer:* Powhatan.

5. From what country did the United States make the Louisiana Purchase? *Answer:* France.

6. What were the original thirteen states of the Union? *Answer:* Connecticut, Delaware, Georgia, Maryland, Massachusetts, New Hampshire, New Jersey, New York, North Carolina, Pennsylvania, Rhode Island, South Carolina, Virginia.

7. Who designed the first United States flag? *Answer:* Betsy Ross.

8. What American city had a great fire reportedly started by a cow—owned by Mrs. O'Leary? *Answer:* Chicago.

9. Who thought he had discovered the Fountain of Youth and where? *Answer:* Ponce de Leon; Florida.

10. What president of the United States was sometimes called "The Rough Rider"? *Answer:* Theodore Roosevelt.

HISTORICAL DRAMA. Brief dramatizations of episodes in local or national history would be appropriate.

207

A DOWN-EAST PARTY

The skippers of the Maine seacoast used to begin the Fourth of July celebration with a "Parade of Antiques and Horribles." In this parade people wore odd or funny false faces and dressed in outlandish costumes. Pitching quoits and boat races were featured.

Why not make this idea the basis for an unusual July recreation event—a picnic or lawn party?

It could be preceded by a maskmaking party in which the participants could fashion their own false faces out of papier-mâché.

For games, play shuffleboard, bull board, horseshoes or quoits, relays and races.

MARINE QUIZ. Work out quizzes appropriate to the sea—names of ships, famous mariners, etc. Some suggestions:

1. What were the names of Columbus' ships? *Answer:* "Santa Maria," "Pinta," "Nina."

2. What great French liner caught afire and capsized at her pier in New York? *Answer:* "Normandie."

3. What is the largest liner? *Answer:* "Queen Elizabeth."

4. What big liner was sunk by a collision with an iceberg in 1912? *Answer:* "Titanic."

5. What British admiral sank the Spanish Armada? *Answer:* Lord Nelson.

6. What famous American of Revolutionary War days said, "I have not yet begun to fight"? *Answer:* John Paul Jones.

7. Who was the villainous pirate in *Treasure Island?* *Answer:* John Silver.

8. What imaginary sea character is noted for having a locker? *Answer:* Davy Jones.

208

9. What pirate of the early days was supposed to have hid a great treasure? Answer: Captain Kidd.

10. What famous sea traveler landed on an island inhabited by tiny people? Answer: Gulliver.

11. What sailor is featured in comic strips? Answer: Popeye.

12. What is the forward part of a ship called? Answer: The bow.

13. What is the after part of a ship called? Answer: The stern.

14. What is the left side of a ship called? Answer: Larboard or port.

15. What is the right side of a ship called? Answer: The starboard.

SEA YARNS. Stories of the sea, fishing tales, etc. "How the Salt Got in the Sea," excerpts from *Treasure Island*, etc.

SEA SONGS. Sing chanteys such as "Cape Cod Girls" and "Blow the Man Down"; songs like "Sailing, Sailing," "Capital Ship," "Anchors Aweigh."

WORSHIP SERVICE. An appropriate worship service could be arranged to close the party. For the scripture read Mark 4:35-41. For singing use "Let the Lower Lights Be Burning," "Sail On," "Master, the Tempest Is Raging," "Jesus, Saviour, Pilot Me," "Stand the Storm."

PLANTATION PARTY

Lay down the shovel and the hoe,
Pick up the fiddle and the bow.
Dress in your overalls or wear your gingham gown,
For the Plantation Party is coming to town.

DECORATIONS. This is an outdoor party, so no special decorations are necessary. If a log cabin set can be borrowed from a local theater, it would add to the atmosphere. Or improvise a log cabin with two-by-fours, brown wrapping paper, and some paint or crayon. A cotton field could be made by the use of white paper or cotton tied on small bushes stuck in the ground. Toy balloons and Japanese lanterns would help.

Program

A quartet singing plantation songs should be on hand to sing at intervals. Stephen Foster songs, spirituals, and work songs would be appropriate.

A string ensemble—violin, banjo, and guitar, perhaps—could add a lot to the enjoyment of the occasion. One of those washboard, tin pan, and harmonica rhythm combinations would make a good feature.

Have a singsong for everyone. Specialize in plantation songs such as "Swanee River," "O Susanna," and "My Old Kentucky Home."

Provide for table games and contests. Tables could be set up on the lawn. Such games as checkers, anagrams, Chinese checkers, dominoes, and caroms could be played. Be sure that there are enough games. Here are some good contests:

WATERMELON FLIGHT. Buy a supply of green watermelon balloons. If none is available locally, order from Slack Manufacturing Company, 124-26 W. Lake St., Chicago, Illinois, or from Rubinstein's, 120 Park Row, New York 7, N. Y. Green sausage balloons, which are cheaper, may be used.

The watermelon flight is achieved by blowing up the

210

balloon and then letting it go. It will make crazy convolutions, darting this way and that. Players could try for distance or height in their flights.

WATERMELON STOMP. Use six to two dozen couples. On each girl tie a sausage or watermelon balloon on the right ankle, so that the balloon will drag on the ground. The couples link arms, the man to the girl's left. Couples mill around, each man trying to stomp and burst the balloons of the other girls, while protecting his own partner's balloon. Where a balloon bursts, the couple to whom it belongs drops out of the game. This continues until only one couple is left. At no time may the man let go of the woman's arm.

WATERMELON SEED GUESSING. Display a glass jar full of watermelon seed. Have guests estimate the number in the jar. The nearest correct answer wins.

WATERMELON EATING. Have several boys eat watermelon with their hands tied behind their backs.

WATERMELON CARVING. Have individuals or groups carve designs out of watermelon rinds. False teeth, faces, houses, and the like are possible.

COTTON PICKING. Make balls of cotton about the size of a golf ball. Space on the ground about five feet apart about five of these balls for each contestant. A small basket or bowl is also provided for each row of cotton balls. The contestant must run to the first ball, pick it up, bring it back, and drop it in the basket. Then he goes to get the second ball, and so on until all the balls are in the basket. The winner is the one who gets all of his cotton picked first.

FOLK GAMES AND DRAMAS. Folk games like "O Susanna," "Brown-Eyed Mary," "Betsy Liner," and

211

"Wait for the Wagon" would be fun. For drama the "Plantation Players" could present some appropriate skit. A take-off on *Uncle Tom's Cabin* would be a good one. Or there could be a dramatic portrayal of some song such as "Ol' Man River," or "Water Boy." There is a burlesque of *Uncle Tom's Cabin* entitled *The Filming of Uncle Tom's Cabin* (Walter H. Baker & Co., 178 Tremont St., Boston 11).

REFRESHMENTS. Serve watermelon. Be sure to provide trash cans or baskets for the discarded rinds.

PATRIOTIC PARTY

DECORATIONS. For this outdoor party use flags; red, white, and blue bunting.

SINGING. Start with the "Star-Spangled Banner." Then sing such songs as the "Battle Hymn of the Republic," "Dixie," "Over There," "When the Caissons Go Rolling Along," "The United States Marines," "I've Got Sixpence," "This Is the Army," and other songs popular during World War II.

PATRIOTIC WHO AM I? Pin the name of a famous patriot on the back of each guest. The guest then tries to find out who he is by asking questions of others about himself and by listening to remarks that they make about him. For instance, if someone says, "How's Martha?" he will be likely to guess he is George Washington. He then reports to the leader who takes the name off his back and pins it on his coat lapel. Some suggestions: Betsy Ross, Molly Pitcher, Benjamin Franklin, Patrick Henry, Paul Revere, Thomas Jefferson, George Washington Carver, Theodore Roosevelt, Woodrow Wilson, Frances Willard, Jane Addams, etc.

212

PATRIOTIC SKITS. These may be impromptu. They will probably be better, however, if some preparation has been made for them. If they are to be impromptu, then appoint one person ahead of time to be responsible for each skit. Possible subjects: "Columbus Discovering America," "The Making of the Flag," "Paul Revere's Ride," "Pocahontas," and many other historical events and people. If there are local events of interest, they may be dramatized too.

PATRIOTIC QUIZ. Conduct a "Battle of the Sexes" quiz with three or four picked men against three or four picked women. These people may be notified ahead of time so as to allow them to make some preparation. Work out a good list of questions. Suggestions: 1. Who was the first person to sign the Declaration of Independence? *Answer:* John Hancock. 2. Who said, "Give me liberty, or give me death"? *Answer:* Patrick Henry. 3. Who was the first president to live in the White House? *Answer:* John Adams, in 1800. A few minutes with a book on American history will reveal an ample supply of questions. Score one point for each correct answer.

GAMES. Line up the men on one side and the women on the other. Then have players in each line call out in turn, "red," "white," and "blue." These colors form three teams that engage in such contests as are planned. Here are two suggestions:

BEANBAG THROW. Make beanbags of three colors—red, white, and blue. Contestants toss at a beanbag board, or they try to pitch the beanbags into a waste basket, or through a hoop decorated in red, white, and blue.

DIZZY IZZY. Wrap or paint three canes or sticks— one red, one white, and one blue. Each contestant takes the cane of his color, places his hands and head firmly on the

213

top while the other end of the cane presses against the ground. In this position he circles around the cane three times and then runs for a designated tree, post, or chair, around which he must run and return to the starting point. Funny things will happen to him

AN AUGUST MERRY-GO-ROUND
(A Lawn Party)

INVITATION:

Come to our August Merry-Go-Round
For there fun and frolic will be found.

DECORATIONS. Lanterns. A miniature merry-go-round if one is available in the community. Arrange the games and exhibits at various places on the lawn.

GUESSING GAMES

WATERMELON SEEDS. Have everyone register a guess on the number of dry watermelon seeds on exhibit in a glass jar.

TREE LEAVES. Mount the leaves of various trees on cards and number them. Have the guests identify the leaves by naming the tree from which they came.

WILD FLOWERS. Mount wild flowers on cards and number them. Have guests try to identify these flowers.

CULTIVATED FLOWERS. Do the same thing with a good assortment of cultivated flowers.

These games can be going on simultaneously as the guests arrive. When they have finished, guests drop their replies in a box provided for the purpose. A committee can check on them. Or guests may check on their own papers as the leader reads the correct answers.

LAWN GAMES

WASHER PITCHING. Sink a small tin can in the ground. Get a dozen or more iron washers about the size and weight of a silver dollar. Paint half of them white or red, to distinguish them from the other half. Players toss these washers at a distance of fifteen or twenty feet, trying to hole them in the can. Each one in the can counts five points. Each washer nearer the hole than any of the opponents' counts one point. Divide into two sides and let each player toss anywhere from two to six washers.

BEANBAG TOSS. Make a beanbag board to represent a huge watermelon. It should have three holes about four inches in diameter. Allow each player three tosses.

DART THROWING. Set up a dart target with the bull's-eye counting twenty-five points, the next circle fifteen, then ten, then five. Allow each player three throws.

FOLK GAMES

By all means, play "Carrousel" ("Merry-go-round"), for it imitates a merry-go-round in action. In addition to being simple, it is plenty of fun. See *Handy Play Party Book*, (Cooperative Recreation Service, Delaware, Ohio), *Singing Games, Old and New* (Campbell Folk School, Brasstown, North Carolina), *Twice Fifty-five Games with Music* (C. C. Birchard & Co., 221 Columbus Ave., Boston 16).

Other appropriate games would be "Sandy Land" (*Handy Play Party Book*), "Chebogah" (*The Fun Encyclopedia*), and "O Susanna."

WATERMELON FEAST

What would an August merry-go-round be like without watermelon! So get 'em ice cold, and cut 'em in generous slices. If someone knows the "Watermelon Song," have it sung by a quartet.

WATERMELON STUNTS. Hide about over the lawn small cardboard watermelons. Each guest must hunt until he finds one. No one should get more than one. On each watermelon is indicated some stunt or game the finder must perform either alone or with a group, as indicated on the card. Numbering the cards will help. Where a group is to perform, all the cards would have the same number. Thus it becomes easy to locate one's teammates. Suggested stunts and games:

FINDING WORDS. Anywhere from three to ten people work fast and furiously to make all the words they can out of the letters in "watermelon."

FALSE TEETH. Three to ten people make sets of false teeth, upper or lower plate, out of watermelon rind. These must be worn. The funnier they look the better.

NECKLACES. Three to ten people, provided with needles, dry watermelon seed, and thread, make necklaces to wear.

INDIVIDUAL STUNTS. Some of the cards could indicate assignments for individuals to perform, such as "Lead the group in a song," "Sing a solo," etc.

A GYPSY PICNIC

Hi, gypsy, ho, gypsy, hey, gypsy, come.
Let's go picknicking, away from hearth and home!

Ask the guests to come dressed in as colorful an ensemble as possible—headbands, kerchief, headpieces, colorful shirts, blouses, and skirts. Select a suitable place for the picnic and arrange a tent or bower for a gypsy fortune-teller.

FORTUNETELLING.   Arrange for several fortune-telling devices. Diligent investigation will probably turn up someone who can read palms and who would be glad to go along for that purpose.

GAMES FOR ALL

SOCCER BASEBALL.   The game is played on a regular baseball diamond, with the regulation number of players, nine. However, more players could be used if desired.

Two pins or stakes (pop bottles, Indian clubs) are placed eighteen inches apart at the home plate. The batter stands behind these pins. The pitcher rolls a soccer football from the pitcher's box and endeavors to knock down the pins. A six- or eight-inch rubber playball will do if a soccer ball is not available.

When the ball leaves the pitcher's hand, the batter can step between the pins and kick the ball. Then he tries to reach first base safely. Continue as in baseball. Three players out end an inning at the box.

A man is out when: (a) The pitcher knocks down a pin in bowling the ball to the batter. (b) The batter knocks down a pin in the act of batting. (c) A fly ball is caught before it touches the ground. (d) The ball is relayed to the baseman before the runner reaches a base. (e) A runner is hit by the ball when running to reach a base.

BUNT BASEBALL.   Played as regular baseball except that the batter bunts invariably. In fact, a player who takes a swing at the ball is out whether he hits the ball or not. Only easy pitching is permitted. If a pitcher throws a

217

hard ball to the batter, it is a base on balls and the batter goes to first. There are six players on a side, no outfielders being necessary.

NATURE FORAGING. Divide into two or more sides. Each group scatters and searches for nature specimens—tree leaves, plants, insects, which they must identify. Allow a limited time; ten or fifteen minutes may be enough.

OTHER GAMES. "Chebogah" is a good gypsy folk game (see *The Fun Encyclopedia*, p. 494).

GYPSY SING. After the picnic supper sit around the campfire and sing. In fact, a lovely gypsy musicale could be worked out for the occasion. Special numbers from *The Bohemian Girl* such as "I Dreamt I Dwelt in Marble Halls" and "Then You'll Remember Me" would be appropriate. "Slumber On, My Little Gypsy Sweetheart" could be sung by the entire group.

A TREASURE HUNT

These are great fun. An adult group would find such an event a pleasing variation from the usual picnic or outing.

In planning, it would be well to keep the following bits of advice in mind:

Plan all details very carefully. Write clues on cardboard and pin firmly to position. Paper crumples easily or blows away. Instruct players to leave clues where they find them. Do not make clues too difficult to interpret or too hard to find. Many a treasure hunt has been a flop because the committee thought it would be fun to hide the clues in unusual places. As a result, most of the participants dropped out before reaching the end of the hunt. If it is planned to keep the group together, insist that people do not run ahead or lag. Have someone read each clue to the entire group. Then proceed together to the next point. Provide a surprise or two along the way. On one such hunt the group was met by a committee at the halfway point. This committee had a bucket of ice-cold lemonade to refresh the hunters. The treasure may be in the nature of refreshments for the party—peanuts, candy, sandwiches. Ice-cold watermelons would be appropriate for this time of year. The hunt may be made by small groups or by couples. In this case a different set of clues would be worked out for each group or couple. A small treasure box (matchbox size) is provided for each group or couple. It may hang on a bush, lie under a rock, or rest in some other place not too difficult to locate. In each box are two papers. One tells where to go for the grand prize (refreshments) and the other indicates some stunt to be performed for the entertainment of the whole group. These stunts may be performed before or after the refreshments, depending on what fits best into the plans. A special prize may be given the couple or group reporting first with its treasure box.

Clues may be done in rhyme or prose. They may require some elementary knowledge of nature lore. Some fun may be added if they are cryptic—in the form of conundrums. Suggestions:

> For your first clue you should go
> To the spot where rosebushes grow.

> Walk due east 'bout thirty paces,
> Where a vine a pole embraces.

219

Hop on one foot to where you see
A park bench under an old oak tree.

Shake hands together all around,
And then move north to a flower mound.

Look for a diamond never mined,
There your next clue you will find.
(This proves to be a baseball diamond)

Move fifty paces and you will be
Right in the shade of an apple tree.

Look in the tree and you will see
Where for you the treasure will be.

Hush, everybody, quiet as a mouse!
The treasure's in the shelter house.

Where the stunt plan is followed, make the stunts easy to do. Suggestions: lead a song, sing a song, recite a poem or nursery rhyme, lead the group in a game, plan a charade, preach a sermon in pantomime.

SUMMERTIME SHOULD BE FUNTIME

There are so many ways to have wholesome fun in the summertime that a group should be ashamed to say that they "can't do anything in June, July, and August." Let's look at some of the possibilities:

A PLAYGROUND. Why not clean off and roll that vacant lot for croquet? Or make a miniature golf or clock golf course? A goofy golf course could be built on almost any sort of lot. Use pieces of abandoned tile pipes, hoops, tin canks sunk in the ground, stovepipes, and old lumber, to make some interesting hazards. Or build courts for ten-

220

nis, volleyball, badminton, and deck tennis. Mass badminton makes a good game. Players used long-handled wooden paddles for rackets. Six players can play on a side, as in volleyball. Some groups light their playgrounds for night use.

PICNICS. Plan at least several picnics for the summer season. Some groups go picknicking every Saturday.

COOK-OUTS. Steak fries, bacon bats, clambakes, fish fries, etc.

CAMPING. Many a local group has its own camping experience. One such group located its camp near enough to the town so that the young people who had to work during the day could come out at night. Daytime camping is good fun for groups that find it impossible to spend the night in a camping location.

HIKE. Penny walks, nature hikes, visits to points of interest, hobo hikes.

BOOK TRAILS. Hike to a lovely spot. Read together and discuss a book, a play, some poetry, or an article.

LAWN PARTIES. Lawns decorated with lanterns make colorful settings for interesting parties.

STORYTELLERS' CONVENTION. Such an occasion lends itself to endless variety. The program may take on an international flavor with stories from many lands. "Uncle Remus" or "Paul Bunyan" stories could be featured.

OUTDOOR MUSIC FESTIVAL. Community singing and special numbers.

OUTDOOR DRAMA. Stunts, skits, or serious drama. For serious drama some of the old miracle and morality plays would be excellent. Why not dramatize the history of a community or church and portray it in a colorful pageant?

CRICKET BALL

The object is to prevent wickets from being knocked down, by hitting ball with hand (volleyball), or bat (indoor baseball), and scoring as many runs as possible by running to first base and back to home base.

Material: Indoor baseball and bat, or volleyball.

Field: Home base area, four feet by four feet. First base area, four feet by four feet, placed thirty feet from home base (corresponding in location to a first base in baseball), if volleyball is used; forty-five feet from home base if indoor baseball and bat are used.

Pitcher's box: Three feet by six feet front and twenty-five feet from home base if volleyball is used; thirty-five feet from home base if indoor baseball is used.

Wickets: Three stakes, two feet long, stuck lightly in ground, one foot apart and one foot back of rear line of batter's box.

Rules: The ball is thrown underhand. Runner stands at right or left edge of home base, within area, and if indoor bat is used, with end of bat touching ground at center of area, until ball is pitched. Catcher stands three feet behind wickets. Pitcher stands in field box. Teams are composed of twelve players, consisting of a catcher, pitcher, baseman, and nine outfielders. Captains may place players where they desire. No strikes, ball, or fouls counted. If a player hits ball he must run. With volleyball, player strikes with hand; with indoor baseball, he uses bat. Fewer than nine outfielders can be used if desired.

A batter is out if the ball is hit in the air and caught before touching the ground; if he is hit by ball thrown by any of the side in the field, or if the ball is thrown to first base and the base touched with ball before the batter reaches the base; or if he misses, or fails to hit, or fouls a ball that knocks down any of the wickets.

A runner is out if he is hit by a thrown or batted ball when between the bases or off base.

Runners must keep one foot in contact with the base area until ball is hit.

More than one runner may occupy first-base area at one time.

All runners on first base may run on a hit ball.

Three outs retire side. Three outs for each side constitute an inning.

If a player should be on base when his turn to bat comes, the captain may substitute another player for him.

A run is scored when player runs to base and returns to home base without being put out.

Teams bat in regular order.

A player on the side of the batter, interfering with a player in the field who is trying to field the ball, is out.

Winning team is the team scoring the largest number of runs in any number of full innings.

HARE AND HOUNDS

An old game is this one, but it is lots of fun. A half dozen to twenty young people divide into two teams. Some spot in the camp is designated as "home." Group One stays at home, giving Group Two five minutes to get started on a twenty-minute tramp that takes the whole group wherever the leader of Group Two chooses. This leader leaves a twelve-inch square of newspaper at head height every hundred feet, so that Group One may follow the trail. Or Group Two may be required to leave torn pieces of paper all along the way in a steady stream. If Group Two gets home without Group One seeing any of its members, Group Two wins. Otherwise Group One wins.

Perhaps interest can be added by requiring each group to be alert to nature interests—identifying trees en route (bringing leaves with them), identifying birds, spotting birds' nests and leaving them unmolested, identifying wild flowers, etc.

CHAPTER VII

Party Games

Party Games

TWENTY QUESTIONS

Two or more play this game. One person goes out of the room. The rest decide on something. The player who left returns to the room and tries to guess what it is by asking questions. He is limited to twenty questions. He probably tries to locate it first. "Is it in the room?" "In the United States?" After he locates it, he probably asks, "Is it animate?" "Is it human?" "Is it a saying?" When he thinks he has discovered it, he names it. If he is correct, another player, perhaps the one who gave him the cue, goes out and the game continues. If he is wrong, he proceeds to ask more questions, unless he has already used up his limit of twenty.

The "something" may be some article in the room. It may be the cap on the captain of the "Queen Mary," the boundary line between Canada and the United States, the beanstalk that Jack climbed, the lamb that followed Mary to school, the school bell, some movie or athletic star, some well-known song, etc.

The procedure can be varied so that the guesser is told whether the thing in mind is animal, vegetable, or mineral.

STAGE SHOW TWENTY QUESTIONS

Select from two to six questioners. They stand on one side of a screen, on the other side of which are displayed, one at a time, certain articles. These articles are visible to everyone in the room but the questioners. They are given twenty questions between them to discover what each article is. The rest of the crowd may offer hints, at their discretion. Suggested articles: a loaf of bread, a toy balloon, a woman's hat, a false mustache, a wig, a grass skirt, an apron, a pencil, a book, a wastebasket, a grapefruit, a penny. It adds to the fun to give the articles, at least temporarily, to the guessers who name them correctly. Particularly is this true if the articles are wearing apparel, in which case the guesser is arrayed in the article guessed.

This game has been used successfully as a banquet stunt.

TWENTY BIBLICAL QUESTIONS

Ten or more can play this game. Send one person out of the room. Then the group decides on some thing from the Bible, such as the slingshot that David used, the ark that Noah built, the golden calf, the jawbone used by Samson, etc. Or they can pick some place, such as Ur, or Bethel, or the lion's den in which Daniel was placed. Or some person, such as Abraham, Moses, Deborah, Sarah, David, Solomon, Mark, Peter, or Timothy. Or they can choose some event, such as the Flood, the crossing of the Red Sea, or Pentecost.

The guesser is called back. He tries to guess what the group has in mind by asking questions that can be answered by "Yes" or "No." He is allowed a maximum of twenty questions. He probably begins by asking, "Is it in the Old Testament?" If the answer is "Yes," he may ask, "Is it a person?" or "Is it an event?" or "Is it a place?" or "Is it a thing?" Having discovered that it is a thing, the line of questioning may try to locate the period in Old Testament history. 'Was it connected with the story of Moses?" "No." "David?" "Yes." "Was it his harp?" "No." "His slingshot?" "Yes."

228

When one questioner is finished, another person is chosen to go out of the room and the game continues.

SCOUTING FOR BIBLICAL WORDS

Ten or more players can participate. The leader has alphabet cards about five-by-seven inches in size. These can be made easily. The game may be played by teams or by individual competition. The leader holds up one card so all can see the letter. The first player to call a biblical name or thing beginning with that letter gets the card or scores a point. If a thing is called, or if there is any doubt about the word called, the caller is required to justify his answer. Thus, if an "F" is flashed and he calls "fiery furnace," he may have to explain that it is the fiery furnace into which the three Hebrew boys were cast.

A variation would be to allow a point for each word called as a letter is flashed. Thus, as the letter "P" is shown, appropriate answers would be "Paul," "Peter," "Philip," "Pilate," "Philippians," "Philistines," "Philemon." In such a case teams may be allowed to consult and then offer their lists. One point would be allowed for each correct answer.

Another variation would be for the leader to call for something specific before flashing the cards. For instance, he may call for "the name of a book of the Bible," or "the name of a person in the Bible." The first person to answer correctly would score a point.

HIDDEN WORDS

Ten or more can engage in this fun. Explain to the group that letters are hidden about the room. These letters are numbered. Each set of six letters spells some six-letter

229

word. Thus, all the letters in the word "battle" are numbered one. Each player is given a number, "1," "2," or "3," etc. He must pick up only letters bearing his number. When he has six letters bearing his number, he tries to figure out what the word is. As soon as he knows what the word is, he reports to the leader.

For a variation divide into four groups, if there is a large crowd. Put up large numbers at the four corners of the room to designate team positions. As soon as a player on team Number One finds a letter bearing that number, he goes to his own headquarters, where a big "1" is on the wall. So it goes until six players have found the letters that are numbered "1." Each team does the same thing. They then place the letters on a table or on the floor and try to find out what the word is. As soon as they do, they report to the leader by whispering the word to him.

When each group has figured out its word, they work out some dramatization of it. The others try to guess what the word is. The team may be required to tell what the first letter is.

For instance, if the word for Group One is "battle," they may put on a mock war.

Some possible words: comedy, church, debate, sailor, tackle, cackle, fencer, senate, picnic, rowing, suitor, sports, etc.

TEN-SCENT GAME

Any number can play this game. Cover ten bottles with crepe paper in the colors indicated. Each player tries to guess what each bottle contains by smelling it. Write answers beside colors on a score sheet.

1. Red—perfume. 2. Blue—vanilla extract. 3. Green—vinegar. 4. Yellow—sour milk. 5. Orange—ammonia. 6.

Pine—rubbing alcohol. 7. Black—peppermint. 8. White—witch hazel. 9. Lavender—camphor. 10. Purple—smelling salts.

SONG ARTISTS

This game calls for five or more players. A blackboard and crayons (if in colors, so much the better) or a large scratch-pad and colored crayons. A player steps up to the board and illustrates some song title. The rest try to guess the title. For instance, he draws a house sitting on a stove.

Someone says, "Home on the Range." That is correct, and then the guesser takes his turn in illustrating a song. Suggestions: "The Old Oaken Bucket," "The Blue-Tailed Fly," "Down in the Valley," "My Old Kentucky Home," "I've Been Workin' on the Railroad," "Mary Had a Little Lamb," and perhaps some current popular songs. After each song is guessed, the group can sing it, if desired.

In a large group divide into sides. Have a representative of each team go to the board in turn. Without telling his teammates what song he is illustrating, he begins his drawing. The first team to guess correctly scores a point.

BOOK TITLE ARTISTS

This is a game for two or more participants. Players draw something to represent the title of a book. For instance, a hat being blown by the wind would be *Gone with the Wind*. An eye, a moving van, and a hoe would be *Ivanhoe*. A person stealing something and a hood would be *Robin Hood*. Three men on one horse would be *Three Men on a Horse*.

Nursery rhymes, poem titles, and fairy stories may be added for variety.

This game may be used as a mixer at a party, with each player drawing something and pinning it on for others to see. Players mix around trying to identify titles and listing them with the names of the artists. After a few minutes, call time and find out what player has identified the greatest number of titles. Have the titles read and verified by the artists.

RHYTHM NUMBERS

Ten or more players are seated in a circle or semicircle. The chairs are numbered. Player Number One starts the game by slapping palms on his knees, clapping his hands together, and then snapping fingers of right hand. This will be done in a one-two-three rhythm. All players follow suit. When everyone gets the proper rhythm, the leader calls his own number on the finger snap. On the next finger snap he calls another number. Thus, slap knees, clap hands, snap fingers and call "one" (his own number); then slap knees, clap hands, snap fingers and call "seven," for instance. Keeping the rhythm, player Number Seven must call his own number on the next finger snap and the number of someone else on the succeeding snap. When a player fails to respond correctly, the game stops and the erring player moves to the foot of the line. All players below him move up one seat, and take the new number of the seat to which they move. The object of the game is to get the top players down. Number One becomes a good target. Each time there is a failure to keep the rhythm the game starts over with renumbered players.

For a variation: Slap hands on knees, clap together, snap right fingers, snap left fingers. When the leader is ready, he begins by calling "Rhythm" on the right-finger snap and another number on the left-finger snap. The player holding that number must call his own number on the next right-finger snap and another number on the left-finger snap. Only the first player calls "Rhythm."

RHYTHM WORDS

This game involves the same number of players and the same formation and motions as in "Rhythm Numbers." The leader calls "Rhythm" on the first snap, and a letter of the alphabet on the second snap. The player to the leader's right must say a word beginning with the called letter on the next snap and another letter on the next. So it goes until some player misses.

Example: First person says "Rhythm," "R"; the second person says "Rat," "C" or "B," and so on until a player fails. The erring player begins the game again with a "Rhythm" and a letter. Only the starters say "Rhythm." After the start there must be a word or letter on every snap.

233

RHYTHM NAMES

This game is played in the same fashion as "Rhythm Numbers" or "Rhythm Words," and is suitable for ten or more players. The only difference is that on the first snap the player calls the first name of some prominent or famous person. Thus, he calls "George" on the snap and the next player to the right must call some famous person whose first name is "George," such as "Washington." Names of historical or fictional personages, stage or movie stars, politicians, athletes, writers, radio performers, etc., may be used. When a player fails to respond, the player missing starts the next round. When a player calls a first name, he must have some individual in mind. However, it is not necessary for the next player to call that particular name. He may call any other prominent person whose first name is the one called. Instead of "Washington," the response might have been "George (Babe) Ruth." When a player responds satisfactorily, the next person to his right calls a new first name, and so on.

SCANDALMONGER

Ten or more can play this game. One person is sent out of the room. The others then make remarks about him that may be complimentary or otherwise. The scandalmonger, chosen by the group, jots these remarks down. The person is called back and the scandalmonger repeats the remarks, pausing after each one to give the victim a chance to guess who said it. "Someone said that you are handsome." "Someone said that you can't add." When the person guesses correctly who made the particular remark, that one must go out of the room while the others talk about him. If the player is unable to guess correctly, the statements may be reread and he may guess again. If he still cannot guess, another player may volunteer to go out as the game continues.

OBSERVATION

Ten or more can play this game to see how sharp their observation is.

Place fifteen or twenty articles on a table—a knife, a ring, a book, a button, a vase, a belt, a bobby pin, a spool, a small bottle, a purse, a pen, a pencil, a paper clip, a hairpin, a flower, a brooch, a penny, a dime, a quarter, an orange, a bean, a needle, etc. Allow all the players to walk by to observe for a brief moment what is on the table. Then they walk out of the room and write down all of the articles they can remember.

A variation on this is to send several players out of the room after they have been told to observe carefully what is in the room. Those remaining in the room remove four or five articles. The players are called back. Each of them is given a piece of paper and a pencil and told to list the things missing.

Still another variation is to send one player out of the room after he has had opportunity to observe the position of each person in the room. Then have two players change positions. Call the other player back and see if he can tell which two have moved.

SCOUTING FOR WORDS

Any number can play this game, and the only equipment needed is a set of alphabet letters. They can be made on stiff cards five by four inches. Color the letters with crayons or poster paint. Two sets of letters would be useful.

The leader stands before the players, calls some category, say, "automobile," and holds up the letter "C." Responses might be "Chevrolet" or "Crosley" or "Cadillac." The first player to answer correctly gets the card. At the end of the game the player with the largest number of cards wins.

Other categories might be biblical names and places, nature (birds, animals, trees, flowers), geography (states, cities, rivers, countries), grocery or department store, literature (authors, books, magazines), music (composers, song titles, instruments, singers, players), etc.

The leader may weave the words into narrative form, such as a trip on the highway, a trek through the woods, a shopping trip, a journey through Bible lands, a visit to the bookstore, attendance upon a musicale, or the like.

The game may be played by sides. If cards are not available, the leader may call the letters instead of showing them. Score points.

SCOUTING FOR FLOWERS OR
FLOWER HUNT

Any number can enjoy this game. Use cards similar to those in "Scouting for Words," and paste on them colored pictures of various flowers. Flower seed catalogues will supply the pictures needed. Flash with cards one at a time and have players call names of flowers. Each correct call scores a point.

Or, make a card set after the fashion described for use as "flash" cards, or use articles and pictures from magazines and catalogues. Number exhibits and place about the room for guests to identify with the correct numbers of the flowers represented, or flash and have players call the answers either in individual competition or by teams. Some sug-

gestions: Bachelor's-button (a button off a man's shirt or trousers). Bluebonnet (a blue bonnet). Buttercup (picture of some butter and a cup). Carnation (a toy automobile or pictures and a map of the United States). Chrysanthemum (a small Santa Claus figure, a copy of an anthem, a jar of Mum). Cowslip (picture of a cow and a petticoat). Dandelion (picture of a stylishly dressed man and a lion). Daisy (page from a calendar and the letter Z). Dogwood (toy dog and a piece of wood. Flag (an American flag). Four-o'clock (clock set at four o'clock). Foxglove (picture of a fox and a glove). Hollyhock (sprig of holly or picture; picture of hawk, or the familiar pawnbroker's three-balls sign). Indian paintbrush (picture of an Indian and an artist's brush). Iris (picture of a rainbow). Larkspur (picture of a lark and a spur). Orchid (picture of baby labeled "ours"). Pansy (a pan and the letter Z). Phlox (pictures of two or more flocks of sheep or birds). Poppy (bottle of pop and a pea). Pink (piece of pink cloth or paper). Snapdragon (a snapshot and a picture of a dragon). Sunflower (picture of the sun and a bit of flour.) Sweet William (a bit of sugar, the printed form used for making a will, and

237

a yam). Violet (picture of a viol and a sign "For Rent").

This same game can be used with birds or animals (a trip to the zoo). Birds: bluebird, blackbird, butterbill, bunting, cardinal, chickadee, crane, flycatcher, Indian hen, ivorybill, kingbird, kingfisher, kite, nightingale, pintail, robin, rail, sandpiper, spoonbill, tern, thrasher, woodpecker, yellowhammer. Animals: antelope, alligator, bear, bat, beaver, buffalo, buck, doe, lion, porcupine.

MY FLOWER GARDEN

Ten or more can participate. One player announces, "I have a flower garden. What are you going to give me to plant in it?" The players in turn must answer with some flower beginning with a letter of the alphabet. These must be given in alphabetical order. For instance, the first player answers "asters," the next, "buttercups," until the whole alphabet is used. If a player cannot answer, and anyone in the group, including the leader, can, he posts a forfeit, redeemed by performing some stunt for the crowd.

MY ZOO

This is played in the same way as "My Flower Garden," except that animals or birds are named. Cue: "I have a zoo. What are you going to give me for it?" "Antelope," "buffalo," "canary," "dove," etc.

MY GROCERY

Similar to "My Flower Garden" and "My Zoo." Cue: "I have a grocery. What are you going to give me to stock it? "Apples," "bananas," "crackers," "doughnuts," etc.

THINGS FOR MY JOB

Ten or more players required. One player goes out of the room. The rest decide what he is to be.

On his return to the room each person mentions something he will need for his job. After he has been all around the room he must guess what he is—a dentist, a carpenter, a doctor, a preacher, a movie star, etc.

For the dentist such suggestions as the following are offered: a white coat, a chair, tooth powder, forceps, drill, etc. For the carpenter: a hammer, a saw, a plane, etc. For the doctor: thermometer, stethoscope, pills, handbag, etc. For the movie star: grease paint, publicity agent, a Hollywood home, etc.

If a player cannot guess what he is, he pays a forfeit to be redeemed by a stunt.

Other suggested jobs: policeman or traffic cop, ballplayer, painter, artist, sculptor, author, lawyer, teacher, aviator, sailor, conductor, gardener, farmer.

BIRD HUNT

Any number can enjoy this pastime. Mount colored pictures of birds on stiff cards five by four inches. Such pictures can be had inexpensively from the National Audubon Society, 1000 Fifth Avenue, New York 28, N. Y. Write the names of the birds on the backs of the cards.

Start the game by telling a story of a hike through the woods and fields where various kinds of birds are seen. Hold up the cards one at a time while the players try to identify the birds. The first player to call the correct name is handed the card. At the close, the player or side with the largest number of cards wins. If no one answers, tell the group what bird it is, put it back in the stack of cards, and hold it up again later.

The game can be varied by numbering the cards. Place them about the room and have the players identify them by writing the names and numbers on paper. Read the correct list to check papers.

MAGIC MUSIC

This game needs ten or more players. Send one player out of the room. While he is gone, hide something about the room—a coin, a button, a ring, or some other small object. The player is called back and is told to find the object. His cues come from the singing of the group. As he draws near the object the group sings louder and louder. As he moves away from the spot where the object is hidden, it sings softer and softer. The object may be in someone's pocket, under someone's foot, on someone's chair, in a vase, etc. Sing some song familiar to the group, such as "She'll Be Coming 'Round the Mountain." Piano music may be substituted for the singing.

CONCERT

Any number can play. One player is the director. The rest are members of the orchestra. Each player chooses some imaginary musical instrument—trombone, violin, bass viol, cornet, saxophone, piano, drum, cymbals, etc., or the director may assign instruments.

Everyone is ordered to tune his instrument just as would be done by an orchestra. Then the director makes believe at beating time as he hums some tune, the livelier the better. All players must pretend to play their instruments with appropriate voice and gesture.

The leader waves his baton for them to cease playing and calls: "Solos." He begins playing some instrument. The player (or players) having that instrument must instantly join the leader in tune and gesture.

Failure to follow suit or coming in at the wrong time incurs some penalty, such as a forfeit or dropping out of the orchestra.

NICKNAMES

Any number can participate. What places, persons, or things are suggested by the following nicknames?

Geographical: 1. The Ould Sod. 2. The Windy City. 3. The Golden Gate. 4. The Eternal City. 5. The Empire State. 6. The Steel City. 7. The Blue Grass State. 8. Little Rhody. 9. The Hoosier State. 10. The Hawkeye State. 11. The Father of Waters. 12. The Land of the Rising Sun. 13. The Queen City. 14. The Old Dominion.

Historical: 1. Old Hickory. 2. Buffalo Bill. 3. Old Ironsides. 4. The Iron Duke. 5. The Little Corporal. 6. The Iron Chancellor. 7. The Maid of Orleans. 8. The Great Emancipator. 9. The Great Compromiser. 10. The Rough Rider. 11. Black Jack. 12. The Happy Warrior. 13. The Lion-Hearted. 14. The Champ. 15. The Little Giant. 16. The Father of His Country.

Sports: 1. Gentleman Jim. 2. The Brown Bomber. 3. The Galloping Ghost. 4. The Manassa Mauler. 5. Big Six. 6. Mr. Inside and Mr. Outside. 7. The Father of American Football. 8. The Red Sox. 9. The Sultan of Swat. 10. Georgia

241

Peach. 11. The California Comet. 12. Harry the Cat. 13. The Four Horsemen. 14. Ruby Robert.

Miscellaneous: 1. Old Glory. 2. Tin-Pan Alley. 3. Union Jack. 4. The Bard of Avon. 5. The Great Commoner. 6. The Swedish Nightingale. 7. The Old Curmudgeon. 8. The Wizard of Menlo Park. 9. The Man of a Thousand Faces. 10. Big Ben. 11. Old Eli. 12. Black Maria. 13. The Fourth Estate. 14. The Waltz King. 15. The Good Book.

ANSWERS

Geographical: 1. Ireland. 2. Chicago. 3. Entrance to San Francisco harbor. 4. Rome. 5. New York. 6. Pittsburgh. 7. Kentucky. 8. Rhode Island. 9. Indiana. 10. Iowa. 11. Mississippi River. 12. Japan. 13. Cincinnati. 14. Virginia.

Historical: 1. Andrew Jackson. 2. William Cody, famed scout and showman. 3. United States frigate "Constitution." 4. The Duke of Wellington. 5. Napoleon Bonaparte. 6. Bismarck, chancellor of Germany. 7. Joan of Arc. 8. Abraham Lincoln. 9. Henry Clay. 10. Theodore Roosevelt. 11. General John J. Pershing. 12. Alfred E. Smith, New York politician. 13. Richard Coeur de Lion. 14. Franklin Delano Roosevelt. 15. Stephen Douglas. 16. George Washington.

Sports: 1. James J. Corbett, champion heavyweight prize fighter. 2. Joe Louis, champion heavyweight prize fighter. 3. Red Grange, football star at Illinois University. 4. Jack Dempsey, champion prize fighter. 5. Walter Johnson, famous pitcher for Washington Senators. 6. Glenn Davis and "Doc" Blanchard, of the Army football team. 7. Walter Camp. 8. Boston, of American Baseball League. 9. George Herman (Babe) Ruth, famous baseball player. 10. Ty Cobb, famous outfielder. 11. Maurice McLaughlin, one-time tennis champion. 12. Harry Brecheen, pitcher for St. Louis Cardinals. 13. Great backfield of Notre Dame, consisting of Layden, Crowley, Miller, and Stulrehder. 14. Robert Fitzsimmons, champion prize fighter.

Miscellaneous: 1. Flag of the United States. 2. The district of New York City where popular music is published. 3. British naval flag. 4. William Shakespeare. 5. William Jennings Bryan. 6. Jenny Lind, famous singer. 7. Harold Ickes. 8. Thomas Edison. 9. Lon Chaney, famous movie star. 10. The clock in the tower of Parliament in London. 11. Yale University. 12. Police wagon. 13. The public press. 14. Johann Strauss. 15. The Bible.

NINE BOOKS OR MIND READING

This game needs ten or more players. Nine books are arranged in rows of three each. One player goes out of the room. One of the players in the room touches one of the books. The "mind reader" comes back and tells which book was touched. The secret lies in the signals of a conspirator in the room. If he brushes his left cheek with his hand, it is the book at top left. If he brushes the right side of his cheek or head, it is top right. If he strokes his chin, it is top center. Left hand on left hip means middle left; right hand on right hip means middle right. Hands held on the stomach means middle center. Left hand at side with forefinger pointing down means left bottom. Right hand at side with forefinger down means right bottom. Hands folded or brushed together mean middle bottom.

In a variation the conspirator holds a book in his left hand. The forefinger points to part of the book that indicates location of the book touched.

243

MAGIC ARITHMETIC TRICKS

One trick: Take four from four and leave eight. After the group has given up, take a piece of paper, tear off the four corners and you have eight corners or points.

Another trick: The leader announces that if the players will allow him to write the third and fifth numbers while they call the first, second, and fourth numbers of five figures, he will give them the total after they have given him the first number of five digits. The only stipulation is that the right-hand digit of the first call must be two or more.

First call	85654
Second call	75683
Leader's call	24316
Third call	97636
Leader's call	02363
	285652

Immediately the first call is made the leader calls 285652 as the grand total. On the leader's call, he calls numbers that add to 9 for each of the numbers in the other players' call. Check the above. The result will always be 2 followed by the first four digits in the first call with a minus 2 on the fifth digit. In this case the last digit was 4 so the answer was 285652. Try it out for yourself before you work it on others.

WHO AM I?

Any number can play. One player starts the game by saying, "Who am I?" He may be any person, living or dead, historical or fictional. The other players try to discover who he is by asking questions that can be answered

"Yes" or "No." Questioners are not allowed to ask if it is a certain person until they have pushed it back by questions that make the answer obvious. Thus, they have found that the person is dead, that he was a man, an American, a figure of Revolutionary days. It is not allowed to begin firing names of men of Revolution days. "Was he a printer?" "No." "A general?" "Yes." "Was he our first president?" "Yes." "Then it's George Washington." "Yes." The player who guesses correctly thinks of another character, says, "Who am I?" and the game continues.

The game can be varied in this way: One player starts the game by saying, "I am someone whose name begins with the letter C. Who am I?" "Are you an English statesman?" someone may ask. "No, I am not Churchill." "Are you a former president of the United States?" another may ask. "No, I am not Coolidge." "An American army officer who defeated the Cheyenne Indians?" "No, I am not Custer." "A character in one of Dickens' novels?" "No, I am not David Copperfield." "A writer?" "No, I am not Cooper." "A scientist?" "Yes." Then the group can ask direct questions such as "Are you a Frenchman?" "Yes." "Did you discover the use of radium?" "Yes." "Then you're Curie." "Yes."

When the player asks if the person is a statesman, writer, singer, or what not, he must have someone in mind whose name begins with the letter called. If the player being questioned cannot think of a statesman, writer, or singer, or whatever the questioner calls, he may challenge the caller. If the questioner answers with a name that fits the category called, then the person who asked "Who am I?" must submit himself to three direct questions, such as "Are you alive?" or "Are you a man?" or "Are you an American?" Then the game proceeds as before, until the person is identified.

This variation of playing "Who Am I?" is a bit more difficult than the first game, but it is possible for those from junior high school and up to get much fun out of it.

WHAT AM I?

Fifteen or more players are needed. On arrival each player has a slip of paper pinned on his back. On the paper may be the name of some animal. The players then mix around trying to find out what they are by asking questions or by listening to remarks made about them. When a player discovers what animal he represents, he reports to the leader. The slip is taken off of his back and pinned on the player's lapel or dress front.

Names of prominent persons may be used instead of animals—people prominent in public life, movie and radio stars, etc. Or names of birds, or trees, or flowers, or other things may be used.

BUZZ

Ten to thirty players are seated in a circle. The buzz number is "5." One player starts by calling "1." The player to his right calls "2," and so it goes—"3, 4, Buzz, 6, 7, 8, 9, Buzz," etc. Wherever "5" appears or where any multiple of "5" appears, the player must not call the number but say "Buzz" instead.

The game can be prolonged and varied by having a different buzz number each time.

BUZZ-FIZZ

The same number can play this game. Players are seated in a circle.

It is announced that on "5," any multiple of "5," or any number in which "5" appears, the player must say "Buzz" instead of the number. On any number containing "7," or any multiple of "7," the player must say "Fizz." Thus, the number would be "1, 2, 3, 4, Buzz, 6, Fizz, 8, 9, Buzz, 11, 12, 13, Fizz, Buzz, 16, Fizz," etc. On a number like "57" the player would have to say "Buzz-Fizz." The same would be true of "35," which is a multiple of both "7" and "5." So it would be "Buzz-Fizz."

Players who make mistakes must drop out or pay a forfeit.

BUZZ BASEBALL

There are eighteen players divided into two teams of nine players each. One team takes the field—they stand or seat themselves in baseball positions: catcher, pitcher, first base, second base, third base, and outfielders. Bases are only a few feet apart.

A player from the "batting" team comes to the "plate," the position in front of the pitcher. The pitcher calls a buzz number, such as "3," for instance. The batter calls "one." His teammates are arranged in a line and they take up the numbering: "2, Buzz, 4, 5, Buzz," etc. If the batting side gets through without a mistake, the fielding side continues the numbering, beginning with the catcher, then the pitcher, then the basemen and outfielders, in order. So it would be "10, 11, Buzz, Buzz, 14, Buzz," etc. If the batting side makes a mistake, the batter is out. He is also out if the fielding side gets through without an error. However, if the fielding side fails to buzz in the proper place, the batter advances as many bases as the number of the fielding side making mistakes.

When three men are out, the teams change sides just as in regular baseball.

Players must count rapidly. If they delay, the umpire may call the batter out, or give him a base, depending on which team is at fault.

COUNTING TO THIRTY

Ten to thirty players are seated in a circle. One player starts the count, beginning with "1." The counting moves to the right or left, as indicated by the leader. On "7," or on any number containing "7," the player whose turn it is claps the palms of his hands together instead of calling the number. On "14," or any multiple of "7," such as "21," or "28," the player whose turn it is hits the backs of his hands together, instead of calling the number.

To complicate the matter further, the direction of the numbering changes each time "7" or a multiple of "7" is reached. Thus, if the numbering is moving to the right, and a player claps on "7," the numbering reverses and moves back to the left until "14" is reached, when it reverses again and moves back to the right. This becomes tricky when "27" and "28" are reached, as can be seen.

If a player calls a "7" or a multiple of "7," the numbering stops and a new start is made, beginning with some other player in the circle. It is a fault also if some player calls a number out of his turn, failing to observe the reverse rule.

The numbering would go like this: "1, 2, 3, 4, 5, 6, clap" (direction reverses) "8, 9, 10, 11, 12, 13, back of hands struck together" (direction reversed) "15, 16, clap," etc.

There are usually screams of delight when the group finally makes it to "30" without an error. When they get really good at it, they can move on to "50" and even "100." But that would require extreme alertness.

If there are more than 30 players, divide into two or more groups to see which group can first count to "30" without an error.

A TOAST TO SIR PUFF-PUFF

Three or more players are needed for this trick stunt that may be done at the table.

The leader says, "Here is the toast to Sir Puff-Puff." He makes one bow. Then he takes his glass and, holding it with the forefinger and thumb, he takes one sip of water. Then he hits the table once with his right forefinger and once with his left forefinger. He hits his right knee with his right forefinger and his left knee with his left forefinger. He stamps once with his right foot and once with his left foot.

The leader repeats, "Here is the toast to Sir Puff-Puff." He bows twice. This time he holds the glass with the first two fingers and the thumb. He takes two sips of water. Each action is done twice—hitting the table twice with his right forefinger, twice with his left forefinger, etc.

The third time the leader says, "Here is the toast to Sir Puff-Puff." He bows three times. He holds the glass with three fingers and the thumb. He takes three sips. All actions are done three times.

Various persons are asked to repeat the toast to Sir Puff-Puff just as the leader gave it. Unless they have been very observant, they will probably do it incorrectly.

If members of the group have difficulty figuring out the trick, the leader may go through it again, making the tip-offs as obvious as he desires.

SCRAMBLED STATES

Give a list of states to each player. The letters in the names of these states are jumbled. Players are given a few minutes to untangle them. Examples: Ningawshot (Washington), Lacirofian (California), Wedalear (Delaware), Gamichin (Michigan), Hadio (Idaho).

STATE ABBREVIATIONS

What state is a father? (Pa.) What state is used in a flood? (Ark.) What state is found in mines? (Ore.) What state is a religious service? (Mass.) What state is not you? (Me.) What state is a doctor? (Md.) What state is an exclamation? (O.) What state is sick? (Ill.) Other similar ones can be found.

ALPHABETICAL GEOGRAPHY

One player calls the name of a country, state, or city. The next player must call a country, state, or city beginning with the last letter in the name just called. Examples: Germany, Yucatan; New York, Kansas, etc.

See "Scouting for Words" (p. 235) and "Capitals" (p. 251).

GEOGRAPHY BEFORE TEN

One player in the center suddenly points at another player and calls the name of some country, state, or island. Before he can count to ten, the person at whom he points must answer with the name of some city, mountain, river, or lake in the particular country, state, or island called.

Players form in line. The leader moves down the line indicating who is to make the response. When a player misses, he goes to the foot of the line.

If a player makes three misses, he may be required to pay a forfeit.

CAPITALS

Ninety-six or less can play this game. Give out the names of the state capitals to half of the group and the names of states to the other half. Or pin outlines of the different states on the state group. Then states and capitals locate each other and are partners for same game to follow. For a small group use only a few states and capitals.

A variation is to give each player a list of states. By the side of each state they are to write in the capital.

Capitals of the various countries in the world can be used in the same manner.

WRONG CAPITAL

Any number of players are divided into two teams which face each other. Number One player on Team A calls a capital but places it in the wrong state, for instance, "Frankfort is the capital of Virginia." Number One on Team B replies, "Wrong. Frankfort is the capital of Kentucky." "Sacramento is the capital of Washington." Number Two on Team A replies, "Wrong. Sacramento is the capital of California." And so it goes, back and forth between the two teams. A player may call a capital correctly, if he desires, thus fooling his opponent, perhaps. A point is scored for each correct answer. One point goes to the opponents for a miss.

251

It may prove more satisfactory for the leader to make out a list of capitals beforehand. In this case he would call a capital, placing it in the wrong state, maybe. The player answering would make the proper correction, if a correction is necessary. A player on first one team and then the other would be quizzed by the leader.

BLIND PROBLEMS

Ten to thirty can have fun with this game. Two slips of paper are provided each player. On one of these slips he writes some problem; on the other he writes an answer, though it need not necessarily be an answer to the particular problem he has written on another slip. The problems are dropped into one box and the answers into another. Now each player draws a problem from the problem box and an answer from the answer box. These drawings are to be done sight unseen.

Players in turn read aloud to the rest of the group the problem and the answer.

Here are some possible results. *Problem:* "What would you do if the English teacher called on you for a book report when you were not ready?" *Answer:* "I'd send it to the cleaners." *Problem:* "What would you do if your favorite suit had an unfortunate experience with a skunk?" *Answer:* "I'd punt out of danger."

OPPOSITES

Any number of players can participate. The leader flashes an alphabet card or simply calls a letter of the alphabet. The first player to call a word beginning with that letter and the word that is its opposite, scores a point for his side.

Thus, the leader flashes an "O." A player calls "odd" and "even" or "old" and "young" and scores a point. Other opposites: fast, slow; rude, polite; smart, dumb; bright, dull; black, white; sour, sweet; ugly, pretty; hard, soft; hot, cold; big, little; tall, short.

GIVEN WORDS

Six to twenty players sit in a circle. Each person whispers to his right-hand neighbor a single word. When everyone has his word, one player begins by asking a question of his neighbor to the left. This player must reply with a sentence in which he uses the word whispered to him. This he does as cleverly as possible, so as to make it fit into his sentence naturally if he can. The other player tries to discover the given word. If he does not guess correctly, he pays a forfeit. In giving words, players give words that are not easy to introduce in an ordinary sentence. The fun comes in the way the players work out answers that include the words.

POLITE CONVERSATION

Any number can play this. Two players are given subjects for conversation. Neither knows what the other's topic is. However, all the rest of the players are informed what the subjects are while the two players are out of the room. In fact, they decide what the subjects shall be.

When the players come back, each tries to bring up his particular subject for conversation. No abrupt introduction of the subject may be made. Each player tries to get to his topic in a natural way.

Subjects should be as ridiculous as possible. "False teeth," "Limburger cheese," "sweet potatoes," "a pig," "an apple a day," "Easter bonnets," and "turkey feathers" are some of the possibilities.

Player A: "Have you ever been in the South (or some special city in the South) at Thanksgiving time?"

Player B: "No, but I have been there during the Easter season."

Player A: "Well, you should be there at Thanksgiving time. Those Thanksgiving dinners are out of this world."

Player B: "I'd like that, but Easter I went to church. You should have seen the Easter bonnets."

Player A: "My mouth still waters from the memory of that turkey, those biscuits, sweet potatoes, and everything."

But Player B got there first with "Easter bonnets."

Send out two more persons and let them try their skill in conversation.

LAWYER'S PUZZLE

Ten or more players are divided into two or more sides. With four teams, for instance, they occupy the four corners of the room.

Each team selects a representative who reports to the leader. Some object is selected, such as the press box in some particular football stadium or baseball park, the chandelier in the room, the church or school bell, etc. Each representative is given the same object. These representatives now go to one of the groups, excepting that no one goes to his own team.

Questions are fired at him by members of the team. These questions are to be answered only by "Yes" or "No." The procedure is much the same as in "Twenty Questions."

As soon as one team guesses correctly, they clap their hands to announce the fact. One point is scored for the winner.

Other representatives are sent out and the game continues.

WHIRR

Two or more players are given one minute to write down all the words they know that begin with the letter "W" and end with the letter "R." Wear, weir, winter, etc.

WORDS

Two players or two teams may play this. One player challenges another to give in one minute all the words he can think of that begin with a given letter. A count is kept. Then the challenger is given a letter by his opponent, and he calls all the words he knows that begin with that letter. It might be just as well to bar the letters "X," "Y," and "Z" as given letters.

TEAKETTLE

Ten to twenty players are seated about the room while one player is sent out of the room. The rest decide on some words which sound alike but have different spellings and meanings. Some examples: rain, reign, rein; in, inn; bare, bear (animal), bear (to carry); pain, pane; sore, soar; so, sow, sew; dear (costly), dear (beloved), deer; fare, fair (a festival), fair beautiful, fair (just); plane, plain (ugly), plain (level land); piece, peace; by, bye, buy; course, coarse.

When the player returns, each person in turn greets him with some sentence containing one or more of the words selected. However, instead of saying the word, they use the word "teakettle" wherever it appears in the sentence. Suppose the group has decided on "by," "bye," and "buy."

"Teakettle the teakettle," someone says, "I went down-town today teakettle myself to teakettle something."

Another player speaks up, "I never go teakettle that place that I don't think what a good teakettle that car is. If I had it, I would be saying 'teakettle, teakettle.' "

If the player guesses the word, the person who gave the tip-off goes out.

Sometimes the guesser is permitted to ask each person one question. The answer must contain the word selected in one of its forms at least, again the word "teakettle" being used to hide it.

THE SNIPPER

Ten or more can play this. In a group of twenty or more two or more "snippers" will keep the game moving.

Players form in a circle with one "snipper" or more in-side. The "snipper" stops in front of some player and spells some three-letter word, after calling it. For instance, he says, "Tag, t-a-g." The player before whom he stands must answer with the names of three objects or things, the first beginning with "T," the second with "A," and the third with "G," before the "snipper" can count to twelve and shout "Snip!" If he calls "tomatoes," "anchors," and "garlic" before the "snipper" finishes, he is safe. The "snip-per" moves on to try another victim with "Cat, c-a-t," or "Dog, d-o-g," or "hit, h-i-t," or some other three-letter word. When a player fails to answer correctly before "Snip!" is called, he takes the "snipper's" place.

ANAGRAM MAKERS

In the game of anagrams, players build words with letters. Then by shifting those letters about they change the words into some other word. In this process all the letters in the original word or words must be used in making the new word.

This game may be played by one player alone. He tries making some anagram words, perhaps starting with single three-letter words. It is really fun. Try it yourself.

Two players may play each other. Each in turn presents a word and the opponent tries to arrange the letters to spell other words. One point may be given for each word made.

A small group may play the game. One player spells the original word. The others write it down. The first player to "anagram" it, or the one making the most words, scores points accordingly.

Two sides may play the game. Either a leader calls out a word on which both sides work or one side presents a word to the other side.

Any word used must have the possibility of at least one other word in it.

Examples: cat (act); ape (pea); art (tar, rat); pat (apt, tap); has (ash); tear (tare, rate); sear (ears, rase); fare (fear); rout (tour); meat (team, mate, tame); seat (sate, teas); face (café); male (lame); pear (pare, reap); sole (lose); scare (races, cares). After such simple ones try longer words like machine (China, me); elementary (met, near, lye); hurricane (Ina, her, cur).

FLOWER ANAGRAMS

Play in the same manner as "Anagram Makers." Or each person may be given a copy of the scrambled flowers and allowed a few minutes to indicate what the flowers are.

Examples: is day (daisy); pops pie (poppies); tuna pie

(petunia); avails (salvia); a rig mold (marigold); (tiller way (water lily); what horn (hawthorn); a rot if shy (forsythia); be tin heel drag (bleeding heart); a Jap coin (japonica); O is tin pate (poinsettia); sore (rose); had ail (dahlia); thy chums ran me (chrysanthemum); I run game (geranium); I call (lilac); sin apes (pansies); one's pies (peonies); O can in tar (carnation); rub pet cut (buttercup).

Try making flower anagrams. Take the name of a flower and rearrange the letters so as to spell a different word, or two or more words.

Then try it out on friends or on the family to see if they can identify the flower. Suggestions: violet, anemone, daffodil, columbine, aster, tulip, forget-me-not, verbena, larkspur, sunflower.

BIBLE ANAGRAMS

This game, for two or more players, is similar to "Flower Anagrams." The only difference is that biblical names are used.

Examples: lie (Eli); line ad (Daniel); us lame (Samuel); loom son (Solomon); on mass (Samson); aha I is (Isaiah); hie jar me (Jeremiah); tan Johan (Jonathan); neb in jam (Benjamin); he ha mine (Nehemiah); had bore (Deborah); a roan (Aaron); nod rim (Nimrod); gin ode (Gideon); grab Eli (Gabriel); he rest (Esther); gin sees (Genesis); slam boa (Absalom); bale (Abel); what met (Matthew). Many others can be devised.

LIVING ALPHABET

For the full alphabet fifty-four players will be needed. Two of them are to act as captains. For a smaller group use only part of the alphabet. In either case work out the list of words beforehand so as to use all the letters that have been distributed.

Two sets of alphabet cards—perhaps five and one-half inches by seven inches. Use white cardboard. Paint one set of letters red, the other green. Crayons may be used in making these letters.

Two teams line up facing each other, on opposite sides of the room. The leader stands at one end of the room, between the two lines. A captain for each team stands at the other end of the room. The captain's job is to get players in proper position to spell the called word.

Each player is given a letter of the alphabet and they arrange themselves in alphabetical order.

The leader calls a word such as "train." The players bearing the letters in the called word rush to the end of the room opposite the leader and arrange themselves (with the captain's help perhaps) in proper position to spell out t-r-a-i-n. The side finishing first scores a point.

Start with easy words. Keep the words within the knowledge and experience of the players. Some suggestions: black, book, break, bum, cat, clerk, dog, dough, extra, fading, foreign, heat, Ireland, joke, march, mouse, New York, price, question, quiz, south, Texas, victory, Washington, water, white, whiz, young, zebra, zero.

Double letters are indicated by the holder waving the letter pendulumlike. When a letter appears in two places, the holder steps in the first place and then moves to the second place and stays there.

The game can be varied by calling out questions in history, literature, geography, the Bible, or other subjects. The players spell out the answers. Example: "What Old Testament character sold his birthright for a mess of pottage?" The first side to spell E-s-a-u scores a point.

For a small group use the letters "A," "E," "H," "M," "N," "O," "R," "S,""T," "U." The following are some of the words using these letters: heart, meat, more, mouth, north, nurse, rate, roast, Rome, rust, sermon, sham, shone, shout, shun, snare, south, stare, storm, stun, tenor, thorn, those, tune.

The game can be varied by placing letters on a table or on two chairs, one set to a chair. Line up players of two teams at a starting line. Call a word to be spelled. Player runs to the set for his team, picks out the letters needed, and spells the word on the table or floor. Or it may be done as a relay, with the first player putting down the first letter of the word, and rushing back to touch off his next teammate. Thus the players run until they have spelled out the called word.

SQUARING WORDS

Here is a game that an individual or a group may enjoy. It is easier to illustrate it than to describe it. All words used must read the same both down and across. It would be easier to try four-letter words first.

Give out definitions of the words in the square and have the players arrange the answers in square-word form.

Examples: I. A weight; to rant; to state positively; nothing other or less than. II. An animal of the deer family; an expression of warning; to rant; a personal pronoun. III. Twelve inches; lubricates; a jar; a former Russian ruler. IV. A city in Italy; a place for baking; to patch; aims. V. A songbird; a fever; impolite; retain. VI. Dispatch; an American lake; refined; a wild animal.

260

I.					II.					III.				
G	R	A	M		H	A	R	T		F	O	O	T	
R	A	V	E	R	A	H	A	V	E	O	I	L	S	
A	V	E	R	E	R	A	V	E	M	O	L	L	A	R
M	E	R	E		T	H	E	M		T	S	A	R	

IV.					V.					VI.				
R	O	M	E		L	A	R	K		S	E	N	D	
O	V	E	N		A	G	U	E		E	R	I	E	
M	E	N	D	S	R	U	D	E		N	I	C	E	
E	N	D	S		K	E	E	P		D	E	E	R	

Here are two five-letter squares: I. An octet; a drone; to shine dazzlingly; a wading bird; inclination. II. Big; wanderer; each; airplanes; a meeting.

I.					II.				
E	I	G	H	T	G	R	E	A	T
I	D	L	E	R	R	O	V	E	R
G	L	A	R	E	E	V	E	R	Y
H	E	R	O	N	A	E	R	O	S
T	R	E	N	D	T	R	Y	S	T

It is fun to try to make these. Begin with some word like "rail," or "home," or "nine," or "lace," and see what can be done to make a square, or several of them. Try it! It's fun!

HIDDEN BIBLE CHARACTERS

This is a game that one person may play alone or copies may be made and distributed to any number. Even a hundred people can try their skill and knowledge with it.

By using letters adjoining in any direction and starting anywhere, see how many biblical characters can be found in the letters of the diagram, using each letter only once. Letters may be joined up, down, across, or diagonally, but they must be letters that are adjacent. A letter may be used only once.

A	E	V	A	J	A	D	S	A	U	I	A	A	A	H
N	D	E	B	O	U	A	H	A	L	A	H	R	M	A
M	I	A	E	S	H	V	S	I	I	S	J	Z	O	M
O	A	C	M	L	I	N	J	L	E	R	E	E	S	L
J	S	E	S	D	B	E	A	E	M	I	N	N	A	E
O	S	E	P	H	E	M	I	H	H	A	E	E	A	O
R	R	E	H	T	S	N	L	A	M	E	H	B	B	J
J	U	Z	E	S	O	O	J	I	A	H	U	E	O	O
O	B	T	D	K	H	O	M	I	N	O	J	H	R	N
A	O	H	H	I	A	N	E	L	A	H	A	L	I	S
E	S	E	E	I	L	N	I	E	L	J	E	T	H	J
S	I	Z	K	E	D	A	B	O	C	A	H	M	L	U
A	A	A	M	L	O	H	R	A	A	O	A	E	S	A
A	C	H	N	H	S	T	A	C	N	M	E	E	H	A
B	R	A	O	A	A	R	H	E	L	I	R	B	E	K

Take a pencil and mark lines lightly connecting the letters in each name discovered. For instance, at the top right in the last two columns will be found H-a-m and A-m-o-s. At the top left is A-d-a-m on the diagonal. In a group give each player a copy. Allow fifteen minutes and then check to see who has the most. When a name is discovered, connect the letters and list the name on a sheet of paper.

The following biblical characters are in the list: Adam, Eve, Ham, Amos, Joab, Joel, Cain, Moses, Rachel, Joseph,

Job, Ruth, Zedekiah, Saul, Abel, Joshua, David, Benjamin, Jacob, Rebekah, Esther, Solomon, Elisha, Isaiah, Ezra, Jeremiah, Nehemiah, Hosea, Naomi, Leah, Esau, Ezekiel, Daniel, Elijah, John, Aaron, Isaac, Abraham, Noah, Lot, Sara, Ishmael.

HIDDEN ANIMALS

C	E	E	P	H	E	A	R
O	A	L	E	L	A	B	C
D	X	M	H	O	W	N	A
I	O	G	O	R	C	T	T
O	L	T	S	G	A	R	M
H	N	E	I	O	E	T	O
S	E	E	P	G	H	N	K
B	M	A	L	G	O	E	Y

Any number can play this game which is similar to "Hidden Bible Characters." Discover the animals by joining letters next to one another in any direction.

There are fourteen animals in this diagram. Can you find them? Ox, elephant, camel, bear, cat, dog, horse, cow, tiger, monkey, sheep, lamb, hog, goat.

HIDDEN FLOWERS

This is played as the two preceding games, the hidden words being flowers. The flowers concealed in this diagram are phlox, tulip, aster, zinnia, rose, petunia, hibiscus, lily, jonquil, gladiola, and lilac.

I	N	I	A	T	R	R	E
E	Z	N	A	S	E	S	O
T	P	I	A	I	L	H	B
U	N	T	L	P	Y	Y	I
I	L	U	L	I	J	C	S
L	X	L	P	N	O	S	U
C	A	O	H	Q	U	I	L
A	L	O	I	D	A	L	G

263

HIDDEN PRESIDENTS

Here is another of the hidden word series. This time the players try to discover the names of presidents of the United States. If used with a large group, mimeograph the diagram of letters and let everyone try his hand at finding presidents.

G	N	T	L	I	G	H	O	R	S	E
R	A	C	O	D	E	T	O	O	O	V
A	T	R	O	L	Y	E	V	I	E	W
T	F	L	E	J	R	G	N	L	H	A
O	C	I	A	S	O	T	T	N	O	S
L	N	C	K	N	L	N	O	S	N	D
N	M	C	K	I	N	E	Y	I	A	A
W	I	N	G	L	D	A	R	R	M	S
L	O	A	I	E	F	H	R	O	J	O
S	R	F	J	E	F	E	S	N	N	H
C	E	V	A	D	O	L	M	N	O	S
L	E	L	N	P	K	N	A	U	R	T

There are nineteen presidents in the list. Try to find at least fifteen of them. Here they are: Grant, Coolidge, Roosevelt, Washington, Hoover, Lincoln, McKinley, Harrison, Taft, Truman, Jackson, Tyler, Johnson, Adams, Polk, Wilson, Garfield, Jefferson, Cleveland.

NOTE: Try making hidden word diagrams. Suggested ideas: historical characters, characters in fiction, vegetables, fruits, movie, radio, and television stars, colleges, football or baseball stars, etc. Make out the list. Count the letters. If there are seven columns, forty-nine letters are needed; eight columns take sixty-four, etc. Be sure there are just enough.

CATEGORIES OR GUGGENHEIM

Five or more players are provided with a pencil and a card or sheet of paper listing the categories, as below.

	M	A	B	E	L
Animals	Moose	Antelope	Bear	Elephant	Lion
Flowers	Magnolia	etc.			
Cities	Macon	etc.			
Rivers	Missouri	etc.			

Each player (or team) is given five minutes to fill in the various categories, with as many under each letter as possible.

At the end of the time limit the leader calls on some player (or team) to read all the animals listed. Ten points are scored for any entry not listed by any other person or team. Five points are scored if two persons (or teams) list the same entry. No points are scored if three or more list the same entry. Thus, players will try to list unusual entries.

Another method of scoring would be to allow one point for each entry and one point extra for each player (or team) that does not list it. It should be decided before the game begins what scheme of scoring will be used.

265

Other categories may be used as desired: birds, books, trees, vegetables, fruits, countries, etc.

A variation is to give each player a blank sheet of paper on which each one writes the letters of a name or thing (each the same name)—the name of a college, such as C-o-r-n-e-l-l, or high school, as W-e-s-t, or church, as G-r-a-c-e, or person, as G-l-a-d-y-s. The leader should decide on this before the game starts. After all players have written the designated letters across the top of the sheet, the leader begins to call categories. For instance, he calls, "Animals." Each player writes the names of animals under the various letters. After a few moments the leader has some player read his list. The scoring is the same as described above.

He then calls another category, such as "Birds." Again he allows a few moments and then calls for listings.

WHAT IS MY THOUGHT LIKE?

Ten to thirty players are seated in a circle. One player thinks of something. He then goes around the circle asking each player what he is thinking. After each player has answered, the questioner tells what was in his thought. For instance, he says, "I was thinking of an ice-cream cone." Now each player must tell why what he mentioned is like an ice-cream cone. That will likely take some tall imagination. It has been "like a song," "a sunset," "a motorcycle," "a pencil," "a rose." So, "It is like a song because it is sweet." "It is like a sunset because it is gone before you know it." "It is like a motorcycle because it runs." "It is like a pencil because it's pointed at one end." "It's like a rose because it comes in various colors."

266

EGG FORTUNE

Six to thirty can play this game. One large paper egg (white or very light color required) for each player, also pencils. Each person is asked to write his initials at the top of the egg. The eggs are collected, mixed, and redistributed, so that each person gets one. The leader then calls out certain questions which the players are to answer with the initials on the egg each has received.

Such questions as the following may be asked: 1. What does he (she) look like? 2. What are his (her) good points? 3. What are his (her) faults? 4. What is his (her) hobby? 5. What does he (she) eat? 6. How does he sing?

Example: Initials T. S. (for Tom Sargent). 1. Looks like "trained seal." 2. Truthfulness, sincerity. 3. Teasing, sad-sack. 4. Telling stories. 5. Tomatoes, sauerkraut. 6. Terribly sweet.

Players write all answers on the eggs. When finished, they pass them to the right-hand person. Each person in turn reads the initials at the top of his egg. The player whose initials they are identifies himself. Then the descriptions are read aloud to the group.

EGG TREASURE HUNT

Divide into small hunting groups. If the group is small, let them hunt as individuals. Have the groups start out at fifteen-second intervals so they will not get in one another's way. Each group is given a large cardboard goose egg on which is written:

> Listen Bo's, follow your nose,
> No use hitchin', go to the kitchen.

In the kitchen they find another goose egg on which is inscribed:

> Listen, you lug,
> Look under the rug.
> Go to the dining room.

In the dining room they find:

> All right, you loafer,
> Look under the sofa.

Under the sofa they find the following advice:

> Listen, stupid, I ain't Cupid,
> Haven't you any sense at all?
> Why not look out in the hall?

> Now you're getting warm, you dope,
> In the window is your hope.

In the window have another large goose egg on which is inscribed in large letters, "APRIL FOOL!" This is the end of the hunt. If preferred, the last egg may direct players to the dining room or elsewhere for refreshments.

Players should be instructed to stay in their groups and to leave the goose eggs where they find them, so that the other groups may also have the fun of discovering them. One player reads the instructions on each goose egg to the group each time.

MILLINERY

Fifteen or more players are divided into small groups and asked to make an Easter bonnet. Provide newspapers, crepe paper, pins, and scissors. The resultant creation should be modeled by someone in the group. If the group is not too large, the crowd could be divided into couples, and each boy could be required to make a hat for his partner. This she must wear, at least for a while, during the evening.

MADAME NOTELLA d'LY

Introduce Madame Notella d'Ly, the great gypsy mind reader. Guests are asked to write questions on slips of paper, fold them once, and drop them in a box. Madame Notella picks one from the box, passes it across her forehead, unfolded, and then calls the question. She then looks at the slip and says, "Oh! That is correct! Now who wrote that question?" A confederate, who wrote a question, but did not put it in the box, speaks up, "I did." The Madame then answers the question, and proceeds to pick another from the box. The trick is that she reads her next question each time she unfolds a paper and pretends to confirm her mind reading. She must be careful not to permit anyone else to see the opened slip. After a few questions have been answered, the leader may announce: "The Madame now will demonstrate her remarkable powers in a new and startling manner. I will blindfold her and then pass through the audience. The Madame will demonstrate how to see with her mind's eye." The announcer then proceeds to hold up various things he finds. The tip-offs are intentionally obvious. "Don't get stuck on this one." "A pin," shouts the Madame. "Watch your step this time." "A watch." "Don't let this one choke you." "A tie." "This one was mint for you." "A coin." "Ring the curtain down on it." "A ring." "Don't wait three months to answer." "A quarter." "Don't let it buck you." "A dollar." There are many tip-offs which can be used.

THE EXHIBIT GAME

Draw or cut out from advertisements the pictures of certain objects, or display the objects themselves.

Provide each guest with pencil and paper or card listing statements regarding the objects. The guests move about the room trying to identify the objects by writing the names of these objects by the proper statements. If desired, the objects may fit into some seasonal theme such as Thanksgiving, Christmas, or Easter. Sample statements and objects:

Reminds you of Humpty Dumpty. *Object:* Egg.

A bald man needs it. *Object:* Rabbit (hare).

For the Easter parade. *Object:* Woman's hat.

Never gild it. *Object:* Lily.

A sound idea. *Object:* Horn.

Beat it! *Object:* Drum.

The four seasons. *Objects:* Salt, pepper, cinnamon, nutmeg.

Man's best friend. *Object:* A dog.

"Like a diamond in the sky." *Object:* Star.

A famous inventor. *Object:* Bell.

On dad's foot. *Object:* Popcorn.

A wild animal with a long sharp nose. *Object:* A candle or taper (tapir).

Two Eastern countries. *Objects:* Toy turkey on a china plate (Turkey and China).

Not the cat's whiskers but the pig's kin. *Object:* Football.

Sauce for the turkey. *Object:* Cranberries.

Keeps the doctor away. *Object:* Apple.

Trees and elephant shave them. *Object:* Trunk.

An act of courtesy. *Object:* Bough (bow).

Washington never told a lie. *Object:* Hatchet or cherry.

270

George threw it across the Potomac. *Object:* A silver dollar.

Member of a famous Christmas octet. *Object:* A reindeer (one of the eight in "The Night Before Christmas.")

A popular tree at the Christmas season. *Object:* A piece of fur (fir tree).

A famous Ibsen play. *Object:* A doll's house (A *Doll's House*).

MERRY CHRISTMAS! HAPPY NEW YEAR!

This is an adaptation of Buzz-Fizz. Ten or more players are seated in a circle. They start numbering around the circle, "1-2-3-4." In place of "5," any number with "5" in it, or any multiple of "5," the player says "Merry Christmas." Thus the numbering would be "1-2-3-4-Merry Christmas-6-7-8-9-Merry Christmas," etc. If a player calls the number instead of "Merry Christmas," he draws his chair into the center of the circle, or he may be required to pay a forfeit.

After playing the game around the circle several times, it may be varied by requiring players to say "Happy New Year" on any number containing "7" or on any multiple of "7." Then "5" and "7" may both be used, so that the numbering would be "1-2-3-4 Merry Christmas-6-Happy New Year-8-9-Merry Christmas," etc.

Watch out for "35" for it calls for both "Merry Christmas" and "Happy New Year." It is a multiple of both "5" and "7."

CHRISTMAS CATEGORIES

Six or more can play this game; if there are more than ten, divide the group into teams. Provide each player or

271

team with a pencil and a category card (see diagram below).

Each player or team is given a few minutes to fill in the card, writing suitable things under each category (dinner, decorations, sports, gifts) opposite the letter for the particular line. If done by teams, one member will write in the answers as the members suggest them.

Christmas	Dinner	Decorations	Sports	Gifts
T	Turkey	Tinsel		Tie
O	Oysters			Oboe
Y	Yams.			
S			Skating Sledding	

Score ten points for an entry no other team has; five points each if two teams have the same entry; no points if three or more have the same entry.

This same idea may be used for other seasons—Thanksgiving (T-H-A-N-K-S), Easter (B-U-N-N-Y), Fourth of July (F-L-A-G), and Valentine (H-E-A-R-T). The categories need not follow too closely the seasonal emphasis. "Historic persons" and "countries" would be suitable for the Fourth of July. "Apparel" would fit Easter.

BIRD RHYMES

Pass out mimeographed sheets with the bird rhymes on them. Players fill them in. Or better, read the rhymes and wait for someone to offer the correct filler. The fillers are all names of birds. All right, let's go!

1. Oh, the birdman said there was no sale
   For a bird as thin as is a ———.

272

2. So he went to town in a Ford, I think,
   And tried to buy a ———.
3. When he got there he heard some sobbin'
   From a girl who wished to own a ———.
4. But he was deaf and did not know,
   He thought she'd asked for a big black ———.
5. And then there was the deuce to pay,
   The girl fussed 'round like a harsh ———.
6. She fumed and fretted and made a howl,
   But he was wise as an old ———.
7. So he, resourceful, without fail,
   Got her to take a ———.
8. Then came a man who was a Dane,
   And said he'd like to buy a ———.
9. And a woman came who made much talk
   About how she'd like to have a ———.
10. Another said from what she'd heard,
    She'd like to see a ———.
11. Still another, in accents pleasant,
    Craved to see the gorgeous ———.
12. And a man with hair just like a brush,
    Said he'd heard and seen a lovely ———.
13. A man whose hair badly needed partin'
    Confessed he'd never seen a ———.
14. He said he guessed he was too narrow,
    But he had no use for an ——— ———.
15. And one little girl who was a darling
    Advised she'd like to have a ———.
16. And a woman with a funny hat
    Was with a man blind as a ———.
17. Together they'd been in the park;
    She thought that it was quite a ———.
18. He shot himself with a blank cartridge,
    And she got as nervous as a ———.

273

19. Now doctor's orders she must follow,
    And pills on pills she has to ———.
20. The birdman spoke to the manager
    About a ——— ———.
21. The manager said, "Bless my soul!
    I'll take a Baltimore ———.
22. Of that the birdman was quite wary.
    He thought he'd prefer a ———.
23. At any rate, it was his boast,
    He'd end it all with ——— on toast.

Answers: 1. Rail. 2. Bobolink. 3. Robin. 4. Crow. 5. Blue Jay. 6. Owl. 7. Nightingale. 8. Crane. 9. Hawk. 10. Hummingbird. 11. Pheasant. 12. Thrush. 13. Martin. 14. English sparrow. 15. Starling. 16. Bat. 17. Lark. 18. Partridge. 19. Swallow. 20. Scarlet tanager. 21. Oriole. 22. Canary. 23. Quail.

CATAPULT

Any number can play this game, for which a cigar box with a hinged top is needed. Fasten two rubber bands to this top, one at each side. Attach these bands also to the

Rubber bands

two front corners of the box. However, first nail or glue a baking powder tin top to the inside box lid. Place a small block of wood, a linoleum disc, or wad of tin foil in the tin. Pull the top back and let it go. The block will fly through the air from ten to twenty feet.

Dress a bottle with a paper pirate hat. You are now ready to bombard Captain Kidd.

Set up a target and try ten shots to see how many times you can hit it. Be careful that wild shots do not damage lamps, vases, or wall.

DIAGRAM FOR SALVO

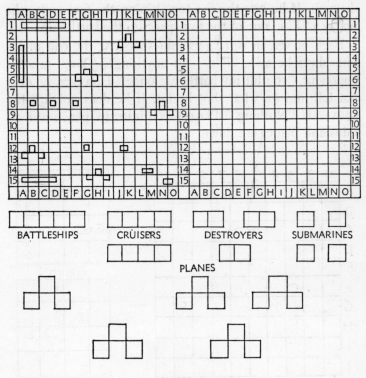

BATTLESHIPS   CRÜISERS   DESTROYERS   SUBMARINES

PLANES

SALVO

Two persons or two teams can play this, or players may be paired for the game. More mimeograph copies of the diagram (see above), and furnish pencils.

Each player or team locates his ships and planes in the left-hand diagram, being careful that opponents do not

275

see their location. In the right-hand diagram each player registers his shots, the first round putting a "1" in each space at which he shoots. On the second round he marks them with "2." Thus, when he begins to hit, he can tell something about the location of the various ships or planes, because he registers his hits in the various ships below the diagram. If he hits the five-ton ship on the first volley, he marks a "1" in one of the five spaces in the battleship.

Each player, in turn, gets four shots. At the end of his four shots he asks, "Did I hit anything?" "Yes," says his opponent, "you hit my battleship once." However, he does not tell him on what shot he hit. If he does not hit, the answer is "Nothing." Players continue to play until all ships and planes are down.

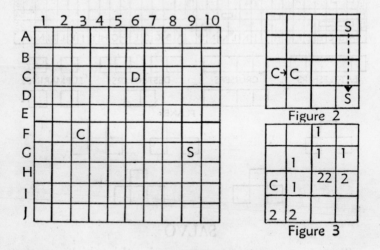

Figure 2

Figure 3

SHIP AHOY

Here is an exciting version of the well-known game called "Ships," "Salvo," or "Battleship." The fact that the ships can move makes the game more challenging. It is said that it is played in the French Naval Academy.

This game is for two players, each equipped with a pencil and paper. It is necessary that the players do not see each other's sheet of paper. Rule paper as in the diagram, but with half-inch squares so shots can be clearly marked.

Ships	Moves	Shots	Hits

C: Cruiser can move one space, or shoot three shots, and it takes three shots to sink a C.

D: Destroyer can move two spaces, or shoot two shots, and it takes two shots to sink a D.

S: Submarine can move three spaces, or shoot one shot, and it takes one shot to sink a S.

Each player places his three ships in any three squares, marking in each square the initials of the ship. Players take turns about in either shooting or moving. A player cannot move and shoot at the same time. When a player shoots, he tells his opponent which square he is shooting into, for example, "I shoot D3." When he moves, he simply states the fact, and draws on his own sheet of paper a line to the new position (see Fig. 2).

The shots a player fires are marked on the bottom of each square into which he fires, while his opponent's shots are marked on the top. In order that players may keep track of the turns from which the shots were fired, it is a good plan to number them. First turn shots are numbered "1"; second turn shots, "2," and so on. In that way recent shots are discernible, and the location of enemy ships discoverable. The player does not shoot in the same spot any oftener than he deliberately intends. With shots and moves so marked, it is a simple matter, too, to check up after the game on puzzling positions which may have occurred (see Fig. 3 for illustration of the recording of shots).

277

Further rules: Because the ships can move or shoot, a great deal more strategy can be employed with well-thought-out tactics to confuse the enemy. However, it is important that the rules be followed carefully, for any variation will throw the enemy unfairly off the track. Notice particularly Rules 1 and 5.

1. A ship can shoot only into any of the *adjoining* squares, not beyond.
2. No more than three shots can be fired at one turn, but these shots can be divided among the ships, or a cruiser can fire all three.
3. After each round of shots your opponent must tell you if you have secured a hit. He does not say in which square the hit was, but must name the ship.
4. The ship which is hit can still fire until it is sunk, but *cannot* move. When a vessel is sunk, the opposing player must be notified.
5. In moving a ship you *cannot* move diagonally across the board.
6. A game is decided when one player loses all his ships. If the game ends with both sides having vessels which are unable to move, the side that has the fewest hits (and hence the strongest ships) wins.

A word of warning: This game has to be carefully played, and players must be familiar with the rules, as one mistake will spoil all the carefully laid tactics employed by the players. This is obvious, because if you have more or less deduced the position of your opponent, it must necessarily be on a basis of accurate information given. Two common mistakes are moving diagonally through squares or firing beyond the adjoining squares which is your allotted range.

A variation is to play this game with animals instead of ships. *E* (elephant) could be substituted for *C* (cruiser); *L* (lion) for *D* (destroyer); *B* (bear) for *S* (submarine). Play in the same manner as "Ship Ahoy."

DESCRIPTIVE INITIALS

Eight or more players are seated in a circle. One player begins the game by introducing the person to his right. In the introduction he must describe that person in words beginning with her initials: "This is Janice Brown, who is just beautiful." Miss Brown then introduces the person to her right: "This is Bob Dorth, who is a big dope" (or "badly damaged," or a "bonny darling"). Thus it goes around the circle. If the group is small and well acquainted, on the first round the remarks may be complimentary. On the second they may be slams.

SPELL IT

From two to twenty-five players each prepare a paper that has twenty-five small squares on it (see diagram). One player starts the game by calling a letter. Each player puts this letter in one of the squares, using his own judgment about where to place it. He must do this before the next letter is called. The next player to the left calls another letter. Again each player writes the letter in a vacant square. This continues, with players calling letters in turn, until twenty-five letters have been called and all of the squares have been filled. The same letter may be called more than once, as the player calling may desire.

279

The aim of each player is to place the letters in the squares in such a way as to make as many words as possible, reading horizontally, vertically, and diagonally.

Score five points for a five-letter word, three points for a four-letter word, and one point for a three-letter word. No score for words of less than three letters. No score for proper names. Count short words written within longer ones unless the shorter and longer words are forms of the same word. For example, if "scat" is one of the words in a line, count both "scat" and "cat." If "cat" is one of the words, do not count both "cat" and "cats." Choose "cats" because it rates two points more than "cat."

OBSERVATION PROVERBS

Ten or more players are divided into two or more teams. Place on a table, in another room perhaps, several objects or pictures—an apple, a piece of money, something gold, the sun, a bird, a stone, a cat, a threaded needle, a horse.

Each team sends an observer who is given thirty seconds to look over the objects or pictures. The observers return to their teams and report the articles they can remember. The teams then write down as many proverbs as the articles call to mind. The proverb must be associated with the object, though the object itself need not be mentioned in it. "A stitch in time saves nine," for instance, might be suggested by a threaded needle. The team that has the most proverbs at the end of three minutes wins.

BEAT THE PAN

Ten or more players can play this game, very similar to "Magic Music" and "The Organ-Grinder Man." One player goes out of the room. The rest decide on something for him to do, such as standing on one foot in the center of the room, or kneeling before someone, or sitting on the floor. He is called back and tries to figure out what he is to do. His only cues come from the beating of a pan. One player is designated to perform this service. With a spoon or a gavel he beats softly when the guesser approaches the spot where he is to perform and loudly when he moves away from it. He beats loudly when the guesser performs the wrong stunt and very softly when he does the right thing. A new player is sent out and a new beater designated for another try at this game.

OLD SAYINGS

Call the first part of the saying. The side or person calling the proper word to finish the saying first scores a point.

As poor as a (church mouse),
As thin as a (rail),
As fat as a (pig),
As rough as a (gale).

As brave as a (lion),
As quick as a (cat),
As bright as a (dollar).
As blind as a (bat).

As pure as (snow),
As neat as a (pin),
As dead as a (doornail),
As ugly as (sin).

As black as (coal),
As green as (grass),
As blue as the (sky),
As slick as (glass).

As rich as (Croesus),
As hard as (steel),
As mad as a (March hare),
As slippery as an (eel).

As stiff as a (poker),
As sly as a (fox),
As fit as a (fiddle),
As hard as (rocks).

281

As flat as a (pancake),
As white as a (sheet),
As brown as a (nut),
As red as a (beet).

As clear as (crystal),
As wide as the (sea),
As cross as a (bear),
As busy as a (bee).

This thing must end
As sure as (death),
Before we all
Run out of breath.

SPLIT PROVERBS

Two or more players write proverbs on cards; one part of a proverb on one card, another part of the same proverb on a different card. Mix the cards on a table and have players see how fast they can match them correctly. There might be two sets, allowing two teams to compete. Examples: Players would match "A stitch in time" with "saves nine"; "All that glitters" with "is not gold"; and "A friend in need" with "is a friend indeed."

JUMBLED INFORMATION

Any number can participate. Make a list of statements in which the information is wrong, but which fits some other part of the list. Try to untangle these statements so as to make them correct. Suggestions:

1. Bread is made of oxygen and hydrogen.
2. The word "miser" stimulates one's brain.
3. Water is composed of flour, yeast, and milk.
4. A hard puzzle in Latin means "wretched."
5. The football player slid to second safely.
6. The base runner caught the punt and ran with the ball.

KNOW YOUR NUMBERS?

This contest will show who knows his numbers. Call the statements, leaving out the number. The first group in which someone calls the correct answer by giving the number fill-in earns a point. Calling the wrong answer subtracts a point.

1. The ——— Bears.
2. A ——— flusher.
3. The House of the ——— Gables.
4. ——— Island dressing.
5. ——— pins.
6. The Gay ———.
7. A ———.
8. A Tale of ——— Cities.
9. The ——— Horsemen of the Apocalypse.
10. ——— Men on Horseback.
11. The Spirit of ———.
12. The ——— Musketeers.
13. The ——— inning stretch.
14. ——— is company; ———'s a crowd.
15. ——— Nights in a Bar Room.
16. "Into the valley of death rode the ———."

17. ——— horse town.
18. ——— in hand.
19. ——— cheers.
20. ——— varieties.
21. Under ——— Flags.
22. Ali Baba and the ——— Thieves.
23. The ——— wise men.
24. The ——— apostles.
25. The ——— Gospels.
26. The ——— tribes of Israel.
27. Judas and the ——— pieces of silver.
28. The roaring ———.
29. Behind the ——— ball.
30. The ——— Commandments.
31. ——— ——— or fight.
32. ——— ages of man.
33. "——— days hath September."
34. ——— poster bed.

283

Answers:

1. Three	13. Seventh	25. Four
2. Four	14. Two; three	26. Twelve
3. Seven	15. Ten	27. Thirty
4. Thousand	16. Six hundred	28. Forties
5. Ten	17. One	29. Eight
6. Nineties	18. Four	30. Ten
7. One	19. Three	31. Fifty-four
8. Two	20. Fifty-seven	forty
9. Four	21. Two	32. Seven
10. Three	22. Forty	33. Thirty
11. Seventy-six	23. Three	34. Four
12. Three	24. Twelve	

The questions can be mimeographed and the numbers filled in. Or the leader can call the question and answers be made verbally. In the latter case the leader may wish to give a clue now and then. For example, he might say whether the question is associated with literature, music, history, the Bible, etc.

MUSIC OF THE NATIONS

Play a few bars of each of the songs suggested or call the instrument or opera named and let the guests identify the country or people it suggests.

"All Through the Night" (Wales); "Aloha Oe" (Hawaii); "Annie Laurie" (Scotland); Bagpipe (Scotland); "Volga Boatman" (Russia); "Blue Danube Waltz" (Austria); "Believe Me, If All Those Endearing Young Charms" (Ireland); Brahms's "Lullaby" (Austria); Czardis (Hungary); "Habanera" from Carmen (Spain); "Celeste Aïda" (Egypt); "Country Gardens" (England); "Drink to Me

284

Only with Thine Eyes" (England); "Eili, Eili" (Hebrew); "Loch Lomond" (Scotland); Harp (Ireland); "Kola Nedrei" (Hebrew); "La Paloma" (Spain); "Londonderry Air" (Ireland); *Madame Butterfly* (Japan); "Merry Life" (Italy); "O Sole Mio" (Italy); "Santa Lucia" (Italy); "Silent Night" (Germany); Balalaika (Russia).

WHAT COUNTRY?

With what country are the following names, words, and terms associated? Use as a sort of quiz program or call the words and score points for the side that answers first.

Rice (China); Thistles (Scotland); Swastika (Germany); Tulips (Holland); Coffee (Brazil); Yodeling (Switzerland); Igloo (Alaska); William Beebe (Galápagos Islands); Harem (Turkey); Jumping bean (Mexico); Pyramids (Egypt); Gaucho (Argentina); Cossack (Russia); Steppes (Russia); John Bull (England); Eiffel Tower (France); Hindu (India); Sugar (Cuba); Kimono (Japan); Maple leaf (Canada); Ski (Norway); Canal (Panama); Tin (Bolivia); Devil's Island (French Guiana); Acropolis (Greece); Mutiny of the "Bounty" (Pitcairn Island); Hula dancers (Hawaii); Diamonds (South Africa); Taj Mahal (India); Beef (Argentina); Shamrock (Ireland); Sombrero (Mexico); Amazon (Brazil); Pineapples (Hawaii); cherry blossoms (Japan); Baseball (United States); Cricket (England); *Jai alai* (Cuba); Dikes (Holland); *Smörgasbord* (Sweden); Vatican (Italy); Windmills (Holland); Vesuvius (Italy); Big Ben (England); Olympics (Greece); Blarney stone (Ireland); Parthenon (Greece); Fez (Turkey).

HANGMAN

Two can play this game. When used in a group, pair off, or divide into two sides.

Draw a gallows (see diagram). One player thinks of a word. He puts down as many dashes as there are letters in the word. Thus for "dime" he would have - - - -.

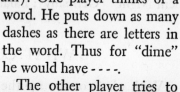

The other player tries to guess the word, one letter at a time. If he calls a letter that is in the word, the opponent must place it on the dash where it belongs. If it appears in the word more than once, he must write it in each place. If he calls a letter that is not in the word, the opponent starts hanging him. He draws the head hanging from the noose. On the next miss he draws the eyes, nose, and mouth; then the body, and so on until the player is hung or the word has been guessed. A good player usually calls the vowels first. If there are none in the word, he knows there must be a "y."

A hanged player is done like the drawing below.

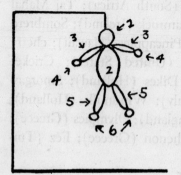

SIMPLIFIED HANGMAN: For small children use no gallows. The word is indicated by dashes, but the first and last letters are placed in their respective places. Thus "dime" would be d - - e.

If the guess is correct, the player puts the letter where it belongs in the word. If the guess is wrong, a cross is placed below any vacant dash. If the word is not completed before all of the blank dashes have crosses under them, the player who thought of the word wins.

MAGIC WRITING

One player goes out of the room. The rest of the group decides on a word to be spelled in what the leader has called "magic writing." The leader uses a cane, umbrella, or stick to make certain marks on the floor. At the same time he talks to the player who is to do the reading. When he finishes, the player announces what the word is.

The secret is this: All the consonants are given by what the leader says, the first letter in each sentence being the tip-off. The vowels are indicated by tapping on the floor: one tap is A, two are E, three are I, four are O, and five are U.

The leader makes various movements with the cane on the floor, pauses for a moment, and says, "Have you got it, so far?" The reader answers "Yes," for that remark indicated that the first letter was H. The leader taps once on the floor and then starts the mysterious movements again. He ends with a flourish as he says, "That's all." The reader announces that the word is "Hat." The one tap told him the second letter was A and the "That's all" told him the third and last letter was T.

Let other players who think they know how to read the magic writing go out; try them to see if they can make it.

MIND READING

This is a variation of "Magic Writing." It is played the same way without using a cane. Again the consonants are given by the remarks of the leader, which should be as natural as possible. The vowels are given by clapping the hands instead of tapping the cane. Here are two examples:

Leader, "Mighty hard word if you're not careful." Claps hands, 1-2-3-4. Pauses and claps hand again, 1-2-3-4. "Now you got it?" Reader, "Moon."

Leader claps hands, 1-2-3. "Can you follow me?" Claps hands, 1-2. Reader, "Ice."

TIME AND PLACE

This is a mystifying magic or mind-reading stunt. It can be done by alert seventh-, eighth-, and ninth-graders. It requires some concentration and a fair knowledge of time zones.

The leader sends a confederate out of the room. The rest of the players then decide on some city and the time of arrival in that city. The confederate is called back and the leader starts calling the names of cities, among them being the name of the city selected. When he is through, the confederate announces the name of the city and the exact time of arrival.

This is one the group will never be able to fathom. The tip-offs come, of course, through the calling of cities.

The first thing the leader does is to tip off his confederate on the hour of arrival. If the hour is one, two, or three o'clock, the first towns named must be in the Eastern time zone. For one o'clock one town would be named and then the caller would skip to another time zone. For two o'clock two towns in the Eastern time zone would be called; for three o'clock three towns.

If four, five, or six o'clock is selected, the first towns called would be in the Central time belt. One such town would indicate four o'clock; two, five o'clock; three, six o'clock.

288

Seven, eight, and nine o'clock would be signified by calling towns in the Mountain time zone.

Ten, eleven, or twelve o'clock call for towns in the Pacific time zone. Thus Los Angeles, Seattle, and San Diego would mean twelve o'clock.

If the leader calls "Boston," "New York," and then skips to another time zone, the confederate knows the hour is two.

The minutes are given immediately following the hour. The minutes are indicated as follows:

0   1   2   3   4   5   6   7   8   9

A   B   C   D   E   F   G   H   I   J

Towns beginning with those letters would be the tip-off.

The matter of A.M. or P.M. is indicated after the minutes have been given. Any town from "A" to "M" would be A.M. Any town from "N" to "Z" would mean P.M.

Here is how it works. The time of arrival is 4:39 P.M. The leader would call Louisville (or any town in the Central time zone.) That would mean four o'clock, for on the next call he switches to another time zone to give the minutes. "Denver, Johnstown." The "D" and "J" mean three and nine. So the mind-reader knows the time is 4:39. The leader next calls "Orlando" (or any town beginning with a letter from "N" to "Z" Now the confederate knows the time is 4:39 P.M.

Next, the leader gives him the name of the city. It comes after any three towns beginning with "San" or "New." Thus San Antonio, Santa Barbara, New York, Rochester, Brooklyn, Chicago, Cleveland. The confederate knows that Rochester is the city for it came immediately after three towns beginning with "San" or "New."

289

The caller should be sure not to name towns that are on time-zone borders, particularly if he thinks the confederate might not be certain whether the town is in one zone or another.

At first it would be a good idea to work out a card chart to hold in the palm of the hand. This chart would look something like this:

Hours:	E T		C T		M T		P T
	1		4		7		10
	2		5		8		11
	3		6		9		12

Minutes:	0	1	2	3	4	5	6	7	8	9
	A	B	C	D	E	F	G	H	I	J

DUMB SPELLING

Two to twelve can participate. Two equal lines of players face each other. Players spell words called by the leader. However, instead of calling vowels, they must make signs that represent them. The right hand lifted is "A." The left hand is "E." Pointing to the eye is "I." The speller makes an "O" with the thumb and forefinger. For "U" he points to someone.

When a player misses he sits down. If the leader desires to speed up the process of setting players down, he may introduce some difficult words, such as hippopotamus or rhinoceros. Begin with easy words like cat and dog.

290

When the players get pretty good at dumb spelling, add other "dumb" letters, such as a whistle for "R," a hiss for "S," a buzz like a bee for "B," and peering into the distance with hand shading eyes for "C."

SPELLDOWN

Ten to twenty players divided into two equal teams face one another. The first player on one team starts the game by calling one letter of the alphabet. The first player on the opposite side adds another letter. Thus it is relayed back and forth from one side to another until some player completes a word. When this happens, the player drops out and the game continues with the starting of a new word. If a player finds he must finish a word, he may fake a letter. If the next player on the opposing side adds another letter, the faking player is safe. However, if the next player challenges him to name his word and he cannot answer, the faker is out. At any time the player whose turn it is may challenge a player to tell what his word is. If the player has an actual word in mind, the challenger is out. Otherwise the player challenged is out.

For example, in c-a-t the player calling "T" is out, for that spells "cat." It doesn't matter if he did have "catalogue" in mind. The moment he finishes any word he is out. It may be agreed beforehand, if desired, that two-letter words do not put a player out.

GOAT

Fifteen to thirty players are seated in a circle. One player starts a word by calling one letter, the next player adds another letter, perhaps with an entirely different word in

291

mind. Just as in spell down, players try to keep from completing a word. If a player does end a word, any word, he becomes a goat and says "Baa-aa." The game goes on around the circle. Each time the "goat's" turn comes he responds with "Baa-aa." Imagine how it sounds when more than half the circle of players have become "goats"!

SHOUTING PROVERBS

Twelve or more players are divided into groups of six each. Each group decides on a six-word proverb, such as "Make hay while the sun shines." Each player in a group is assigned one word in the proverb. The leader counts, "One, two, three," and each player in the group shouts his word at the same time. The other groups try to guess the proverb. The group may be required to repeat its proverb several times. Each group, in turn, shouts its proverb in this manner. Some six-word proverbs: "Two heads are better than one," "He robs Peter to pay Paul," "Absence makes the heart grow fonder," "The early bird catches the worm," and "A stitch in time saves nine."

OPPOSITE ANSWERS

Fifteen or more players sit in two equal rows facing one another. A questioner walks up and down between the rows. He stops suddenly in front of some player, points his finger, and asks a question. The person questioned is not supposed to answer. The answer must come from the person directly opposite. If the person questioned answers, or if the opposite fails to reply before "It" can count to ten, the guilty player takes "It's" place.

MOUTHPIECE

Ten or more players are seated in a circle by couples. One of these players is the lawyer or "mouthpiece." The player to the lawyer's right is his client. One player inside the circle is the district attorney. The purpose of the district attorney is to get a "client" to answer a question, any question. He steps up to a "client," points his finger, and snaps out some question, such as "Do you like candy?" or "Do you play tennis?" or "Can you swim?" If the "client" makes the slightest effort to reply, he becomes the new district attorney and the questioner takes his seat in the circle. All questions must be answered by the "lawyer" or "mouthpiece" immediately, or the "lawyer" becomes the district attorney. The district attorney's success will depend on his ability to surprise the person being questioned, and to ask questions that will likely bring a quick reply.

PARTNER ANSWER

Ten or more players are needed for this game, which is played the same as "Mouthpiece," except that whichever one of the players is questioned, the partner must answer. The game can be varied so that the player to the left of the one questioned must answer.

COFFEEPOT

This is an old favorite that has given much amusement through the years. Fifteen to forty players are seated in a circle. One player goes out of the room while the others think of some activity.

The player returns and asks questions, trying to discover

what the activity is. In asking his questions he substitutes the word "coffeepot" for the activity. Thus, he may ask a player, "Do you coffeepot?" All questions must be answered truthfully.

Suppose the activity selected is "playing baseball." The player must answer "Yes" if he plays baseball. Succeeding questions may be such as, "Do you coffeepot in the house?" "Do you coffeepot at night?" "Do you coffeepot in summer?" "Do you coffeepot in winter?" "Do you coffeepot alone?" "Do you coffeepot in a car?" He continues to question until he guesses the activity. The person who gives him the cue takes his place.

Players may answer the questions by "Yes" or "No," or they may offer more information if they choose.

HIDDEN PROVERB

Ten to thirty players—if more, form two or more groups —sit in a circle. One person is sent out of the room. The group chooses a well-known proverb, such as "Make hay while the sun shines." Starting anyplace in the circle (moving clockwise) each person takes a word of the proverb, that is, the first person takes "make," the second, "hay," the third, "while," and so on until each person in the circle has a word.

"It" is called back. He may ask any person any question he wishes. That person must answer, using somewhere in the reply the exact word he got from the proverb. Thus, "What did you have for breakfast?" "Coffee and doughnuts. That baker sure does make the best doughnuts." "When did you have breakfast?" "Oh, quite a while ago." "What did you do last night?" "I went over to see Mary.

294

When I got there I said, 'Hey, Mary, let's go to a show.'
She said, 'Hay is for horses, but O. K., let's go!' "

"It" may ask questions of each person in succession or
he may skip about the circle, as he chooses. He may also ask
one person more than one question, if he thinks he has
discovered a key word. He keeps asking questions until he
discovers the proverb. The person who answers the last
question is "It." Keep the game moving.

TUNE MATCHING

Here is a good mixer for fifteen or more. Give each player
a tune to hum. Four or five are given the same tune. At the
signal to start all players begin to hum as they move about.
Those humming the same tune get together. They continue humming until all four or five (as announced) are
discovered. Then each group sings its song. "Home on the
Range," "O Susanna," "When Irish Eyes Are Smiling," are
good tunes.

SOLEMN COUNT

Four or more can play this game, which may be used as a
forfeit, a stunt, or a contest between team representatives.
Each player, in turn, is to sing any song he chooses. After
the first three words, he must say solemnly, "One." After
the next three words of the song, he says, "Two," and so on
through the song, saying the numbers in order. If he smiles,
calls the wrong number, or skips any phrase of three words
without counting, he is out. The singer finishing perfectly
or reaching the highest count without a mistake is the winner. Thus, Mary had a (one) little lamb, little (two) lamb,
little lamb (three), etc."

I LOVE MY LOVE

Ten to twenty players seated in a circle. The leader starts off, "I love my love with an A, because she is amiable. Her name is Amy and she comes from Ames." The next player takes the letter "B," and so on through the alphabet, each player in turn telling why he loves his love, what the name is, and what the city. The reason, the name, and the city must all begin with the letter given. Players who are unable to respond may be required to pay a forfeit, to be redeemed later.

THE MINISTER'S CAT

Ten to thirty players are seated in a circle. One player starts the game by saying, "The minister's cat is an amiable cat." The next player to the right repeats the statement, substituting in the place of "amiable" some other adjective, such as "anxious" or "angelic" or "artful." Each succeeding player makes a similar remark, using a different adjective, until no one is able to think of a different descriptive word beginning with "A." The player who fails pays a forfeit. The game continues with the players using the letter "B," etc.

SPELL IT

Twelve or more players are divided into two sides. Provide each side with cards about eight-by-eight inches. On these cards are letters of the alphabet, one set to each team. One team thinks of a six-letter word and selects from their set the letters for that word. Six players from the opposite team are lined up, either standing or sitting. The opponents put the six letters in their hands, one letter to each of the six. The letters are mixed up so they do not spell anything. The contestants cannot look at their cards until the signal is given and the word is announced. Without moving from their places they must switch their cards with one another until they have the word spelled properly. Time is kept by a watch and then the other team tries. The team taking the shorter time wins.

The game can be varied by lining up six players from each team. Give the players the letters in the word, one letter to each player. The team first arranging the letters correctly wins.

ENCYCLOPEDIA GAME

One player chooses a simple, well-known subject, such as bread, umbrellas, shoes, cotton, silk, etc., and reads the description of the subject from an encyclopedia. However, where the name of the subject appears, he substitutes the word "blank," and wherever the description gives a hint that is too obvious, he skips the word or says "blank." The object of the game is to see who can first guess the subject being described.

Historical characters or geographical locations can be used in this same manner.

ROTARY CHECKERS

Make board out of cardboard or three-ply wood about fifteen inches square. Use marbles of various colors for counters.

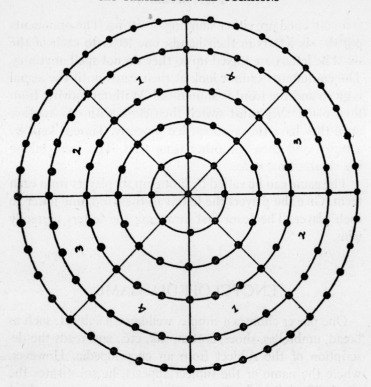

The game may be played by two or three or four players. The object of the game is for each player to move his ten marbles from a section of the board to the one with the same number on the opposite side of the circle. Each player plays toward an empty point.

Moves are made along lines only. A marble of an old color is placed in the center hole and remains there during the entire game.

An open jump: A marble may move as many holes beyond (up to five) another marble as there are empty spaces in the line. This play may be used across the board or around the circle. When an open jump is taken, that is the only play for that move.

298

A series of single jumps in straight line, or in zigzag fashion as in Star Checkers, can be made provided each jump is taken on a straight line or circle.

Single moves can be made.

In case one is in an opponent's point and preventing him from winning the game, the offending marble must be moved.

CHAPTER VIII

Dramatic Games and Stunts

Dramatic Games and Stunts

PANTOMIME CAPERS

Pantomime capers are one-man charades. Familiar sayings, song titles, book titles, trades or other forms of work (sweeping, driving, planting, knitting, making a pie, etc.), names and other ideas are presented in pantomime, while the rest of the players guess what is being represented. The pantomimist begins by saying, "I am presenting a familiar saying," or whatever of the categories he is using. Then he goes through the motions of pitching hay, perhaps. He stops, looks up, and mops his brow. Someone guesses that the saying is "Make hay while the sun shines." Other old proverbs such as "It never rains but it pours," "A stitch in time saves nine," "A fool and his money are soon parted," would be easy to do in this fashion.

Sometimes the game is given a comic turn. Players offer certain burlesque or ridiculous interpretations: A player holds his open hand at the back of his head. He explains that this represents an Indian looking backward. The hand is held on top of the head, palm up and fingers moving. This is an absent-minded professor scratching his head. The player goes through the motions of typing. He takes hold of his nose and moves his head to one side. He types a bit more and moves the head in the other direction. He explains that this is a moron typing.

DOUBLE UP SPEECH

Two persons perform in this stunt. At least one rehearsal before the performance is needed to work out the angles. One of the performers makes a speech, quotes a well-known poem or nursery rhyme, or sings a song. The other performer stands directly behind this person, as well hidden as possible. He puts his arms out under the armpits of the other person, who holds his own hands back of himself. The front person makes the speech while the hidden performer makes the gestures. He goes through the usual motions of a speaker or singer and throws in some extras for good measure. For instance, he takes the other fellow's handkerchief out, wipes his forehead or nose, takes out his watch and holds it up to note the time, rubs his chin, picks his ear, takes off his spectacles, puts them back on, twirls his watch fob or chain, scratches his nose, etc. All this time the performer is going ahead with his speech, poem, or song. This can be very funny. Try it!

DRAMATIC PI

Give out numbered letters, one to a person, to ten or more players. Each set of letters forms a word. All Number Ones get together, figure out what word their letters spell, and arrange to dramatize the word for the rest to guess. All other numbers do the same thing. Thus, the Ones find out that their word is "fight." They stage a battle royal. The Twos discover that their word is "style." They put on a style show. The Threes find that their word is "teach." They present a school scene.

304

MOTHER GOOSE DRAMA

Give to each of several groups some Mother Goose rhyme for dramatization. Perhaps you can buy a ten-cent book of these rhymes and distribute the pages so that each group will have the rhyme and possibly a picture illustrating it. Pantomime the action and have the rest guess what rhyme is being presented.

ALPHABET DRAMA

This may be a dramatic reading by one person. He repeats the alphabet from "A" to "Z" several times with dramatic voice and gesture. Ask several people to perform. One is to make a political speech, one to preach a sermon, one to make a prosecutor's speech before a jury, one to give a reading. In each case they are to repeat the letters in the alphabet.

Or pick a cast of two or three persons. Give them a few moments to prepare a play in which the characters simply repeat in order the letters of the alphabet. You may decide on the dramatic situation to be portrayed. For instance, a husband late for supper. The angry wife. She speaks angrily, "A-B-D-C-D-E-F?" "G-H-I-J-K," is the quiet explanation of the husband. "L-M-N-O-P-Q," sarcastically responds the doubting wife. "R-S-T-U-V-W-X-Y-Z," replies the husband in his most persuasive manner. Then with a smile he holds out a jewel box with an eager "A-B-C?" The wife responds this time with a delighted "D-E-F-G." Sequences are easy to work out. Keep them brief.

Select several small casts and ask each one to produce an alphabet drama.

305

ALPHABET ROMANCE

Characters

K.T., The Maid	L.C., The Daughter
M.A., The Mother	P.T., Her Suitor
P.A., The Father	M.D., The Doctor

Note: As each character enters, a person at the side of the stage holds up a sign bearing the name of the character.

Enter K.T., dusting furniture as she hums some tune. Sees candy box on table. Delighted "O!" Looks around to see if anyone is looking. Opens box. Closes it with disgusted "M. T."

Enter M.A., followed by P.A. M.A. knits. P.A. reads newspaper.

Enter L.C., skipping to a chair. Opens magazine, reads and utters a romantic "O!"

Doorbell rings. K.T. goes to door. Returns with announcement, "P.T."

P.T. enters. L.C. rushes to meet him with "O, P.T." "O, L.C." They sit down.

L.C. speaks to M.A. and motions for her to leave. M.A. walks over to P.A. and motions for him to go also. P.A. shakes head. M.A. takes him by the ear and they exit.

P.T. holds L.C.'s hand. She sighs, "O, X T C (ecstasy)." P.T. says, "O, L.C., B. P.T.'s M.R.S." L.C. replies, "C. M.A., P.A." Then she calls excitedly, "M.A., P.A.!" M.A. and P.A. enter.

P.T. speaks to M.A., "M.A., L.C. B. P.T.'s M.R.S.?" "O. K.," replies M.A.

With some gentle shoving from L.C., P.T. approaches P.A., who is frowning, and says, "P.A., L.C. B. P.T.'s M.R.S.?"

P.A. shouts an angry "N O!" and shoots P.T. (The

gun may be a pipe, a pencil, a toy pistol, or simply his fore-finger.) At this moment someone pops a sack off-stage and P.T. drops to the floor.

L.C. frantically calls "K.T., S. O. S.! S. O. S.! M.D., M.D.!"

K.T. rushes off stage and returns with the M.D. He opens his case, takes out a saw, a bicycle pump, and other equipment, as desired. Examines the prostrate P.T. and solemnly pronounces his verdict: "T.B."

The whole cast shouts, "O. G.!"

Curtain.

MOTHER, MOTHER, MAY I GO?

Provide each person with a paper napkin. One person demonstrates the stunt, then asks the entire group to re-peat it with him. The lines are given in singsong fashion, gradually getting faster each time the girl speaks.

Characters

GIRL (high, light voice) uses napkin as bow in her hair.

MOTHER (a bit lower voice, slightly affected speech) uses napkin as bow on her shoulder.

FATHER (deep voice) uses bow as mustache.

GRANDMOTHER (shaky, high voice) holds bow at throat.

KID BROTHER (loud and disgusted voice) bow to throat.

GIRL: Mother, Mother, may I go
                   Down to the corner to meet my beau?

MOTHER: No, my darling, you may not go
                   Down to the corner to meet your beau.
                   But ask your father if you may go
                   Down to the corner to meet your beau.

307

GIRL: Daddy, Daddy, may I go
         Down to the corner to meet my beau?

FATHER: No, my darling, you may not go
         Down to the corner to meet your beau.
         But ask your grandmother if you may go
         Down to the corner to meet your beau.

GIRL: Grandmother, Grandmother, may I go
         Down to the corner to meet my beau?

GRANDMOTHER: Yes, my darling, you may go
         Down to the corner to meet your beau.
         Tell your mother she had fun,
         She had beaux when she was young.
         Tell your father just the same,
         He was the one who changed her name.

GIRL: Thank you, Grandmother, now I may go
         Down to the corner to meet my beau,
         Whoops-tee-doodle, won't we have fun?
         Hurrah! Hurrah! Life's just begun.

KID BROTHER: Aw, baloney!

TREES

"Ladies and gentlemen! Mr. ——— will now sing *Trees* for us!" The pianist plays the introductory bars of the song with a flourish. The better this is done, the better the effect. As the pianist finishes the introduction and starts the song, the singer shouts, "Timber -r -r."

308

THE VIPER

Two or three badly frightened persons, at proper intervals, dash through the room crying, "The viper is coming! The viper is coming!" When the last person has warned the guests of the viper's approach, there is a moment's pause. Then slowly through the door comes a pathetic-looking figure, hair disheveled, a bucket in one hand, and a mop in the other. She looks around, as if a bit bewildered, and then says: "I am the viper! I have come to vipe the floor!" Corny? Yes, but it can be exceedingly funny.

THE LION HUNT

(As presented by James McGiffin)

This is a little icebreaker which is usable with a group of any size for just fun and nonsense.

Directions: Have the group sit in a semicircle or where they can see leader. In case of a large group, the leader should be in an elevated position. Each member of the group is seated with hands on knees, palms down.

The group will follow the leader in doing everything that he does as he proceeds with the story.

Whenever the leader uses the name "Mrs. Lion Hunter," everyone puts his right hand to his mouth and makes the Indian call in a high pitch. When the leader says "Mr. Lion Hunter," the group does the same as above, only using a lower pitched Indian call.

The leader is the narrator.

Story: One day, Mrs. Lion Hunter (Indian call) said to Mr. Lion Hunter (Indian call), "Why don't you go for a lion hunt?" Mr. Lion Hunter (Indian call), said, "O. K."

309

So Mrs. Lion Hunter (*Indian call*) opened a door. (*Extend both arms sideways to shoulder levels, then bring both arms together in front and clap hands once signifying opening and closing of door.*) Then Mr. Lion Hunter (*Indian call*) starts on his hunting trip (*leader and group slap knees left and right alternately, imitating walking.*)

As he proceeds, the leader can build his story with reference to the beautiful day, the flowers, the birds, etc., as he walks along. Continuing, the leader mentions that they are approaching a bridge over a stream, and everyone, following his example (*thumps his chest instead of slapping knees*). After crossing the bridge, they proceed on toward the woods. They finally reach a stream which will have to be jumped. (*Everyone raises his arms and jumps in standing position.*) They continue on through the meadows until they come to a lake which is crossed by swimming. (*Everyone rubs hands together in unison.*) When they supposedly reach the other side of the pond, they (*shake themselves like a dog shakes off water*) and continue on their march. The leader now takes them up a hill (*slapping of knees gets slower and slower*) and pauses halfway up the hill (*everyone pants as if out of breath*). After a while they continue their climb of the hill and pause at the top. (*Everyone stands up, turns around once with right hand to forehead, scanning the horizon.*) Then they run down on the other side. (This effect is created by *slapping knees faster.*) Then they climb another hill. (Action for the group is same as for the first climb except at first pause for breath *everyone reaches right hand down and drinks from a running brook.* The more noise made the more fun.) They finally proceed on up the hill until they reach the top and then stand and gaze around at the horizon in search of the lion which, lo and behold, is right there! The hunter, realizing that he has left his gun at home, turns

310

and flees down the hill looking back over his shoulder, exclaiming that he must go faster, and the group under the direction of the leader goes through, in reverse, the procedure followed in finding the lion, until they arrive home. The tempo is increased by the leader as the lion gets closer and closer. Conclusion: "Oh, Mrs. Lion Hunter (*Indian call*), open the door!" She did, and Mr. Lion Hunter (*Indian call*) got into his cabin safe but tired out, and a much wiser hunter.

OTHELLO: GRAND UPROAR

(Adapted from a production by an English mission girls' school in Jerusalem)

PROLOGUE: Chorus, sung to the tune of "Long, Long Ago."

ALL: Come now, enjoy this, our tragical show
Of Desdemona, of Othello!
It's sure to move e'en your hard heart of stone,
Poor Othello, poor Desdemona.
They loved each other clean to distraction;
He grew so jealous, he stopped her heart's action;
Then stabbed himself to his own satisfaction,
Poor Othello, poor Desdemona.

OTHELLO: (Sung to the tune of "Long, Long Ago.")
I am the hero who lived long ago;
I'm Othello, I'm Othello.

311

I showed my temper and caused lots of woe,
I'm Othello, Othello.
Ne'er was a spouse so loyal as she was,
Ne'er was villain so cruel as he was,
Ne'er were two lovers so luckless as we was,
I'm Othello, Othello.

DESDEMONA: I am the heroine who died in disgrace,
I'm Desdemona, I'm Desdemona.
Died with a pillow stuffed in my face,
I'm Desdemona, Desdemona.
Guileless was I, and innocent also,
Hated by one who thought I was false. Oh,
I loved him truly and worshiped him also,
I'm Desdemona, Desdemona.

IAGO: I am Iago, the villain, you know.
I'm Iago, I'm Iago.
I caused unlimited sorrow and woe,
I'm Iago, Iago.
Oh, how I tortured the man and his wife so,
Till he at last took the poor lady's life, oh,
Then he stabbed himself quite dead with a
        knife, oh,
I'm Iago, Iago.

EMILIA: I am the lady in waiting, you see,
Emilia, Emilia.
Iago finds it a cinch to use me,
Emilia, Emilia.
I found the kerchief that caused so much sad
        woe,
I found the villain and made him so glad.
        Oh,

312

Pre → Ping Pong — Judy

leader — Louise

music — Sharon Linder

donations — Anna Mae

Shadow show —

games?

refreshments → ice cream bars —
Louise — Judy

business —

xy speaker —

Little I guessed that my husband was bad
    though,
Emilia, Emilia.

OTHELLO: (Sung to the tune of "Silver Threads Among
    the Gold.")
Good-by, darling, I must leave you,
Though it breaks my heart to go;
Something tells I am needed
At the front to fight the foe.
Here's a token at the parting
And to you I'll e'er be true,
See the ships are in the harbor,
Adieu, adieu, adieu, adieu.

(Othello gives her a red kerchief)

DESDEMONA: (Sung to the tune of "Silver Threads Among
    the Gold.")
Thank you for the handkerchief, dear,
Darling, I will miss you so,
It will wipe my tears of grief, dear,
How I hate to see you go.
I will cherish it with loving care,
And never lose it, that I swear;
How I love you, I declare,
Without you all life is bare.

DESDEMONA: (Sung to the tune of "Forsaken.")
Forsaken, forsaken, forsaken am I,
Like a stone on the pathway, neglected I lie,
Sadly gaze I out yonder where goes Othello
And then with my kerchief I mop tears of
    woe,
And then with my kerchief I mop tears of
    woe.

(Rings water out of a wet washrag hid in her
  kerchief)

(Enter Emilia)

EMILIA: (Sung to the tune of "Yankee Doodle.")
Othello has gone to sea
But do not feel so badly,
It will not bring him back to thee
To look so glum and sadly.
Othello has gone away
Gone away this very day,
Othello will fight they say,
Till he has conquered Turkey.

(Exit singing)

Scene 2

HOME FROM THE WARS

(Enter Othello at one side, Iago at the
  other)

OTHELLO: (Sung to the tune of "Spanish Cavalier.")
I'm home from the wars, from the wars I've
  returned,
To greet my dear wife, Desdemona,
And if you should ask, she's waiting I know,
Dressed in her nicest kimono.

IAGO: (Sung to the tune of "My Bonnie Lies Over
  the Ocean.")

314

Othello, I'm glad you've come home, sir,
It's time you came back to your wife,
I'd hate for you longer to roam, sir,
Lest it should cause trouble and strife.
Beware, take care,
Lest it should cause trouble and strife, and
strife,
Beware, take care,
Lest it should cause trouble and strife.

I saw her this morn at the window,
I saw the red rose in her hair,
I wonder for whom she was watching,
She looked so adorably fair.
Beware, take care,
She looked so adorably fair, so fair,
Beware, take care,
She looked so adorably fair.

I think that I saw her give Cassio
A smile as she stood on the stair,
I think that she gave to him also,
The rose that she took from her hair.
Beware, take care,
The rose that she took from her hair, her
hair,
Beware, take care,
The rose that she took from her hair.

(Exit Iago)

(Enter Desdemona)

DESDEMONA: (Sung to the tune of "Maryland, My Maryland.")

You find me waiting here for you, Othello,
my Othello,
I've loyal been to you and true, Othello, my
Othello,
Since you've been gone, I've been so sad,
This handkerchief was all I had
To cheer me when I felt so sad, Othello, my
Othello.

OTHELLO: (Sung to the tune of "My Bonnie Lies Over
the Ocean.")
My head it is likely to bust, dear,
My head it is likely to break,
If ladies weren't present, I'd cuss, dear,
It is such a horrible ache.

DESDEMONA: There, there, there, there,
We'll wrap it up tight in this handkerchief,
There, there, there, there,

OTHELLO: (Spoken) Take it away! (Tosses handkerchief away)

(Exit Desdemona and Othello, Desdemona
still singing, "Oh, who will ease now my
grief?" Enter Emilia, who finds handkerchief on floor)

EMILIA: (Sung to the tune of "Juanita.")
Down on the floor here
A nice handkerchief I see.
Sure 'tis the same one
Iago begged of me.
How oft old Iago

316

Bade me steal it when I could.
But I still refused him;
It was quite too good.
Found it, I've found it,
Finding's keepings, so they say,
Found it, I've found it
He shall have it today.

(Enter Iago. Emilia gives him the handkerchief)

IAGO: (Sung to the tune of "I've Been Working on
the Railroad.")
I've been hunting for this kerchief
All the livelong day,
I've been wishing I could find it,
Just to prove the things I say.
Now I'll make Othello jealous,
Cause much sorrow, grief, and pain,
Now I guess that I have fixed him
When he meets his wife again.

(Exit Iago, followed by Emilia)

Scene 3

(Enter Othello and Desdemona)

OTHELLO: (Sung to the tune of "Oh, Where Has My
Little Dog Gone?")
Oh, where, oh, where has my red bandanna
gone?
Oh, where, oh, where can it be?
Oh, why, oh, why have you hid it so long?

317

Oh, where, oh, where can it be?

DESDEMONA: (Sung to the tune of "Long, Long Ago.")
It's safely tucked away and will e'er cherished be
Dear Othello, dear Othello,
As a gift and a token of thy love to me,
My Othello, Othello.

OTHELLO: (Sung to the tune of "Skip to My Lou.")
I believe you're lying now to me,
I believe you're lying now to me,
I believe you're lying now to me,
To whom did you give it when I was out at sea?

DESDEMONA: (Sung to the tune of "Miserere.")
Oh, why do you hurt me so-o-o-o-o and cause me grief and woe-o-o-o-o?
I'd never deceive you, you must surely know.
Oh, oh, oh, oh! Poor Othello, now I must go.

(Exit Desdemona. Othello paces back and forth)

(Enter Iago)

IAGO: (Sung to the tune of "Ach, Die Lieber Augustine." Waving the bandanna.)
Oh, I've found the kerchief, the kerchief, the kerchief,
Oh, I've found the kerchief that she gave away.

318

> She tossed it, she waved it, she gave it to Cassio,
> Oh, I've found the kerchief that she gave away.

(Exit Iago)

OTHELLO: (Sung to the tune of "Maryland, My Maryland.")
> How mad I am,
> How mad I am,
> Nobody knows how mad I am.

(Exit Othello)

Scene 4

(Enter Desdemona)

DESDEMONA: (Sung to the tune of "Old Black Joe.")
> Gone are the days when my heart was young and gay,
> Gone are the joys, they have fled so far away,
> Sadly I sigh for the days of long ago,
> I hear his angry footsteps coming,
>   O-thell-o.
> He's coming,
> He's coming and my head is bending low,
> I hear his angry footsteps coming,
> Othello.

(Desdemona falls asleep on couch)

(Enter Othello)

319

OTHELLO: (Sung to the tune of "Clementine.")
O my darling, O my darling,
O my darling Desdemona,
Thou'll be lost and gone forever
From my heart and from my home.
Fair thou wert and very charming,
But thy heart was like a stone,
So I fear I must dispatch thee,
Though it leaves me sad and lone.

(He smothers her with a cushion)

(Enter Emilia)

EMILIA: (Sung to the tune of "Juanita.")
'Thello, Othello,
Have you killed that lady true?
'Thello, Othello,
I'm ashamed of you.
Over that kerchief,
What an awful fuss you've made,
Got madly jealous,
When 'twas just mislaid.
Desdemona dropped it
Once when you were cross and mad,
Finding it I gave it
To my husband bad.
Iago, Iago,
Used it then with wicked art.
Iago, Iago,
What a wretch thou art!

(Enter Iago. Exit Emilia)

320

OTHELLO: (Sung to the tune of "Hot Time in the Old Town.")

Me, oh, my! I've killed my sweetheart true.
I hope I die! Oh, I don't know what to do,
I'd better kill myself and bring my score to two;
There'll be a funeral in Venice tonight.

So, please, oh, please, oh, please just watch me fall,
I've killed the one that I loved the best of all,
So now I stab myself—believe me, that is all;
There'll be a funeral in Venice tonight.
(Stabs self and falls)
(Curtain)

[Courtesy of Wilma Minter.]

POOR MARY

(A Shadow Show)

1. Mary was contrary,
   Contrary as could be;
   She ran away from home one day,
   She wanted liberty.

2. She ran across the ocean,
   She skipped across the sea,
   Until she came to No-Where-Land,
   The land of Timbuctee.

321

3. There she saw a cannibal
   Hiding behind a tree;
   She ran as fast as e'er she could,
   She cried, "I sure must flee."

4. The savage shot at Mary,
   His arrow it did fly,
   And stabbed poor Mary in the heart,
   So she did up and die.

5. He carried her away with him,
   Her blood did fall deep red;
   And where a drop of blood did drip,
   There sprang a flow'r instead.

6. The savage chopped up Mary,
   In tiny little bits;
   He fried and ate her greedily,
   And then she gave him fits.

Directions: Verse 1: Mary in a tantrum, shaking first, tearing her hair, jumping up and down.

Verse 2: Mary running, then skipping.

Verse 3: Mary peers, hand over eyes. Savage peeping from behind a tree (someone waves branch). Mary runs, the cannibal pursues.

Verse 4: Savage shooting. Mary has a paper or cardboard arrow which she holds so that the shadow makes it appear to be through her body. Mary falls.

Verse 5: Savage picks her up and carries her off. Mary drops paper for drops of blood. Giant flowers spring up. These can be made of newspapers.

Verse 6: Savage chops vigorously. Appropriate sounds.

Holds skillet as over a fire. Eats greedily. Holds stomach as if in misery.

YE OLD PLANTATION DRAMA

How about setting up a "spontaneous drama" on the spot, casting it, and then having the cast enact it? Actors say and do what they feel is the appropriate thing for the moment. For the cast there could be the aged father and mother, Little Nell, their only daughter, the villain, and the hero. Give the cast ten or fifteen minutes to get ready. Then "Bingo," the play is on.

Scene 1. The Old Homestead. Nell's family in dire straits. The villain holds the mortgage and the upper hand.

Scene 2. The Village Post Office. Nell looks for a letter from a long-lost brother. It never comes. The hero offers consolation.

Scene 3. The Action. The villain demands Nell's hand. He gets rough. The hero arrives in time to stop him. Curses.

Scene 4. The Climax. The hour when the mortgage is due is at hand. The villain is mean and gloating. Just before the hour arrives, the hero rushes in with the letter from the long-lost brother. It contains a check ample to pay off the mortgage. "My hero!" More curses!

SHADOW SHOW GAME

Ten or more persons are needed. Draw a sheet over a doorway. Place a light six to eight feet back of it so that the shadows of persons between the light and the sheet will be cast on the sheet. Performers should be fairly close to the sheet. Try out the arrangement to see that the proper effect is obtained. Suggested shadow shows:

The Hospital: Doctor, nurse, patient. Examination. Administering anesthetic. Operation. Exaggerated equipment.

The Dentist: Drilling. Pulling tooth. Appropriate sounds.

Fishing: Pulling in an enormous fish or bird cage.

The Nap: Nodding. Big fly bothering. Snores.

The Spanking: Mother, boy. Large paddle. Appropriate sound effects—whack of paddle, yells of boy.

The Barber Shop: Haircut, shave. Exaggerated effects.

The Make-Up: Girl primping.

The Fight: Appropriate sound effects.

The Quarrel: Finger shaking, tongue out (use long cardboard tongue)

BIRD, BEAST, OR FISH

Twenty or more players are divided into teams of equal numbers. Designate these groups as Team One, Team Two, Team Three, and Team Four. The leader stands at center, while the teams occupy the corners of the room.

Each team sends one player to the center, where the leader whispers to them the name of a bird, a beast, or a fish. The players rush back to their groups and act out the word in pantomime. No sounds are allowed.

The representative first tips off his team whether the word is a bird, a beast, or a fish. Thus he flaps his arms like wings and they know it is a bird. Or he walks on all fours and they know it is a beast. Or he goes through the motions of swimming and they know it is a fish.

Now he tries to convey to them what particular bird, or beast, or fish it is. This requires some imagination on the part of the actor, and the guessers, as well.

As soon as the group guesses the word the actor is portraying, he rushes back to center to report to the leader. The one who gets back first scores one point for his team.

Each player on the team should have opportunity to go to center. Then total the scores of the teams.

The leader should make up a list of names before the game. Some suggestions:

Birds: Cuckoo, duck, eagle, hen, kingfisher martin, mockingbird, nightingale, owl, parrot, peafowl, robin, rooster, woodpecker.

Beasts: Bear, beaver, camel, deer, elephant, giraffe, gnu, goat, hippopotamus, kangaroo, mule, opossum, rabbit, tiger.

Fish: Drumfish, eel, flounder, flying fish, jellyfish, perch, red snapper, sailfish, sardine, shark, smelt, starfish, sunfish, swordfish.

IN THE MANNER OF THE ADVERB

Ten to thirty, or more, can play. One player thinks of an adverb. The rest of the group then ask him to do certain things "in the manner of the adverb."

Suppose the player thinks of the adverb "slowly." One of the other players says, "Walk across the room in the manner of the adverb." He moves slowly across the room. Another suggests that he sing in the manner of the adverb. The next player tells him to shake hands with someone in the manner of the adverb. The next asks him to recite "Mary Had a Little Lamb" in the manner of the adverb. Each time he responds appropriately. The player who guesses what the adverb is then thinks up another word and the game continues.

Suggested adverbs: Angrily, bashfully, politely, quickly,

reverently, madly, sadly, laughingly, quietly, lazily, moodily, harshly, roughly, crazily.

DUMB CRAMBO

Ten or more players are divided into two groups, one of which leaves the room. The other group decides on a word to be guessed. Those outside then come in and are told a word that rhymes with the one to be guessed. The guessers go into consultation and then proceed to present in pantomime what they suppose the word to be. This they continue to do until they guess the right word, or decide to give up. When they present a wrong word, the other side signifies that it is wrong by shaking the head. When they guess the word they are applauded.

For example, they are informed that the word rhymes with "ho." The guessers consult, listing possible words, such as "beau," "dough," "flow," "grow," "hoe," "know," "no," "row," "sow," "sew," "tow," "woe." They act out "beau," with Pa, Ma, the girl, the boy, the pesky little brother and all. Their opponents give them time to put on their performance and then shake their heads. The guessers then go through the motions of mowing a lawn. That's not it. They do "row," "sow," and "woe." When they do "woe," the opponents applaud.

The other side then goes out and their opponents select a word. Thus the game continues.

Suggested words: Pin, style, fight, kick, bear, car, gun, press, vain, yearn.

INDIVIDUAL DUMB CRAMBO

Five or more players form a circle. One player begins the game by saying, for instance, "I am thinking of a word that rhymes with ear." Persons in the group try to guess the word. Instead of calling out their answers, they act out the words they have in mind. Someone says, "Is it a . . . ?" and pantomimes by putting his fingers to his head like horns. "No," says the leader, "it is not a deer." "Is it a . . .?" and the questioner shades his eyes with one hand and looks intently in some direction. "No, it is not peer." Other words are acted out, such as "fear," "gear," "tear," "hear," "clear," "jeer," "near," "veer," until finally someone gets it by acting "queer." The person who guesses correctly becomes the leader and calls another word. In the beginning, at least, only one-syllable words should be used. Suggested words: Style, sash, tree, kite, bend, pert, tie, rock, ban, pine, yearn.

DRAMAGRAMS

Four or more players divide into two teams. Each team decides on a book title, a proverb, or a song title. One team sends a representative to the opposing side. This representative is told what the title or saying is. Perhaps it is shown to him written on a sheet of paper. He then goes back to his team and tries to tell them through pantomime what it is. They ask him if it is a book title. He nods. They ask, "How many words?" He holds up three fingers. He next holds up two fingers to indicate that he is showing them the second word in the title. He holds his hands up high. Then he indicates width by holding his hands out. Next he holds up three fingers to indicate that he is presenting the third word in the title. He goes through the motions of casting and then reeling in a fishing line. Someone guesses *The Big Fisherman.* The same technique can be used in presenting a song title or a well-known proverb.

Teams take turns in sending representatives to the other team.

CHARADES

Six or more can play this old favorite that offers opportunity for much creative fun. Divide into two or more groups. Each group in turn acts out some word while the rest try to guess what it is. Often the word is broken up into syllables and presented a syllable at a time, such as sax(sacks)-o (owe)-phone. The presentations may be as elaborate or as simple as desired. The group presenting the charade announces the number of syllables in the word and the number of scenes used in the presentation. Here are some examples:

Dictionary: "Four syllables and two scenes." *Scene 1.* A teacher or dramatic coach correcting a performer's diction, "You must pronounce your words so that every syllable is heard and understood." *Scene 2.* Performers talk about the "airy" condition of the room, "Nice breeze blowing."

Harmony (Harm-mow-knee): "Three syllables and three scenes." *Scene 1.* "You're hurting me." *Scene 2.* Mowing lawn. *Scene 3.* Football or basketball player with injured knee.

Action (Act-shun): "Two syllables and two scenes. *Scene 1.* A brief dramatic episode. *Scene 2.* Shunning someone.

Allegheny (Alley-gay-knee): "Four syllables and three scenes." *Scene 1.* Group bowling, "Set 'em up in the next alley." *Scene 2.* A merry group having fun. *Scene 3.* Concern about an injured knee.

Antedate (Aunty-date): "Three syllables and two scenes." *Scene 1.* Aunty arrives for a visit. *Scene 2.* Class answering questions about important historical dates, or boy dating a girl.

Suggested words: Address, adhere, admit, backslide, bagpipe, balsam, bandage, bellow, bifurcate, biological, blowpipe, canary, caption, carpentry, classic, courage, dilate, furlong, gallop, gangster, graduate, greenback, guidance, harpsichord, hoodwink, hydraulic, inconsiderate, infancy, investment, liable, libel, manageable, mansion, misfortune, misinform, monotony, peerage, satire, sausage, spinster, supine.

BIBLE CHARADES

Build charades around biblical characters. Suggestions: Aaron: a run. Abel: able; a bell. Amos: a muss. Andrew: Anne drew. Cain: cane. Daniel: Dan yell—Dan, "Rah! Rah!" Deborah Deb-owe-raw. Eli: Yale graduate or Boola Boola. Genesis: Jenny-sis. Haman: Hay-man. Isaiah: I say, "Yah." Luke: not very warm. Mark: on the mark. Matthew: Matt-hue; Matt-hew. Noah: Know-ah. Philemon: File-lea (nice meadow), mon (hoot mon). Samson: Sam's son. Samuel: Sam-you-well. Silas: Sigh-lass. Sisera: Sissy-rah. Solomon: Solo-man.

GEOGRAPHICAL CHARADES

Plan some charades using geographical locations and names—states, rivers, cities, countries, lakes, etc. Some suggestions: Aden: A-den. Amsterdam: Am-stir-dam. Arkansas: Ark-can-saw. Baton Rouge: Bat-un-rouge. Boise:

Boy-see. Buffalo: Buff-halo. Champaign: Sham-pain. Cicero: Sissy-row. Constantinople: Constant-tea-know-pull. Dearborn: Deer-born. Delaware: Della-wear. Hartford: Hart-ford. Hot Springs: Hot-springs. Houston: Hew-stun. Maryland: Mary-land. New Jersey: New-jersey. Paterson: Pat-her-son. Pine Bluff: Pine-bluff. Sioux Falls: Sue-falls. Syracuse: Sear-accuse. Washington: Washing-ton. Way-cross: Way-cross.

CHAPTER IX

Riddles

Riddles

The following are some of the uses that may be made of riddles for social occasions:

Getting partners. The questions may be given to half of the guests and the answers to the other half. Questions and answers try to discover each other. A master list should be in the hands of the leader. After a reasonable time he reads the correct answers.

Icebreakers. At a supper or banquet place a riddle at each plate. Guests share riddles with those near them.

Contests. Divide guests into two or more groups. The leader calls out the riddle. The first group in which someone answers correctly scores a point. Or select five or ten persons, and give to each of them a riddle with the answer. Have them propound their riddles, one at a time, to the rest of the group.

Here are some good riddles for good fun:

1. Why is a quarrel like a bargain? It takes two to make it.
2. What part of London is in France? The letter *n.*
3. What is always behind time? The back of a watch.
4. What has plenty of teeth but cannot eat? A saw.
5. What is everyone doing all of the time? Growing older.
6. What word, by changing the position of a single letter, becomes its opposite? United—untied
7. Why is bread like the sun? Because it isn't light until it rises.

8. Why is an empty room like a room full of married people? There isn't a single person in it.

9. What is the beginning of eternity, the end of time and space, the beginning of the end, and the end of every place? The letter e.

10. Why is a beehive like a spectator? Because it is a bee-holder (beholder).

11. Why is pouting like a ragged coat? It is a bad habit.

12. If the letters of the alphabet were invited out, what time would U, V, W, X, Y, and Z go? After tea (T).

13. If a tough piece of meat could speak, what English poet would it likely name? Chaucer (Chaw, sir).

14. Why is an angry boy just about to start a fight like a clock at 59 minutes and 59 seconds past 12 o'clock? Because he is just ready to strike one.

15. What's the difference between a mirror and a girl who chatters constantly? One reflects without speaking, while the other speaks without reflecting.

16. Why is a bowl of flowers on the table like a speech made on the deck of a ship? Because it is a decoration (deck oration).

17. When is a door not a door? When it is ajar.

18. What relation is your uncle's brother to you if he is not your uncle? Your father.

19. Why is a steel ocean liner like losing one's fortune? Because it is a hardship.

20. What is the difference between a butcher and a flashily dressed flirt? The butcher kills to dress, and the flirt dresses to kill.

21. What is the difference between a person late for a train and a teacher in a girl's school? One misses the train and the other trains misses.

334

22. Where did Noah strike the first nail in the ark? On the head.

23. What shape is a kiss? Elliptical (a lip tickle).

24. Why is a bad cold a great humiliation? Because it brings the proudest man to his sneeze (his knees).

25. When are old clothes like corpses? When they are mended (men dead).

26. Which is the largest room in the world? The room for improvement.

27. When is a young girl not a young girl? When she turns into a drugstore.

28. Why is a newborn baby like a donkey's tail? Because it has never been seen before.

29. What miracle happened when Mr. Stone and Mr. Wood stood on the corner and a pretty girl passed by? Stone turned to Wood and Wood turned to Stone. Then they both turned to rubber. The girl turned into a beauty shop.

30. Why is a thief called a jailbird? Because he has been a-robbin' (a robin).

31. What is the difference between a man going upstairs and one looking upstairs? One is stepping up the stairs, while the other is staring up the steps.

32. Why are chickens the most profitable of livestock? Because for every grain they eat they give a peck.

33. What is it that every living person has seen but will never see again? Yesterday.

34. Thirty-two white horses on a red hill,
Now they go, now they stand still. Your teeth.

35. What does a man love more than life?
Hate more than death or mortal strife;
That which contented men desire,
The poor have, and rich require;
The miser spends, the spendthrift saves,

And all men carry to their graves? Nothing.

36. Why is a defeated team like wool? Because it's worsted.

37. Why do pianos bear the noblest character? Because they are grand, upright, and square.

38. What was the first bet ever made? The alphabet.

39. What's the difference between a mouse and an attractive girl? One harms the cheese, while the other charms the he's.

40. "His mother was my mother's only child." What relation was the man to the woman who spoke those words? Her son.

41. Suppose there was a cat in each corner of the room; a cat sitting opposite to each cat; a cat looking at each cat; and a cat sitting on each cat's tail. How many cats would there be? Four.

42. A girl had an aunt who was in prison. She sent her an animal whose name urged her to escape. The aunt sent back a fruit that brought the message that escape was impossible. What was the animal and what the fruit? Antelope; cantaloupe.

43. As I was going to St. Ives,
I chanced to meet nine old wives;
Each wife had nine sacks,
Each sack had nine cats,
Each cat had nine kits.
Kits, cats, sacks, and wives,
Tell me how many were going to St. Ives. One.

44. A duck before two ducks; a duck behind two ducks; and a duck between two ducks. How many ducks were there in all? Three.

45. How long did Cain hate his brother? As long as he was Abel (able).

46. Why is a man's nose in the middle of his face? Because it is the center (scenter).

47. What time of day was Adam created? A little before Eve.

48. When is a window like a star? When it is a skylight.

49. What colors are suggested by the winds and the storms? The winds blew (blue) and the storms rose.

50. What is the difference between a gardener, a billiard player, a precise man, and a church janitor? The gardener minds his peas, the billiard player, his cues, the precise man, his *p*'s and *q*'s, and the church janitor, his keys and pews.

51. Which can see most, a man with one eye or one with two eyes? The man with one eye, because he can see all that the man with two eyes can see, and in addition he can see the other man's two eyes, while the man with two eyes can see only the one of his one-eyed companion.

52. What occurs once in a minute, twice in a moment, but not once in a thousand years? The letter *m*.

53. What are two modern miracles? The deaf-mute who picked up a wheel and spoke, and the blind man who picked up a hammer and saw.

54. Why is the heart of a tree like a dog's tail? It's farthest from the bark.

55. Why is the letter *i* the happiest of the vowels? Because it alone is in bliss while *e* is in hell and the other vowels are in purgatory.

56. What is the difference between stammering and stuttering? Stammering is w - - - when y---you c--can't s--start. Stuttering isssss whwhwh-when yyyyy-you cccccan't st-st-st-st-stop.

57. The Bishop's Riddle: Once there was a bishop who claimed that wherever he went, night or day, he was accompanied by (see if you can guess them!):

(1) Two playful animals (calves).
(2) A number of animals of the rodent family (hares —hairs).
(3) A member of the deer family (hart—heart).
(4) Some whips (lashes).
(5) Two military weapons (arms).
(6) Two hotel steps (inn steps—insteps).
(7) The senate, when it takes a vote on a hotly contested issue (ayes and noes—eyes and nose).
(8) Ten Spanish gentlemen (ten dons—tendons).
(9) Two places of worship (temples).
(10) Two students (pupils).
(11) Two coverings for kettles (lids).
(12) What the king leaves for his offspring (crown).
(13) Two percussion instruments (drums).
(14) Two established measures (hands and feet).
(15) Two head coverings (caps—kneecaps).
(16) What a carpenter needs (nails).
(17) A couple of fish (soles).
(18) Some shellfish (mussels—muscles).
(19) Two lofty trees (palms).
(20) Two kinds of flowers (tulips and iris.)

58. When is a girl's hat not a girl's hat? When it becomes a girl.

59. Where were the first doughnuts fried? In Greece.

60. Why is a river rich? Because it has two banks.

61. Graveyard Riddles: If you lived in a graveyard,

(1) With what would you open the gate? (With a skeleton key.)
(2) What would you do if you got a bad cold that settled in your throat? (Start coffin.)

338

(3) How would you identify in three letters a plaintive poem? (L-E-G, elegy.)

(4) What kind of jewels would you wear? (Tombstones.)

(5) Where would you keep them? (In a casket.)

(6) How would you get money? (Urn it.)

(7) What would you eat? (Pyre cake or buries.)

(8) How would you move things about? (By carrion them.)

(9) What would you do getting ready for a play? (Rehearse.)

(10) What would protect you from the sun? (The shades.)

(11) Supposing a woman told you she was going to call? (You would specter.)

(12) What would be your disposition? (Grave.)

Indexes

INDEX OF DRAMATIC GAMES AND STUNTS

ALPHABETICAL INDEX

I hear a ghost, 107
I love my lover, 296
I'm looking for a wife, 152
Impromptu circus, 18
Impromptu debate, 114
Impromptu pantomimes, 147
Individual dumb crambo, 327
In the manner of the adverb, 325
In the shade of the old apple tree, 79
Invisible ink fortunes, 96
Irish quiz, 169, 185
Irish sculpture, 171
Irish shenanigan party, 177
Irish wake shenanigans, 180
Irish washerwoman, 171

July lawn party, 203
Jumbled book titles, 49
Jumbled information, 282

King April entertains, 187
Kiss the blarney stone, 183
Know your numbers? 283
Kung hi, 63

Lawyer's puzzle, 254
Let's go bear hunting, 68
Let's have a circus, 13
Lincoln penny, 165
Lion hunt, 309
Literary quiz, 49, 52
Living alphabet, 258
Love letters, 162
Lucky handshaker, 156

Madame Notella d'Ly, 269
Magic arithmetic tricks, 244
Magic music, 240
Magic writing, 287
Man, gun, tiger, 65
Marine quiz, 208
Masquerade party, 120
Mental test, 195
Merry Christmas, 271
Midget witches, 91
Milk bottle top toss, 205
Millinery, 268
Mind reading, 243, 287

Minister's cat, 296
Monkey, 164
Moother Goose drama, 305
Mother Goose party, 69
Mother Goose rhymes, 71
Mother, Mother, may I go? 307
Mouthpiece, 293
Muffin-pan polo, 29
Murder, 87
Museum of the dead, 97
Music memory test, 118
Music of the nations, 284
Musical chairs, 58
Musical contest, 205
Musical flop, 59
Musical mixer, 57
Musical party, 56
Musical quiz, 119
Musical Valentine, 148
My favorite book, 51
My flower garden, 238
My grocery, 238
My sweetheart, 154
My zoo, 238
Mystery music, 59
Mystery party, 72

Name a book, 52
Naming presidents, 205
Nature foraging, 218
Necklaces, 216
Neighborhood Halloween party, 101
Nicknames, 241
Nine books, 243
November parade of time party, 122
November party, 125
Number quartets, 66
Number quiz, 67
Number refreshments, 68
Numbered chairs, 67
Nut toss, 107
Nuts to crack, 107

Observation, 235
Observation proverbs, 280
Ocean wave, 32
Old sayings, 281
Old witch is dead, 87
On the double, 181

349

1. Let Ruth know
   Margie
   Dearborn
   Kinnicins
   Edith

2. food { diplomas
        Potato chips   punch   buffet
        drink

3. Registration card.

4. wrap books

5. Tell Rosie
   Tell Paul

6. decorations
   armchair
   ruler
   School colors
   green & green
   dunce hat

   Centerpiece